SouthernLiving

Curtains, Draperies & Shades

DESIGN: SALLY ALTIZER

Cascading draperies and Roman shades set a tone of enveloping comfort and establish this guest room's color scheme.

Oxmoor House

DESIGNER: JOSEPH MINTON

While this elegant bedroom incorporates four styles of window coverings, harmony reigns thanks to a thoughtful choice of fabrics.

Cover
Design: ***James Boone, Vasken Guiragossian.*** Photography: ***Meg McKinney Simle,*** Southern Progress Photo Collection. Architect: ***William Poole.*** Design: ***Mary McWilliams.***

10 9 8 7 6 5 4 3 2
First printing January 2000

ISBN 0-376-09069-3

Library of Congress Catalog Card Number: 99-65009

Printed in the United States

Southern Living® *Curtains, Draperies & Shades* was adapted from a book by the same title published by Sunset Books.

Book Editor
Christine Barnes

Special Consultant
Dorothy Perry

Contributing Editor
Fran Feldman

Coordinating Editor
Linda J. Selden

Consulting Editor
Jane Horn

Editorial Coordinators
Bradford Kachelhofer, Vicki Weathers

Design
Joe di Chiarro

Illustrations
Susan Jaekel, Mary Knowles, Sally Shimizu

Photo Styling
JoAnn Masaoka Van Atta

Special Contributors
Linda Bouchard, Bridget Biscotti Bradley, Barbara Brown, Tishana Peebles, Jean Warboy

Photography
Philip Harvey (with additional photography by ***Jean Allsopp,*** 1, 6, 40 bottom, 89 (both), 102 bottom; ***Colleen Duffley,*** 113 top; ***Sylvia Martin,*** 11 left, 14 right, 38, 67 (both), 86, back cover top right and top left; ***Emily Minton,*** 2, 12 bottom right, 66, 70, 87, 108 bottom, back cover bottom left; ***John O'Hagan,*** 85 bottom; ***Laurey Weigant,*** 37 bottom left and right).

Our appreciation to the staff of *Southern Living* magazine for their contributions to this book.

Window Dressing

Even when the view is outstanding, most windows need to be covered to ensure privacy, temper light, and provide insulation. Window treatments also make a strong decorating statement, enhancing—and sometimes transforming—a room. How to plan and sew window treatments that are both practical and beautiful is what this book is all about.

Whether you're a novice or an experienced sewer, you'll find a wide array of projects from which to choose. Begin by becoming familiar with your options; then use the principles of color, pattern, texture, and design to plan your treatment. Whether you're making a simple pair of tab curtains or a formal swag with cascades, you'll find detailed instructions and illustrations to guide you every step of the way.

We're grateful to the following for their help in preparing this book: Ado Corporation; American Cancer Society Designer Showcase; Bernina; Marti Caires; Calico Corners; Carol Fabrics; Curtain Call Window Coverings; Heidi Emmett; Fabricut; Freudenberg, Pellon Division; The Gardener; Angelo Garro of The Renaissance Forge; Gingher Inc.; Harding's Interiors; Cynthia Jaggi of Springs Window Fashions Division, Inc.; Kirsch; Kravet Fabrics, Inc.

Also, Lensol Fabrics, Inc.; Bill McDougald of Southern Living magazine; Marin Designer Showcase; Murtra Industries, U.S.A.; Nicole Patton Interiors; Norbar Fabrics Co., Inc.; Dick Perry; Restoration Hardware; Robert Allen Fabrics; San Francisco Decorator Showcase; San Francisco Symphony Design House; Schumacher; Shears & Window; Sydney Davis Fabrics; Jeanne Tepper of BJT Design Studio; Jill Van de Wege; Waverly; and Wroolie & LoPresti.

Special thanks to Jeanne Tepper for selecting the fabrics in "A Fabric Collection."

Special Features

Decorating Basics

Decisions, decisions, decisions! Every aspect of home decorating, whether it's sewing window treatments or choosing a wall covering, means making decisions. And for many people, that can be very intimidating, especially considering the time, money, and effort involved.

The information in this chapter will help take the guesswork out of making decorating decisions. Become familiar with the various window treatment styles; study the guidelines for using color, pattern, and texture; and read up on some basic decorating principles. Then you'll be ready to create treatments that will enhance your decorating scheme and work wonders for your windows.

Good design emanates from a pleasing blend of color, pattern, and texture. Apple green glazed walls provide a smooth backdrop for a sumptuous scalloped valance and generous puddled side panels. Silk, cotton, gilt, and wood mingle successfully in the formal eclectic scheme.

DESIGN: DIANE CHAPMAN INTERIORS

If you're tired of staring at a bare or poorly dressed window, it's hard to resist the urge to buy some fabric, set up the machine, and start sewing. But, like any project, a successful window treatment relies on some thoughtful decision making.

First, become familiar with the various styles and terms so you'll know how to tell a curtain from a drapery and a valance from a cornice. Then, let an awareness of your functional and decorative needs guide you to choosing the treatment that's right for you.

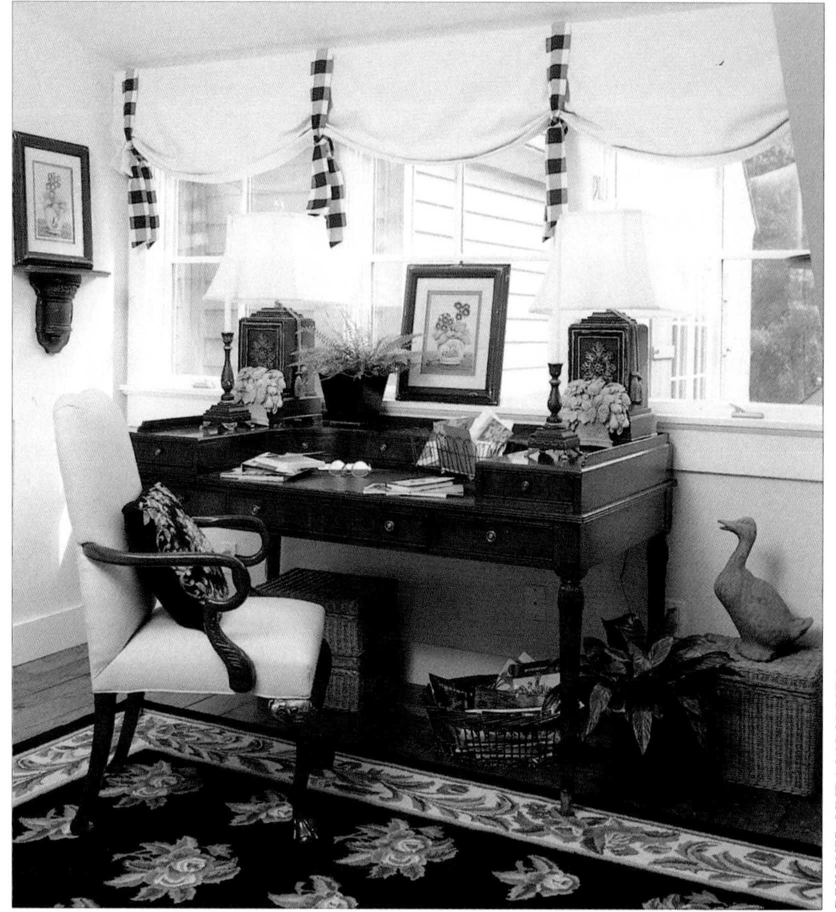

DESIGNER: LINDA WOODRUM

Black-and-white gingham ties hold up a stagecoach valance made of simple white canvas and create a pleasing scalloped edge.

Coming to Terms

If you haven't kept up with window treatment fashions, you're in for a pleasant surprise. Familiar styles have been joined by a collection of innovative top treatments, from graceful shaped valances to traditional swags and cascades. Here's a brief look at your options.

Curtains. By definition, curtains are gathered on a rod or attached to a rod by tabs, ties, or rings (some people call the latter style draperies). If the curtains open and close, it's by hand.

In general, length sets the style with curtains. Café curtains cover only the lower half of the window, ending at the sill or apron. With cafés, use a generous amount of fabric so they don't look skimpy. For other short curtain styles, end the panels 5 inches below the window opening.

Full-length curtains lend themselves to both elegant and informal schemes. Bishop's sleeve and extra-long curtains that puddle on the floor impart a luxurious mood; in contrast, simple floor-length curtains tied back high create a casual effect.

Curtains combine well with other treatments. If you like the look of stationary curtain panels but you want some privacy, pair the curtains with miniblinds or a pleated shade. For a more finished effect, top them with a cornice or valance.

Draperies. Long considered staid and predictable, today's draperies offer a variety of intriguing pleat styles and decorative hardware.

Strictly speaking, draperies have pleated headings that attach to rods by means of drapery hooks. As with curtains, however, terms are blurred, so you may hear full-length panels with rod-pocket headings referred to as draperies.

Pinch pleats, the traditional drapery heading, consist of three shallow folds tacked at the base. Variations of that basic style include goblet, reverse pinch, and butterfly pleats.

Though most draperies hung on conventional or decorative rods are meant to be opened and closed, draperies can also be stationary. Pleated side panels tie back beautifully because the pleats form consistent folds.

Shades. Shades offer an enormous array of versatile styles.

Moreover, shades are as hardworking as they are good-looking, ensuring privacy, controlling light, and conserving energy.

Roman, balloon, and cloud shades all raise and lower by means of cords threaded through rings sewn to the back of the shade. From the front of a flat Roman shade, you see crisp, tailored folds. A variation, called a soft-fold Roman shade, has extra fabric in the folds to keep the shade rounded even when it's lowered.

Pleats in balloon shades create billowy poufs at the lower edge. The shirring at the top of a cloud shade and an optional ruffle at the bottom add softness.

Because they're inexpensive and easy to make, roller shades are popular in informal areas and in children's rooms. Top them with a simple valance or cornice.

Valances. Some valances, such as rod-pocket, Roman, and balloon, look like short versions of their longer counterparts. Others are more innovative, sporting shaped, poufed, or rolled lower edges.

Running swags trimmed with knotted rosettes introduce color and pattern to expansive windows. Custom roller shades feature set-in antique lace and tassel pulls.

Deep swags and narrow cascades complement the window's shape and character. Small crystals sewn to the fringe embellish the treatment.

DESIGN: WEST VALLEY COLLEGE INTERIOR DESIGN DEPARTMENT

Used alone, valances bring a whisper of style and color to windows. Placed over another treatment, they not only conceal the heading but also lend a decorative flourish. Arched, tapered, or scalloped valances crown curtains and draperies, adding flowing lines and visual interest. Box-pleated valances provide a classic top treatment for tailored draperies. In children's rooms, dress a blind or roller shade with a skirt or stagecoach valance.

The lower edges of valances offer unlimited possibilities for trimmings, from ruffles and piping to contrast banding and fringe.

Cornices. Because their edges are so clearly delineated, cornices add architectural interest. The effect depends, in part, on the shape of the lower edge: straight cornices are simple and tailored; those with scallops are more formal.

When used on more than one window in a room, cornices unify the space and create a pleasing visual rhythm. They also display the fabric's design over a flat area.

In addition, cornices serve two very practical purposes: they cover the heading and hardware at the top of the undertreatment, and they block cold drafts coming from the window.

Swags and cascades. Among the most impressive of all window treatments, swags and cascades bring distinction and classic form to windows. Once found in only the most opulent settings, today's versions adapt to informal decorating schemes as well.

Challenging to make and mount, traditional and cutout swags look like flowing lengths of fabric. Usually, they're accompanied by cascades. For a more formal look, put swags and cascades over long side panels or sheers.

Easy-to-make running swags can be wrapped around a pole,

DESIGN: CHERYL DRIVER OF HILARY THATZ

Oversize headings, twisted cord trim, and a contrast lining on the leading edges enhance these voluminous shirred panels, interlined for extra body. The treatment hangs from rings on a decorative wood pole.

draped in decorative swag holders, or held in place with knots or tabs.

Taking Stock

No matter how beautiful your window treatment, if it's not appropriate for your home, it won't be successful. Take some time to consider the larger picture.

Your home's style. Whether your room is completely bare or you're simply replacing an old window treatment with a fresh, new one, your home's style will affect the style of the treatment.

A home with lots of traditional character will probably suggest a window treatment, such as classic swags in a Georgian-period home or tab curtains in a country-style house. In a home with a less distinctive style, you can probably choose nearly any window treatment, letting the fabric and hardware set the mood.

Don't ignore your furnishings. Your window treatments need to work with them, too.

For windows that face the street, give some thought as to how the treatment will look from outside. Though all windows need not have the same treatment, it's best not to mix too many styles.

Window style and placement. If your windows are plain, you may want to downplay the window treatments and let the furnishings take center stage. Noteworthy windows, on the other hand, demand distinctive treatments.

Look at the space surrounding your windows. Ideally, you should be able to stack treatments off the window. Where space is limited, choose a treatment that stacks compactly. If you have beautiful molding around the opening, an inside-mounted treatment will allow it to be seen.

To coordinate different size windows in a room, use the same fabric but different style treatments. For example, hang flat Roman shades on a bank of small windows and mount pleated draperies made of the same fabric on French doors. Or, in a bedroom, dress the windows with balloon shades and put a same-fabric balloon valance over miniblinds on the bathroom window.

Practicality. Active rooms call for casual treatments made of durable, soil-resistant fabrics; formal rooms allow for delicate fabrics and trimmings.

If you open and close the window often, be sure the treatment won't get in the way. A simple valance or cornice over a pleated shade that raises and lowers easily may be your best bet.

Functional Considerations

It's obvious: windows are designed to admit light and air and allow views of the outside world. But windows and their treatments play a myriad of other roles, ranging from purely decorative to hardworking.

Understanding how windows and their coverings function can help guide you to treatments that both express your style and meet your needs.

Light. The primary function of windows is to provide natural light. In fact, "lots of light" is a wish frequently expressed by people who are planning new construction or a remodel. Light gives life to a room, creating a mood, enhancing colors, and revealing textures.

How much light actually enters a room depends on many factors: the number of windows; their size, shape, and location in the wall; buildings or plants outdoors; and the color of the room's furnishings, walls, floor, and ceiling.

To admit the maximum amount of light into the room, choose a treatment that stacks back completely, exposing all of the window glass; if you want to add a valance or cornice, it should extend just a few inches into the window opening.

To filter light and control glare, your window covering choices include sheers, laces, and casement fabrics. Many of these light-screening fabrics create interesting textural patterns when light passes through them.

Densely woven, heavy, dark fabrics eliminate most, if not all, light. The most effective light-blocking treatments are curtains, draperies, and shades lined with blackout linings.

Remember, too, the sun's potential to damage fabrics and furnishings. Lined window treatments last longer than unlined ones; they also protect furnishings. Even a sheer undertreatment can block some of the sun's destructive rays.

Climate. To take advantage of refreshing breezes, choose treatments that completely clear the window when it's opened. Fabric is also a factor: heavy fabrics block the flow of air more than lightweight ones.

Most window treatments, even those not designed for energy efficiency, have an insulating effect, particularly if they're lined. The space between the fabric and the window—a dead-air space—prevents air currents, cold or hot, from circulating. Tightly woven fabrics form a more compact barrier than loosely woven ones.

Pleated draperies with deep folds capture more air than sheer curtains. Cornices and board-mounted valances and swags enclose the tops of treatments, blocking cold drafts. Combination treatments insulate windows and inhibit heat loss.

Privacy. Any window in your home has the potential for allowing people to see inside. Where privacy is important, treatments made of sheer, lace, or lightweight fabrics let in some light during the day while at the same time providing privacy; at night, you'll need a heavier window covering that closes completely.

For maximum privacy, consider combining a hard window treatment, such as blinds, pleated shades, or shutters, with a soft fabric treatment.

Noise control. Open or closed, windows allow noise to penetrate a room. But window treatments can reduce noise from both outside and inside the house. The same dead-air space that insulates against heat loss and heat gain also acts as a buffer for noise.

In general, the softer and more generous the treatment, the more sound it will absorb.

Combining a shirred valance with a pleated shade offers both the softness and color of fabric and the practicality of a shade.

DESIGN: PHILLIP H. STIDHAM, HOME DEPOT

View. When the view deserves to be seen, choose a treatment that clears the glass completely. Curtains and traversing draperies are obvious solutions; shades that stack work just as well. Windows with great views are not the place for low tied-back curtains or deep top treatments.

When choosing fabric for a window with an outstanding view, take one of two approaches. One approach is to use fabric that repeats the color and pattern on the wall so as not to distract the eye from the view beyond. The second is to frame the window with a distinctive treatment, much as a picture frame enhances a work of art. Just make sure the treatment doesn't steal the scene.

When the view is unattractive, the window treatment can play a prominent role. Fabrics with intriguing colors and patterns attract more attention than plain ones. Combination treatments put the focus on the window, not the view.

For a view you never want to see, a treatment you can close that's made of a sheer or semisheer fabric will let in light but obscure the view.

Bringing the outdoors in. When you're inside, windows are an important connection to the outside world. To strengthen the link between interior and exterior spaces, choose neutral fabrics and understated treatments that clear the windows. On French or sliding doors, use treatments that stack back completely so you can easily open doors and pass through.

COLOR, PATTERN, TEXTURE & DESIGN

A well-planned window treatment combines basic design elements—color, pattern, and texture—with subtle design concepts to create a beautiful, balanced effect. Understanding the theory that underlies those design elements and concepts will help you achieve the look you want on your windows, as well as in the entire room.

A Primer on Color

No matter which window treatment style you prefer, your initial decisions will be about color. A familiarity with color terms and principles will help you make those decisions.

Color terms. *Hue* is just another word for color. Every hue has a "visual temperature." Yellow, red, and orange are warm and lively; they're often referred to as advancing colors because they seem nearer than they are. Blue, green, and violet are cool and tranquil; they're often called receding colors because they appear to be farther away.

Intensity is the degree of purity, or saturation, of color. Though both seafoam and hunter green are technically green, they vary in their intensity, or strength, of color.

Value is the amount of light and dark in a color; color with white added is a *tint,* color plus black a *shade.*

The color wheel. All color combinations and variations come from the color wheel (see at right). Though the color wheel can't dictate schemes, it can help you visualize what will happen when you combine various colors.

At first, the color wheel may seem off-putting. Just remember that almost no one uses these colors in their full strength over large areas; instead, most colors used in decorating schemes are altered or combined in ways that soften their visual impact.

Primary colors—red, yellow, and blue—are the source of all other colors. Primaries are powerful, usually too powerful to use full strength on such large areas as windows and walls.

Secondary colors lie midway between the primary colors on the wheel because they're formed by combining primaries: green comes from blue and yellow, orange from yellow and red, and violet from red and blue. Secondary colors are less strong than primaries.

Intermediate colors result when you mix a primary color with an adjacent secondary color. Blue (a primary) and violet (a secondary) combine to make blue-violet, an intermediate.

Complementary colors are those opposite each other on the wheel. Red and green are complements, as are blue and orange, yellow and violet.

Complementary colors are stimulating and full of surprises. Used in their full intensity, they seem harsh. But when a small amount of one color is added to its complement, the result is a pleasing, less intense version of a predominant color. The inner wedges on the color wheel show tints that have a bit of complement added.

Neutral colors—white, black, and gray—are the noncolors. Low-intensity warm colors are also considered neutrals. Light neutrals, often used in understated window treatments, put the focus on other elements in the room.

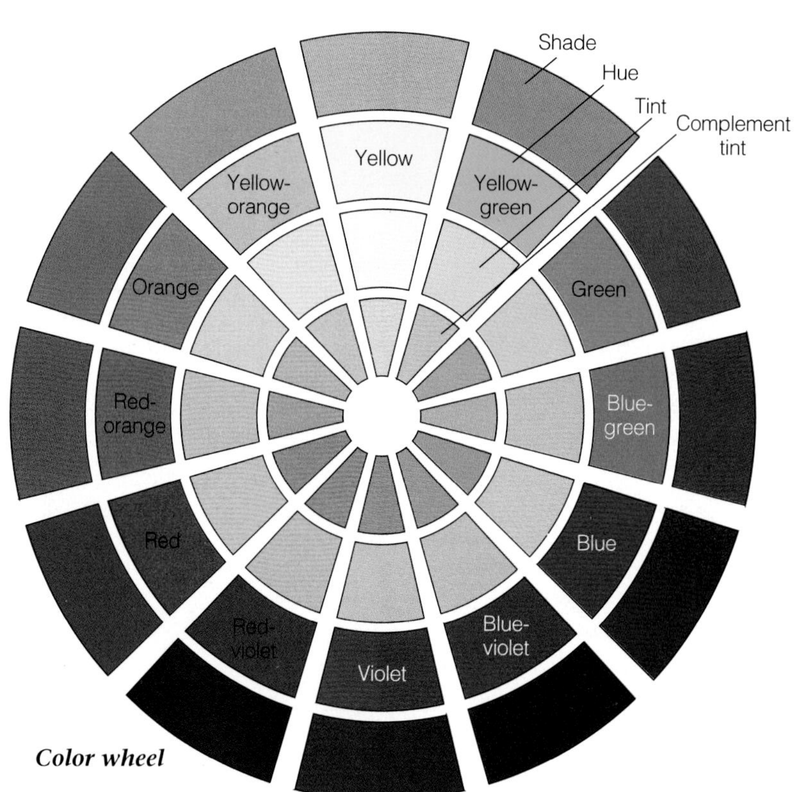

Color wheel

DESIGNERS: TODD YOGGY AND DAVID CROW

Handsome lined-wool draperies in an oversize plaid display a lively version of contemporary red and green. This popular decorating scheme, which balances warm and cool hues, is repeated on the walls and in the area rug.

Gemstone colors from all around the color wheel contribute vitality to a contemporary cotton print. The pattern shows clearly down the face of the soft-fold Roman shade.

Combining colors. Whether you're taking your color cues from a fabric you like or you're starting from scratch with your favorite colors, understanding the three basic types of color schemes will help you develop your own. Again, keep in mind that the colors used are almost always softened versions of what you see on the color wheel.

Monochromatic schemes consist of one color in a variety of intensities and values. Because colors have so much in common in monochromatic schemes, rooms appear unified and harmonious. To keep them from looking boring, spark the scheme with small dashes of bright color.

Complementary color schemes are those based on colors opposite each other on the color wheel. They tend to be richer than monochromatic schemes because they balance warm and cool colors.

Those combinations can be startling or subdued: instead of violet and yellow, think about a quiet room with a soft amethyst swag and creamy walls. One of the most favored color combinations in home decorating, pink and soft green, is really just a subtle version of the strong complementary combination of red and green.

Within the complementary category are more complex combinations. A *triad* consists of any three colors equidistant on the color wheel, for example, yellow, red, and blue. In decorating, this triad emerges as the historically popular combination of wheat, brick red, and slate blue.

A *split complement* is also composed of three colors—one primary color plus the color on each side of its opposite. Yellow plus red-violet and blue-violet is one example of a split complement. Though you'd never dream of using these colors full strength, imagine a floral chintz pattern in butter cream, berry, and periwinkle.

To avoid the clash of pure opposing color, always vary the intensity, quantity, and value of complementary colors.

Analogous, or related, color combinations are composed of two or more colors that lie next to each other on the color wheel. This combination results when you start with a favorite color and add related colors to it.

Characteristics of color. Understanding the qualities of color will make it easier for you to visualize color in window treatments.

In general, light colors are expansive, dark colors more contracting. To increase the sense of space and light in a dull room, use pale tints of warm or cool colors on windows and walls. To make a large room seem cozier, use rich, dark shades that draw in space.

Repeat colors used at the windows in other places in the room to unify and balance the scheme.

DESIGN: HEIDI EMMETT. WINDOW TREATMENT: DELTA PI DESIGN

Stylized patterns on a knotted swag and companion wallpaper border combine naturally because they share colors. A contrast lining on the swags and knots accents the treatment.

Color is also affected by the direction of light. Windows facing south and east let in warm, cheering light. Indirect northern light is softer and cooler, and light from the west is harshest of all.

You can use your awareness of light to guide your color choices. For example, a room facing north will feel more cheerful bathed in warm color, while cool hues tone down the bright light in a west-facing room.

An additional thought on color: If the room's scale can handle a window treatment that's bold or brightly colored, fine. There's nothing like a little color to enliven a scheme. But remember that you'll probably be living with the treatment for a number of years. Low-value, less-intense colors may "wear" better visually than strong ones.

Tips on using color. The following hints will help you choose and combine colors:

■ *To develop a color sense,* look through decorating magazines and pull examples of fabrics, window treatments, and rooms that appeal to you. Though they may seem unrelated at first, you'll gradually see a pattern to your preferences.

■ *Take your color cues* from the colors you love. Also, ask your family about their color likes and dislikes, since they'll be living in the scheme you create.

■ *Where rooms adjoin,* blend colors from one space to the next, creating color unity. Color that jumps is visually distracting. If, for example, one room is predominantly celadon and the adjacent room is rose, have some of the other color in each room.

■ *If you must work with existing furnishings,* don't see them as a constraint. It's actually easier to build a scheme on what you have than to start from scratch.

■ *Color changes* throughout the day. If possible, buy a yard or so of the fabric you're considering, pin it to the wall, and look at it in different lights.

Also, keep in mind that the impact of color is intensified when it's used in large quantities. The color that's just right on a pillow may overwhelm the room when it appears on a full-length window treatment. In such a case, use it for a valance or simple swag.

■ *Add a shot of unrelated bright color* to enliven a decorating scheme.

Pattern Principles

Pattern enriches any decorating scheme, adding depth, movement, and visual interest. But pattern also raises perplexing questions about where to use it and how to combine different patterns.

You can develop pattern confidence by following some basic pattern principles. There are no hard-and-fast rules, but observing how

DESIGNER: GINGER MENZIES KELLY

The bold pattern of these handsome fabric panels are in perfect scale to this graceful arched library window.

patterns appear at windows and how they interact throughout a room will make the job of selecting and combining patterns easier.

Pattern styles. Though the variety of patterns available is endless, you'll probably find yourself drawn to one or two particular styles. Make sure that your preferences are in keeping with the style of the room and its windows.

Ever-popular *naturalistic* patterns are realistic renderings of natural forms, typically flowers; they're usually used in formal, traditional settings.

Stylized patterns simplify and repeat natural designs to capture their essence; paisley motifs, stylized plant forms, are one example. Stylized patterns occur in both formal and informal schemes.

Abstract patterns, popular in contemporary settings, are loose, artistic interpretations of realistic designs; large, splashy florals are typical abstract patterns.

Nonrepresentational designs made up of stripes, plaids, and hard-edged shapes are referred to as *geometrics*. They're seen in contemporary settings as well as in traditional schemes, where geometrics, such as stripes, often combine with naturalistic patterns.

Keeping things in scale. The size of a pattern should correspond to the scale of the room and its windows.

Small-scale patterns are often used in cozy rooms, where their design is clearly retained and seen. Save large-scale patterns for spacious rooms; because they seem to take up space, such patterns can create the impression that a room is smaller than it actually is.

Combining different patterns. Patterns that share at least one color combine easily. One pattern may have all the colors in a scheme, another may contain just one hue plus white, while a third consists of two of the colors.

Richly patterned silk scarf swag drapes alluringly over Art Deco brass holdbacks. Underneath, a bronze metallic sheer adds shimmery color and softens the view.

DESIGN: DIANNA COPPERSMITH, INTERIORS OF MARIN. WINDOW TREATMENT: DOMINO DESIGNS. WALL MURAL: ROBERTA AHRENS

Similar patterns of different scales also combine well, such as small checks and larger plaids. Again, a common or analogous color will help tie the look together.

In fabric, a strong pattern or motif works best with a contrasting smaller pattern, such as floral clusters surrounded by twining leaves or ribbons. This concept can be applied to window treatments, too: think of a large floral print swag with cascades lined in a neat stripe.

For decorating purposes, you can approach pattern combinations in three different ways. The first is simplicity—unpatterned walls, windows, and furnishings, seen, for example, in the clean Shaker style as well as in more formal schemes. When you adopt this approach, let subtle textures come into play.

Another approach is to use pattern throughout—on the windows, on the walls, even on the furnishings. This all-out mix of patterns, tricky to pull off successfully, relies on making careful choices. One of the easiest-to-accomplish combinations consists of light and airy patterned walls punctuated by darker, more densely patterned window treatments, both of which maintain at least one common color.

DESIGN: KIMBERLY BRAGG INTERIOR DESIGN. WINDOW TREATMENT: PAT LEPE, INTERIOR WINDOWS OF SONOMA

In an example of asymmetrical balance, a bell swag (best left to professionals) crowns a delicate voile curtain scooped to the side.

A pouf valance is the focal point of this charming nursery. Its soft folds and fresh pastel color scheme stop the stripes from dominating the room.

A third approach, perhaps the most popular strategy, is to combine pattern with plain color for a balanced look. Keeping walls plain while dressing windows in pattern draws attention to the window and the window treatment.

How to use pattern. Keep in mind these additional tips when you work with pattern:

■ *Consider the impact* of pattern placed on different surfaces. A fabric hanging as a full-length gathered or pleated window treatment will look entirely different when used flat on a Roman shade.

■ *To keep a room from looking too busy,* introduce visually restful solids.

■ *When you combine patterns,* try to maintain a consistent mood. For example, a formal moiré fabric won't work with a stylized country chintz, even if they share a common color.

■ *Avoid combining too many patterns* in one area. A good rule of thumb is to use only one bold pattern in a room and use it on a large surface so that it predominates. Then add two or possibly three smaller-scale patterns, distributing them around the room to avoid pattern clusters.

The Role of Texture

Shimmering faille, nubby woven wool, and tasseled fringe—all window treatment materials possess texture, from distinctive to subtle.

When the texture is smooth, light is reflected and colors appear lighter and more lustrous; smooth fabrics, such as antique satin, often appear formal and refined.

When there's more texture, fabric appears duller because the texture absorbs rather than reflects light. Window treatment fabrics with noticeable texture—coarse canvas or loosely woven casements, for example—tend to be casual, though you'll find exceptions to this rule.

How much texture you use at your windows depends, in part, on the style of the room and how you've used color and pattern in the space. A monochromatic color scheme with very little pattern allows for more texture than a scheme with bold color and pattern. A masculine study, for example, is a good place for neutral, subtly textured fabrics, such as cotton/linen blends.

For a beautiful blend of rough and smooth surfaces throughout a room, try to introduce enough texture to create interest, but not so much that visual chaos results. And remember, patterned fabric, even if it's smooth, has a visual texture, too.

Design Concepts

Color may be first and foremost when it comes to decorating, but the design principles are just as important. Though these basic concepts deal with intangibles, they're useful in making subtle decorating decisions.

Balance. A room is balanced when a sense of visual equilibrium exists. To achieve balance, you need to think about the impact, or visual weight, of elements in a room. Rough textures and bold patterns, for example, possess visual weight and attract attention. Small-scale furnishings and fabrics in light, cool colors lend little visual weight.

Balance in a room can be symmetrical or asymmetrical. Symmetrical balance occurs when half of something is the mirror image of the other half. This type of scheme tends to be quiet, restful, and often formal. Few rooms are completely symmetrical, but there are often symmetrical elements, such as identical windows flanking a fireplace.

Asymmetrical balance is active and much more common than symmetrical balance in decorating schemes. On a window, asymmetrical balance is achieved with a one-way rod-pocket curtain tied back high over a sheer that's tied low to the opposite side. The same principle is at work in a pattern that balances visually heavy motifs with a grouping of lighter ones.

Rhythm. The deliberate repetition of elements constitutes rhythm. This repetition brings a sense of unity and continuity as your eye moves easily from one motif or area to another.

A geometric pattern with a strong directional design is an example of rhythm in fabric. A continuous running swag that covers more than one window creates rhythm in a room, as do identical treatments on a series of windows. More subtle rhythm comes from repeating the same or similar lines elsewhere in the room.

A constellation of just-for-fun hardware includes (1) iron holdback, (2) star holdback, (3) ivy holdback, (4) spear finial, (5) star holdback, (6) sun holdback, (7) olive branch finial, and (8) leaf holdback. Most holdbacks can be used as swag holders.

Emphasis. Every room needs a focal point; without it, the overall design looks monotonous. The starring role may go to a work of art, a noteworthy piece of furniture, or a distinctive wall covering.

When the windows are outstanding, consider emphasizing them. Voluminous curtains that puddle on the floor, goblet-pleated draperies, scalloped cornices, formal swags with cascades, and decorative hardware (shown above) can all turn a window into the focal point of a room.

Harmony. When both unity and variety exist in a window treatment or a room, harmony results.

If you have several windows of different sizes, you can unify them by using the same fabric on all the windows, an approach commonly used in rooms with both windows and French doors.

Variety—in just the right amount—contributes vitality and excitement to a room's design. It can be subtle, as in slight variations in color, or it can be startling, as with a strong accent color or accessory.

One way to establish harmony is to unify window treatments, wall coverings, and furnishings with a common color while varying the surface design from plain to patterned.

Scale. The window treatment needs to be scaled for the room. A treatment that's too large will make the window appear massive; a treatment that's too small will get lost in the room.

Before You Sew

How do you measure a window? How much fabric will you need? Is it important to line your treatment?

These questions and more are answered in this chapter. It describes the sewing tools you'll need and the techniques you'll rely on to measure for yardage, choose appropriate fabric, join widths, and make hems. Tips for handling patterned fabric will make easy work of matching repeats and cutting lengths.

So take the time to become familiar with the fundamentals. Your project begins right here, before you sew.

Successful window treatments start with the right ingredients. All the makings are here—attractive fabrics, handsome decorative hardware, and distinctive trimmings.

GETTING STARTED

Whether you're draping a wall of windows or sewing a single shade, you'll undoubtedly have to handle much more fabric than for most sewing projects, so you'll need plenty of room and probably some special tools.

Space to Work

Staking out and organizing a special work area is worth the time it takes, even if it steals some living space for a while. A sewing room with a large table and special nooks and crannies for supplies is ideal. But if you don't have the luxury of a sewing room and table, you'll still need a large, flat surface on which to measure, cut, and sew.

As an alternative to a table, consider a piece of plywood or a hollow flush door. As a base for either one, you can use a pair of sawhorses or a table (protected with a blanket). If you choose sawhorses, you'll need rigid plywood ¾ to 1 inch thick. Plywood supported by a table can be ½ inch thick.

It's best to pad your work surface. For details, see the facing page.

Tools of the Trade

The following list includes all the tools necessary for making window treatments, as well as some that are very useful though not essential.

Measuring tools

A spring-return 12-foot or longer *steel tape measure* assures easy, accurate measuring of windows and fabric. For measuring fabric, a 60-inch synthetic tape is convenient, but it's not designed to measure windows. Avoid cloth tapes—they tend to stretch.

A *carpenter's square*, available at hardware stores, is essential for squaring off the ends of yardage. A 12- by 24-inch square is better than a smaller one—the longer your first line, the easier it is to extend it accurately. Look out for any rough edges that might snag fabric.

A 32- by 40-inch piece of *matte board* (used for framing artwork) is a lightweight alternative to a carpenter's square. If you place the short side parallel to the selvage, you'll get an even longer crosswise line than you would with a square. Make sure the corners are square.

A metal or wood *straightedge* (be sure a wood one is straight) is useful for marking and extending cutting lines. The surface must be perfectly smooth. Available in a variety of sizes, a clear *quilter's ruler* is especially helpful in marking hems.

Handy for measuring and marking fabric, a *cardboard cutting board* can also be used as a guide when pleating swags.

To mark cutting lines, hems, and pleats, you'll need a *fabric marker*. Your choices are many, from traditional chalk to pens and pencils used by quilters. Experiment on a sample swatch first: some markers leave permanent marks after pressing. A regular number 2 lead pencil is suitable for light fabrics.

A *hem gauge*, a 6-inch ruler with an adjustable slide, aids in measuring seam allowances and lower and side hems.

Cutting tools

Easier on the hands than regular scissors, *bent-handled shears* allow

Tools for making window treatments include (1) carpenter's square, (2) quilter's ruler, (3) fray preventer, (4) steel tape measure, (5) metal straightedge, (6) fabric markers, (7) push pins, (8) dressmaker pins, (9) bent-handled shears, (10) embroidery scissors, (11) thread clips, (12) seam ripper, (13) quilter's pins, (14) T-pins, and (15) hem gauge.

the fabric to lie flat while you cut. Choose an 8- or 9-inch-long pair; they're lightweight and the blades cut quickly. Use your shears only on fabric (paper will dull the blades in short order).

Pinking shears, available with saw-toothed or scalloped blades, are useful for finishing seam edges so they resist raveling.

Four-inch-long *embroidery scissors* are handy for clipping threads while sewing. Even more convenient to use are *thread clips,* which snip threads in a snap.

Ironing tools

A *steam iron* is the most versatile ironing tool because it adjusts conveniently to a wide variety of fabrics. To steam out wrinkles and freshen up window coverings after they're hung, try a *hand steamer;* it can also be used on hard-to-reach places.

Since you'll need a larger surface than most ironing boards offer, consider padding a *large table* or piece of plywood instead, especially if you'll be pressing great quantities of fabric (cover the surface as described at right).

Keep a *plastic spray bottle* handy near the ironing surface for extra moisture. But be careful: Too much water can waterspot the fabric, particularly if it has a finish. Test a sample first.

Sewing tools

A strip of *masking tape* laid down on the throat plate of your sewing machine serves as a handy guide for keeping seams and hems straight. For hints on using tape, see page 33.

Always use *sewing machine needles* that are compatible with the weight of your fabric. Check the needle package and your sewing machine manual for guidance. To machine-tack pleats, be sure to use a sturdy needle—size 16 or 18—since it may have to penetrate as many as 30 layers of face fabric, lining, and stiffener.

A packet of *hand-sewing needles* in assorted sizes should take care of most hand-sewing jobs. But tacking pleats by hand will require a special heavy-duty needle. For this job, buy a packet of *repair needles.*

Fine, sharp *dressmaker pins* (number 20), 1¼ inches long, are best but are sometimes hard to find. Longer, larger *quilter's pins* hold medium-weight and heavy fabrics securely; just be sure not to try to sew over them.

Stronger than dressmaker or quilter's pins are *T-pins,* useful for holding plush or open-weave fabrics, which tend to swallow pins with small heads. T-pins come in two sizes: numbers 20 and 24 (large). *Push pins* are useful for pleating swags and temporarily securing shades, valances, swags, and cascades to mounting boards.

A *seam ripper* speeds the task of taking out any imperfect rows of stitching.

A bead of *liquid fray preventer* laid along the raw edges of fabric dries clear and prevents fraying. Use the liquid on the edges of a roller shade. It's also useful along the edges of ravel-prone fabrics if you don't plan to finish the seams.

Padding A Work Surface

Covering your work surface with padding prevents your fabric from slipping and sliding and allows you to anchor the fabric as you're working.

Covering a table. Drape enough blankets or cotton (not polyester) batting on the table so you have at least a ½-inch thickness. Starting at one end, pull the corners tightly and fasten them underneath with safety pins. Repeat at the other end. Tape any dangling edges.

Cover the padding with an unpatterned sheet or canvas. Smooth and fasten as you did the blankets. If you're using canvas, you can spray the surface with water; as the canvas dries, it will shrink tightly over the padding.

Padding a plywood sheet or a door. Begin by layering blankets on the floor to a thickness of ½ inch. Center the plywood or door on top. Starting at the middle of one long side, fold the blankets over the edge and secure them with four staples placed about 2 inches apart. Repeat on the opposite side, pulling tautly. Do the same on the remaining sides.

Return to the starting point and continue pulling and stapling the blankets in 12-inch segments on both sides of the center until you've worked to the corners. Miter the corners and staple.

Lay an unpatterned sheet or canvas on the floor; center the padded wood on top. Fasten as you did the blankets. If you're using canvas, dampen as described above.

WINDOW MATH

The key to making treatments that fit your windows perfectly is careful measuring and calculating. It's a challenging but critical job—a miscalculation of even an inch or two could leave you short yards of fabric. The instructions in this section will guide you.

Read the following sequence to get a feel for the entire process involved in making window treatments. Then you will be ready to measure your window and determine the yardage needed for your project.

■ *Choose your window treatment project* and the type of fabric from which you'll make it (see the next chapter for projects and pages 25–32 for fabric guidelines).

■ *Decide on the type of hardware* you'll use (for hardware information on your particular treatment, look in the project chapter starting on page 35). Purchase the hardware after you've measured your windows, but don't install it until your project is completed.

■ *Measure your windows* according to the instructions that follow and record the measurements in the spaces below the window diagram (shown at right). Guidelines are included to help you determine how much coverage you need above, below, and on the sides of the window.

■ *Fill in the window treatment work sheet* on page 22 to determine the yardage required. (The work sheet applies to all treatments except swags and cornices; you'll find measuring and calculating instructions for those treatments in the project section.) Fill in every box that applies; put a slash through those that don't.

■ *Purchase the fabric* and any trimmings and notions.

■ *Make the window treatment,* determine where on the window it goes, and install the hardware and treatment.

The Professional Approach to Measuring

No matter what your window treatment, carefully following a series of simple steps will produce a custom job. This approach is the one used by professionals, who work directly from the window measurements rather than from the hardware.

Taking window measurements

Measuring a window opening is straightforward (see drawing below). Be sure to use a steel tape when you make your measurements and write them in the spaces provided.

If your treatment will be mounted inside the window, you need measure only the width of the opening (A) and the length (B). But if your treatment will hang outside the opening, as most do, you'll have to determine not only the width and length of the opening but also the area to be covered to the left (C) and right (D) of the opening and from the top (E) and bottom (F).

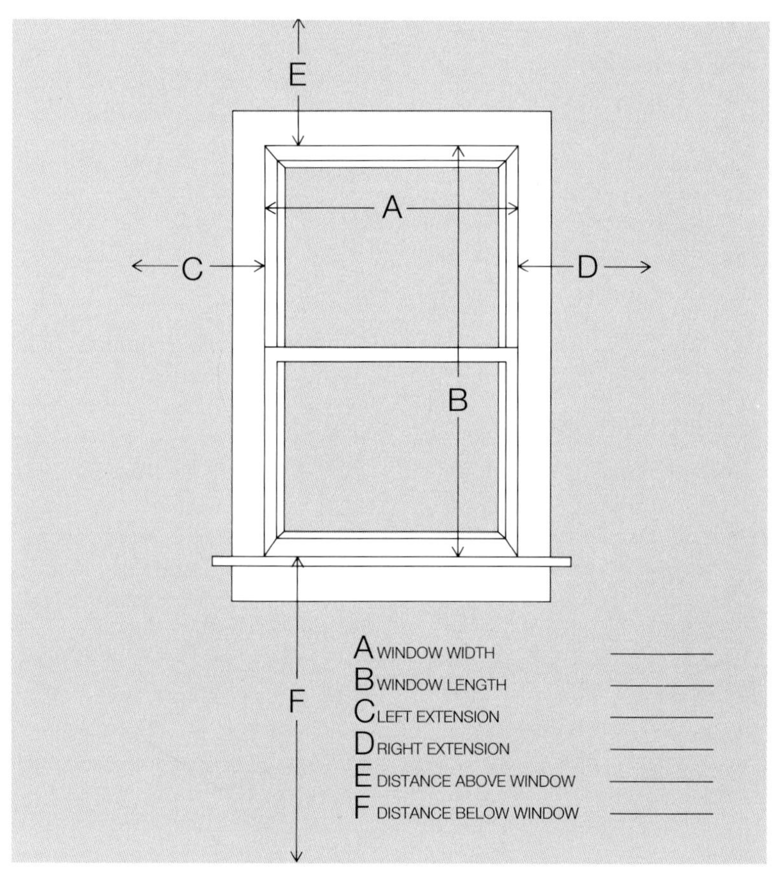

The amount of coverage around the opening will depend on the treatment's style and scale and whether it goes over or under another treatment.

Extensions depend on how much light control and privacy you want (see page 9). For treatments that, when opened, don't clear the window completely, extensions can range from 2 to 10 inches. For traversing draperies or curtains that open completely, see the information on stackback, at right.

Shades usually extend 1 inch beyond the trim board on each side or 2 inches beyond the window opening if there's no trim board. If treatments are being teamed, the extensions must be sufficient to allow the top treatment hardware to clear the undertreatment at the top and sides.

Distance above the opening is typically 5 inches, which prevents the top of the treatment from being seen from the outside. You may also begin a treatment just below the ceiling, at the bottom of crown molding, or halfway between the ceiling and window opening. Valances typically begin 8 inches above the opening.

Distance below the opening varies, depending on the window and the look you want. In general, treatments are most pleasing to the eye when they end in line with either the window or the floor. When the lower edge falls midway between, the effect is visually disturbing.

Apron-length treatments should end 5 inches below the opening so the hem doesn't show from the outside. Floor-length treatments should end ½ inch short of the floor (where there's a deep carpet, lay a piece of cardboard on top to use as a base when you measure). There are two exceptions: if you use an open-weave fabric or live in a particularly humid area, leave an inch between the treatment and the floor.

In double treatments, the inner treatment should be ½ inch shorter than the outer one, unless the inner treatment is a sheer; in that case, make it ¼ inch shorter.

Using existing hardware

If the hardware already on your windows is in good condition and meets your needs, you can reuse it. Take the following measurements and use them to fill in the window treatment work sheet on page 22.

1. Measure rod or pole from end to end for rod or pole size.

2. Measure from front of hardware to wall for return. For draperies, measure overlap when treatment is closed.

3. *For rod-pocket curtains or valances,* measure from top of rod or pole to where treatment will end; add desired depth of heading, if used. Add take-up allowance (see page 23, step 7). To ensure correct length, pin or baste hem, hang, and adjust as necessary. Then stitch final hem.

For tab curtains, measurement will depend on length of tab.

For draperies on a standard traverse rod, measure from top of rod to floor; subtract ½ inch. *For draperies on a decorative rod,* measure from bottom of rod or rings to where treatment will end. *For curtains on*

Allowing For Stackback

Curtains or draperies that open to expose the entire glass area—or most of it—need room to stack beyond the glass. This area is called the stackback.

For most fabrics you'll need to allow one-third the width of the glass area (or the area you wish to expose) for the stackback. For a two-way draw treatment, place half the stackback on each side of the glass. For a one-way draw, the entire stackback goes on one side. The drawings below illustrate stackback for two-way (at left) and one-way (at right) draw treatments.

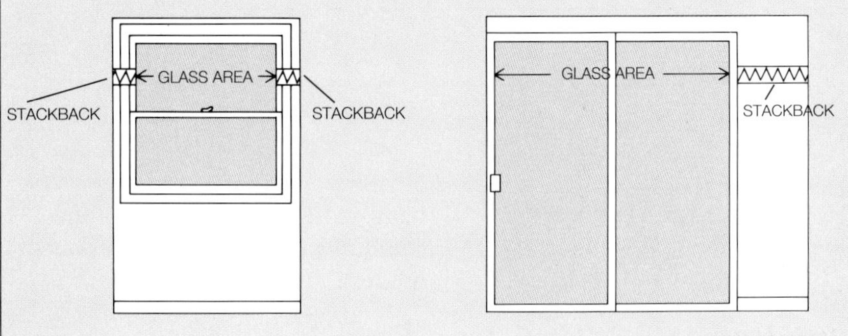

Window Treatment Work Sheet

NUMBER OF WIDTHS

Left Extension	Window Opening	Right Extension	Rod, Pole, or Board Size	Return + Overlap* + Return	Finished Width	Fullness	Side Hems	Total Width Required	Usable Fabric Width	Number of Widths
+	+	=	+	=	x	+	=	÷	=	

* For draperies only

TOTAL YARDS

Distance Above	Opening	Distance Below	Finished Length	Top Allowance	Hem	1" Ravel Allowance	Cut Length or Repeat Cut Length	Number of Widths	Required Fabric in Inches	Inches Converted to Yards	Yards Needed
+	+	=	+	+	+	=	x	=	÷	36 =	

LINING

Finished Length + 5"*	Number of Widths	Inches Converted to Yards	Yards Needed
x	÷	36 =	

* For curtains and draperies only; for other treatments, see individual projects.

RETURN SIZE CHART

Treatments on Window	Return Size*
1 Treatment	3½"
2 Treatments	5½"
3 Treatments	7½"

* May vary; check manufacturer's instructions.

rings, measure from bottom of rings to where treatment will end.

Yardage Calculations

Though the process may seem laborious, only careful calculating will ensure that you'll have sufficient fabric to complete your project. Using the window measurements you just made, follow the steps below, filling in the window treatment work sheet (above) as you go.

To determine allowances for fullness, hems, headings, and pockets, turn to the project you're making (see the next chapter) and look under "Calculating yardage."

Determining number of widths

Number of widths is arrived at by adding to the finished width—the width of the treatment as it will hang, closed, at the window—the amounts needed for side hems and fullness.

1. Add left extension (C), width of window opening (A), and right extension (D) to get rod, pole, or board size.

2. To that figure, add returns—distance from front of hardware to wall—and overlap.

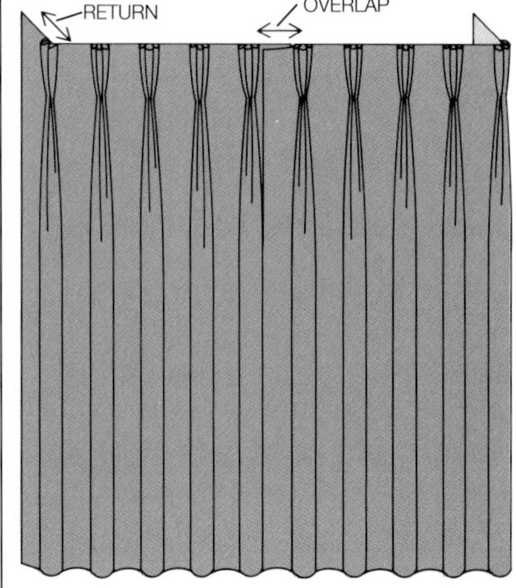

For return size for one or more treatments on a single window, see chart above. For traversing draperies only, add 1½ inches to each panel for overlap.

3. Multiply finished width by desired fullness, usually 2½ times for medium-weight fabrics and 3 times for sheers.

4. Add side hem allowances for total width required.

5. Divide total width by usable fabric width (less selvages and seams) to arrive at number of widths needed. Most fabrics and linings come 48 or 54 inches wide. If lining is a different width than fabric, calculate number of lining widths separately.

Sheers, often 118 inches wide, are meant to be fabricated without seams, with selvages running parallel to floor—"railroaded" is professional term; if you're using such a fabric, divide total width by 36 inches for yardage.

6. If number of widths determined in step 5 isn't a whole number, you must round it off. For any treatment with horizontal fullness, round off to next whole number if fractional part is ½ or greater (for example, 3.7 widths rounds off to 4); round off to smaller whole number if fractional part is less than ½. (Fabric width lost this way doesn't significantly reduce fullness.) If, however, your number is 1 plus any fraction, round up to 2; otherwise, you would split one width.

Most curtains and draperies open at center; each half of the treatment is called a panel. When you have two panels, divide total number of fabric widths in half to determine how many widths will make up each panel. For example, a pair of draperies that requires 5 widths of fabric will have 2½ widths in each panel. With draperies, never use less than half a width (anything narrower is difficult to pleat).

For Roman or roller shades, always round up to next full width.

Determining total yardage for unpatterned fabric

Total yardage is based on cut length (the finished length plus headings, hems, and a ravel allowance) multiplied by the number of widths. For information on calculating cut length and total yardage for patterned fabric, see at right.

Continue on the second line of the work sheet.

7. Add length of window opening (B) to distance above (E) and below (F) opening to arrive at finished length.

For curtains on flat rods, add ½ inch to finished length to allow for take-up (1 inch total on a sash curtain); for wide, flat rods, add 1 inch; for round rods, add diameter of rod.

8. To finished length add top allowance and lower hem allowance (see individual project for specific figures) plus a 1-inch ravel allowance to get cut length.

9. Multiply cut length by number of widths to get total length, in inches. Divide result by 36 to arrive at number of yards to buy. Add about 5 percent more (a minimum of a yard) for flaws.

Determining total yardage for patterned fabric

If you plan to use a fabric with a printed or woven design, you'll probably have to buy extra yardage since, with few exceptions, the repeats in the pattern must be matched when you make your window treatment.

The calculations are the same as those for unpatterned fabric up to the cut length figure. It's this measurement that needs to be adjusted to account for the pattern repeat on your fabric.

Must patterns match? A tiny pattern repeat—a dot or small floral pattern, for example—may not need to be matched for gathered styles, such as rod-pocket curtains. But don't let the size of the repeat fool you. Even the smallest patterns can look mismatched after the fabric has been seamed.

To see if small repeats will need matching, unroll enough yardage while you're in the store so you can lay two sections of the fabric side by side, selvages aligned. Matching motifs in the pattern, arrange the fabric sections to make the pattern continue across the two widths. Now shift one section slightly.

If you can't see any difference in the pattern, you can calculate total yardage according to the directions for unpatterned fabrics. But if the pattern fluctuates jarringly, base your calculations on the size of the pattern repeat (see below).

Measuring the repeat. To calculate the extra yardage for matching patterns, you must measure and record the height of the pattern repeat, called the vertical repeat.

■ *Vertical repeat.* Sometimes, the vertical repeat is printed on the selvage, but rather than rely on that figure, do the calculations yourself. Simply measure lengthwise from the same spot on one motif within the repeat to the same spot in the next identical motif. That distance is the vertical repeat.

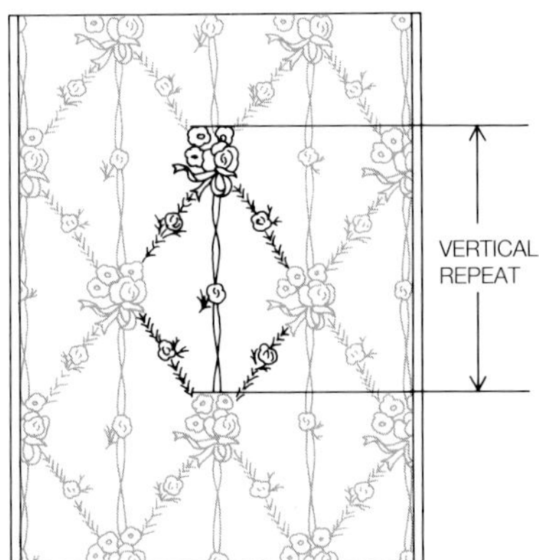

■ *Matching widths.* Most patterned fabric, particularly home decorating fabric, is designed so that horizontal repeats match at or just inside the selvages.

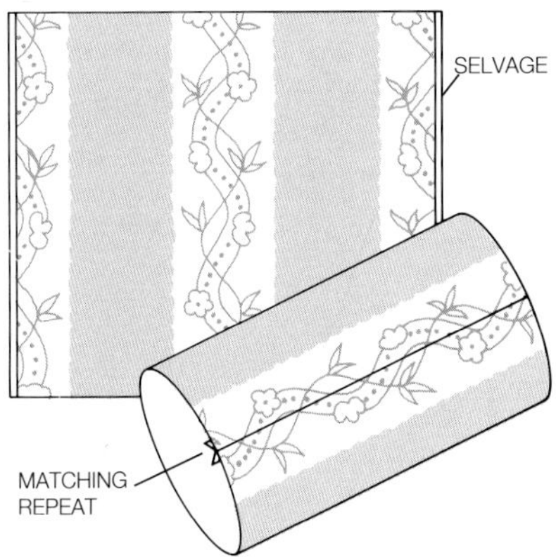

If the pattern matches farther into the width, you'll lose fabric when you stitch widths together. Check to see where patterned fabric matches before you buy it. If the distance from the inner edge of the selvage to the point where you'll stitch is more than an inch, don't buy the fabric.

Pattern placement. To make seams inconspicuous, repeats on each fabric width should match those on adjoining widths, repeats on each panel should match, and the pattern on all the windows in the room should also match.

You have some flexibility in where the pattern repeats fall on the finished treatment. The usual approach is to place full repeats at the lower hem and allow the top of the treatment to end anywhere on the repeat. If you place the top of a full repeat at the top of the treatment, the pattern will be lost in the pleats or gathers.

When treatments are different at the top or bottom, place a full repeat at the bottom of the longest treatment. On the shorter treatment, place the pattern so the eye reads the repeats at the same level in all treatments.

Repeat cut length and yardage calculations. To adjust the cut length figure for your pattern repeat and determine total yardage, follow the steps below.

1. Follow directions for steps 1–8 on pages 22–23.

2. Divide cut length measurement by vertical repeat size. Round up to next whole number if result contains a fraction to arrive at number of pattern repeats needed for each cut length.

3. Multiply that number by vertical repeat to determine, in inches, repeat cut length.

4. Multiply repeat cut length by number of fabric widths to get total length in inches. Divide by 36 to convert to yards.

Those few crucial inches. To make sure that pattern repeats will fall in the right place when your window treatment is made up, it's crucial to start measuring total yardage at the correct point in the pattern, rather than at the cut end of the yardage on the bolt. Usually, the cut end coming off the bolt is the bottom of the pattern, that is, the motifs run toward the center of the bolt. Study the pattern and look for arrows on the selvage to determine which way is up.

To have full repeats fall at the bottom of the treatment, unroll enough yardage to find the full repeat that would end at the lower fold. Measure below that for the hem allowance; begin to measure total yardage there.

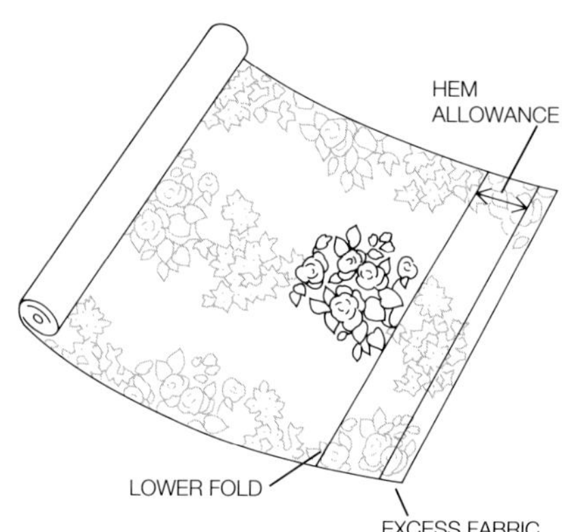

Why Line?

The benefits of lining window treatments far outweigh the added cost and time. A lining increases insulation, provides a greater degree of privacy, and extends the life of the window treatment by protecting the face fabric. It also improves the appearance of most window treatments by adding extra body.

Most lining fabrics for window treatments are made of cotton, cotton/polyester, or polyester/rayon blends. Sateen, a type of strong, tightly woven fabric, comes in white and a range of off-whites. Challis lining is lighter and less polished than sateen. Fade-resistant colored linings are also available, usually by special order. For a uniform appearance from the outside, use the same color lining for all window treatments.

For energy efficiency and light control, insulating, also called thermal, and blackout linings are laminated with vinyl or layered with foam acrylic (the effect is often referred to as flocked or sueded).

Interlinings, which resemble flannel, add body and insulating qualities to window treatments and effectively block noise and light. Because interlined treatments are heavy, they must be securely hung.

Choose a lining fabric that's compatible with the face fabric. Hold the two together to check whether they drape well as a pair. For a light, airy fabric, consider a separate lining drapery or curtain so it doesn't spoil the look.

Most lining fabrics are 48 or 54 inches wide. If the lining is the same width as the face fabric, the seams joining fabric widths will fall in the same place, and your calculations for lining yardage will be the same as for the face fabric; for lining that's narrower than the face fabric, you'll have to calculate yardage separately. Turn to the window treatment work sheet on page 22.

SELECTING & PREPARING FABRIC

Crucial to the success of a window treatment is the fabric from which it's made. But selecting a suitable fabric from the dizzying array available in fabric stores and sample books can be tiring and frustrating. That's why it's important to know what to look for in a fabric and how to prepare it so it will hang evenly and drape smoothly.

Shopping Tips

You'll probably find the best fabric selection, as well as the most knowledgeable salespeople, in stores that specialize in fabrics for home decorating. Other good sources include full-service fabric stores, which often have home decorating fabric sections, and interior decorators, who have access to fabrics from a number of sources.

Take your time. You'll be making a sizable investment in money and time, and the fabric you finally decide on is likely to hang in your home for years.

Looking at fabric

Choosing fabric involves more than simply picking a color or pattern that you like. Here are some guidelines.

Appearance. Undoubtedly, your first consideration as you browse among bolts of fabric will be appearance. When you shop, take along paint chips and fabric swatches to compare colors, textures, and patterns with those of your walls and furnishings.

But don't use this as a substitute for looking at a fabric sample in your home. Background color and lighting can alter a fabric's appearance, sometimes drastically.

You may be able to take an entire bolt of fabric home with you for a day or two. Or you may want to buy a yard or so and hang the fabric by the window you're planning to cover; this also allows you to test the fabric to see how easily it sews and whether it wrinkles readily or waterspots.

When you're buying fabric off the bolt, unroll several yards and gather one end in your hand. Does it drape well? Does it have the necessary weight for the treatment you're considering? Does the design or texture hold its own, without getting lost in the folds?

Stand back several feet so you can see how the fabric looks from a distance.

Grain. To drape properly, fabric must have as straight a grain as possible, that is, its crosswise threads should run perpendicular to its lengthwise threads.

If the fabric is warped (the term used to describe fabric when it has gone through the mill press crooked and is slightly bowed), the repeats may match but the panel will not be square once the widths are seamed. Also, the seams will not hang straight.

You can initially judge the straightness of grain just by looking closely at the crosswise threads near one selvage; they should be perpendicular to the selvage.

For a more reliable test, unroll about a yard and a half of the fabric and fold the cut edge to one selvage, forming a triangle. Grasp the diagonal fold and pull very gently. If the grain is straight, the fold should stretch slightly, without puckers or twisting, and bounce back when you let go. You should be able to feel the threads pulling in two different directions.

At the same time, check the fabric to see if it's likely to stretch out of shape as you work with it. Often, you can judge this just by pressing or pulling it gently with your hand as the fabric lies on a flat surface.

Be very careful when selecting a patterned fabric. In nearly every case, the print will be slightly off-grain, veering at an angle from the crosswise threads. Usually, the misalignment isn't severe enough to be noticeable. But if you're not sure, take a closer look.

To check patterned fabric, fold the fabric back a few inches, wrong sides together, aligning selvages. If the print runs evenly along the fold, it's fairly well aligned with the fabric grain. But if it wanders across the fold, the print is badly off-grain. Because it's virtually impossible to straighten the grain, don't buy any fabric whose pattern is off by more than ½ inch in each width.

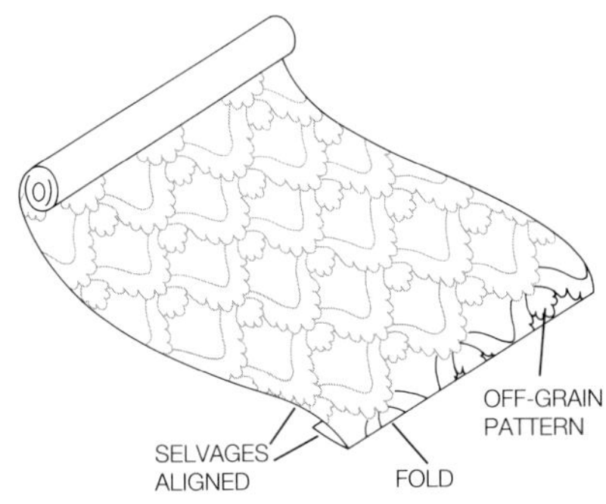

Practicality. Once you've narrowed your choices to several bolts of fabric you like, ask yourself some practical questions.

- *Will the fabric meet* your functional needs (see page 8)?

- *Is the fabric stable* or will it shrink or stretch during climatic changes? Loose weaves and fabrics with heavy weft (filling) yarns have a greater tendency to sag, shrink, or ripple from temperature and humidity changes than firmly woven fabrics with equal warp (lengthwise) and weft yarns.

■ *Is the fabric durable?* Some fibers, particularly synthetics, hold up better than others under repeated use and handling, an important point if the treatment will be opened and closed often. The tighter the weave or thread count (number of threads per inch), the stronger the fabric. Most home decorating fabrics have a higher thread count than fashion fabrics.

■ *Will the fabric resist fading?* Bright colors fade more than subdued colors and solids more than prints. The dye process used also determines resistance to fading. For natural fibers, vat-dyeing is best; for synthetics, solution-dyeing. Surface-dyed or printed fabrics have the least resistance to fading.

Finishes. Finishes added to fabrics prevent wrinkles and mildew and discourage insects. The most appreciated finishes, however, are those that repel stains and soil. Silicone finishes seal fibers, allowing you to wipe away water-base stains. Fluorochemical finishes repel both water and oil-base stains and last through several dry cleanings.

Check the fabric selvages or ask a salesperson for information on any finishes.

Cost. If you're on a tight budget, it's better to choose a less expensive fabric than to skimp on the yardage. Luxuriously draped, such a fabric can look as elegant as one that's much more costly.

You can save money by buying seconds—fabrics that have minor defects, though sometimes they're simply overruns. Some outlets sell seconds clearly marked as such; others mix seconds with first-quality fabrics and sell them at the same price. If you see flaws on a fabric and it's not marked as a second, ask about it.

When comparing prices for the same pattern, make sure the fabric is the same. Often, a fabric house will take a pattern used on a costly fabric and "downprint" it on a less expensive one. That's why you may see what looks like the same print priced differently at two outlets. The less expensive version may have a lower thread count; it may also be narrower, requiring more widths for the treatment.

When figuring total cost, remember to add in the lining and any trimmings.

Buying & preparing fabric

Once you've selected your fabric, buy all you need at one time (plus an extra ½ yard for sample pressing and stitching), and, if possible, buy it all from one bolt. If the amount of fabric left on a bolt is too little for your project, have a full bolt (or more, if needed) special-ordered. Though it will take extra time, it will ensure that color and pattern won't vary.

Checking color. If you're using fabric from two different bolts, hold the fabrics together and examine them in different light; look for any perceptible differences in the colors. If you can't see any, you're probably safe.

But to ensure the best results, don't mix fabric from different bolts at the same window. For example, if you have three windows, buy enough from one bolt to make treatments for two of them; then, from another bolt, buy all of the fabric for the third window. To do this, you'll need to think in terms of cut lengths instead of total yardage when the fabric is being measured. Mark the pieces so you won't mix them up while you're sewing.

Matching patterns. Check that any yardage cut from a second bolt begins at the correct point in the pattern (determine this the same way you determined the starting point for measuring the first cut length). Again, it's best to buy one bolt that has adequate yardage for your entire project.

Inspecting fabric for flaws. If you're buying fabric off a bolt, inspect the fabric carefully for flaws or inconsistencies in color or weave as the salesperson counts off the yardage. If you're not able to examine the fabric at the store, you'll need to look it over carefully before you begin measuring and cutting. Always buy 5 percent more fabric (a minimum of a yard) than you need to account for any flaws.

Preshrinking and cleaning your fabric. Though home sewers usually preshrink garment fabrics, it's not always a good practice when making window treatments. Preshrinking can wash away the fabric's protective finish; in addition to losing its fresh, crisp appearance, the fabric will lose some of the properties the finish provides.

As a rule, dry-clean treatments made from home decorating fabrics. A fabric labeled washable can be washed in warm water and dried in a machine; remove the treatment and hang before it's completely dry.

Choosing thread

All-purpose cotton-wrapped polyester, the most commonly used thread, works well for natural-fiber fabrics and blends. Readily available in a wide range of colors, it combines the best qualities of polyester and cotton; it's particularly good for heavy fabrics, because it's so strong.

Polyester thread is often used for synthetic fabrics, though it stretches slightly when sewn and, on tightly woven synthetics and blends, can sometimes cause puckering. To avoid this problem, loosen the tension on your machine or use cotton-wrapped polyester thread instead. You can't use polyester thread in a serger.

Colorless nylon monofilament thread is ideal for blind-stitching hems. And because it's clear, sturdy, and not bulky, it can be used on all types of fabric. Use number 6 nylon thread for machine-tacking pleats; for blind-stitching hems, use number 4.

When matching thread to fabric, choose thread that's a slightly darker shade than the fabric. For prints, match the thread to the predominant color. If you plan to zigzag seam edges together on an unlined treatment, match the thread to the wrong side of the fabric, which is often lighter than the right side.

For serging a lined treatment, use thread that matches the face fabric for the stay stitch (the main stitching) and off-white for the other spools. For an unlined treatment, the other threads should match the back of the face fabric.

How to Cut Lengths

To cut your fabric into the lengths required for your project, you'll need the cut length or repeat cut length measurement from your window treatment work sheet (see page 22); a large, flat work surface; a carpenter's square or a matte board; a straightedge; and a pencil or fabric marker. Use one of the following methods, depending on whether your fabric is unpatterned or patterned.

Unpatterned fabric

For fabric with no discernible pattern, you'll need to square off one cut end of the yardage; then you can begin cutting lengths.

Squaring off the fabric. Lay the fabric, right side up, on a flat surface.

A good way to create a cutting guide is to pull a crosswise thread, if possible. Cut into the fabric beyond the selvage near one cut end. Pick up one thread and pull it across the width. If the thread breaks, cut farther into the fabric next to the thread and pick it up again.

Pressing Professionally

Your iron will be your constant companion as you sew. Keeping the fabric wrinkle-free is well worth the hot and steamy time it takes. In addition to pressing seams, headings, and hems as you work, you may need to press your fabric before cutting it if it's wrinkled or folded.

Always test a sample of the fabric first to find out how much heat, moisture, and pressure from the iron are needed to produce smooth results without affecting the fabric's original character. Fabrics vary widely. Some, such as moiré, may waterspot and should be pressed with a dry iron; others, such as linen, need steam to smooth their wrinkles.

Safe ironing temperatures vary according to the fiber content of the fabric. If your fabric is a blend, let the most delicate fiber determine the heat level to use. For example, a 75 percent cotton/25 percent polyester blend should be pressed at a medium-low setting.

It's safest to start testing with a low temperature setting. Gradually increase the temperature until the fabric responds.

Keep these pointers in mind as you press:

- *Keep the iron's surface clean* by scrubbing it (when the iron is cool and unplugged) with a solution of baking soda and water.
- *A press cloth* helps prevent scorching and iron shine. Use a piece of muslin that's been prewashed to remove sizing.
- *For fussy work*—pressing ruffles, for example—set the temperature slightly lower than normal for the fabric.
- *Protect a heat-sensitive fabric* (any fabric that requires the "low" setting on the iron) by covering the ironing board with extra padding, such as flannel or another soft fabric.
- *Press seams lightly* on the wrong side, or the seams will show on the right side. Never press the right side if the fabric is embossed (moiré), glazed (chintz), or highly textured (damask or brocade).
- *Don't press folds too hard;* a razor-sharp crease is not desirable and may break down the fibers.

If you couldn't pull a thread, align the short blade of the square along one selvage of the fabric, close to one cut end, at the point where you'll be able to mark a line across the full width of the fabric. Using the other blade of the square as a straightedge, draw a line perpendicular to the selvage.

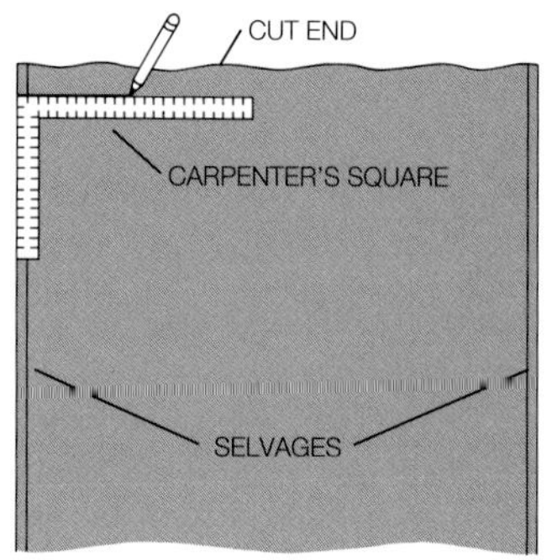

Remove the square and use a straightedge to extend the line 12 inches at a time to the opposite selvage. (Lining up your straightedge with the drawn line and extending the line only 12 inches at a time keeps it straight.) With the square, check that the line meets the opposite selvage at a perfect right angle. Cut along the line.

Cutting lengths. Measure down each selvage a distance equal to the cut length; clip selvages at this point. Using a straightedge, draw a line across the fabric between the clips. With a carpenter's square, check each corner for square.

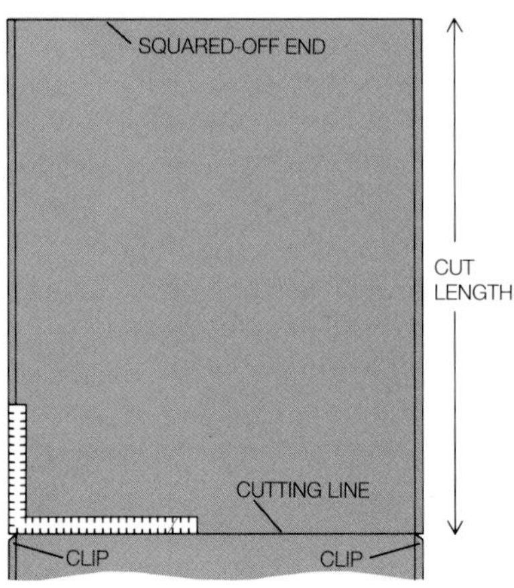

Cut along the line; this is the first squared-off length.

Continue to measure, mark, and cut until all lengths are cut. To avoid sewing one width to another upside down, make a small notch in the selvage at the lower right corner of each length.

Patterned fabric

Virtually all prints and some woven pattern repeats run slightly off-grain. When you cut print fabric for window treatments, follow the lines of the pattern rather than the grain of the fabric.

Once all the widths have been seamed, you can then square off the bottom edge.

Squaring off first end. On a flat surface, lay out several yards of fabric, wrong side up. At the cut end, bring the selvages together in the center, forming a tube. Look to see where the motifs—a flower, a leaf, a geometric shape—match.

Mark the matching points on each selvage where you started measuring total yardage when you bought the fabric. Unfold the fabric, turn it right side up, and, using a straightedge, connect the marks to make your cutting line. Cut along this line.

Cutting lengths. To cut the first length, follow the instructions for unpatterned fabric (see at left), substituting your repeat cut length figure for the cut length.

To cut additional lengths, tape the uncut fabric down, right side up. Lay the first cut length, right side up, on top, carefully positioning it so the motifs in the pattern repeats match perfectly.

Mark the cutting point on each selvage; remove the top piece and use a straightedge to mark the cutting line. Then cut along the marked line. Repeat for each successive length.

To avoid confusion when you sew widths together, mark pieces by making a small notch in the selvage at the lower right corner of each length.

Squaring off joined widths. If, after joining widths, the top and bottom edges aren't square, you'll need to square and trim the bottom. (The top edge will be squared when you measure and mark the hem, the finished length, and the top allowance.)

With the panel right side up, lay a carpenter's square along the selvage on the short edge. Mark a line perpendicular to the selvage; extend the line 12 inches at a time to keep it straight. You'll have a thin triangular segment left at the bottom.

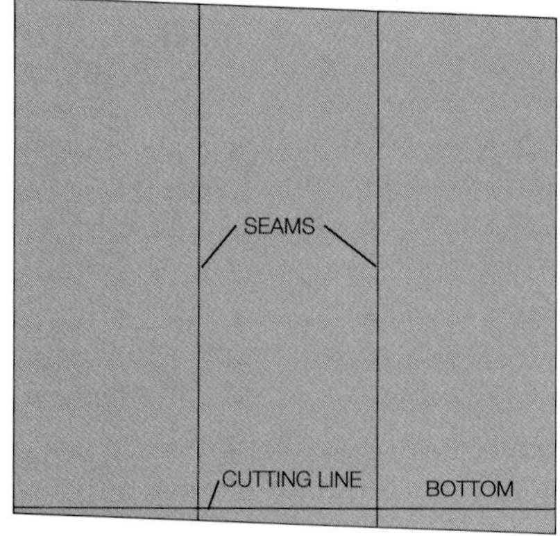

Before you cut on the marked line, be sure you'll have enough fabric at the top. With some patterned fabrics, the repeat cut length will provide the extra fabric you'll need to square the bottom and still give you the required inches at the top.

Measure the hem allowance plus the finished length from the marked line. From this point, measure the top allowance and check to be sure that it doesn't go beyond the shorter edge. If it does extend beyond, you'll need to decrease slightly the depth of your hem and/or heading.

FABRIC COLLECTION

Fiber, whether natural or man-made, is the raw material from which fabric is made. Often, two or more different fibers are blended in one fabric to bring out the best aspects of each fiber.

Natural fibers

Natural fibers are favorites with home sewers because they're beautiful and easy to handle.

Cotton, the most versatile of all fibers, dyes well and blends easily with other fibers. Stable, durable, and relatively inexpensive, cotton comes in a wide range of weights, textures, colors, and patterns. Decorator cotton fabrics are usually treated to resist wrinkles and soil. Cotton is susceptible to fading and sun rot and is flammable.

Linen is strong and smooth, with a stiffer feel and appearance than cotton. A relatively expensive fiber, it's somewhat resistant to mildew and sunlight. Linen wrinkles easily unless blended with a more stable fiber, such as cotton or polyester, and can also stretch in humidity unless blended with a nonabsorbent synthetic. Linen burns easily.

Silk, a very costly fiber, drapes beautifully and dyes in jewel-like hues. Because it's weakened by sunlight, consider silk only for windows that receive little direct sun, even when the treatment is lined. Silk will burn unless treated.

Wool is a strong, resilient fiber that's most stable when blended with synthetics. It drapes well and has superior insulating qualities. Wool will fade and rot in the sun; it also attracts moths and shrinks unless treated. Wool does not burn easily. It's fairly expensive.

Synthetic fibers

Man-made fibers, whether used alone or blended with natural fibers, lend strength, durability, and stability to fabrics.

Acetate drapes well and possesses a silklike luster. Often blended with cotton or rayon for formal fabrics, such as moiré, acetate is by nature a weak fiber, fading and changing color over time. Acetate burns and melts. It's relatively inexpensive.

Polyester is resilient, sunfast, and wrinkleproof. It also resists mildew and doesn't shrink. Blending polyester with natural fibers produces a more stable fabric. A moderately priced fiber, polyester melts when exposed to high heat.

Rayon, which is derived from cellulose, drapes nicely and blends well with other fibers. It's often mistaken for a natural-fiber fabric. Vulnerable to sunlight, rayon is inherently weak and will shrink, stretch, and burn if not treated; it also wrinkles easily. It's a moderately priced fiber.

Sateen (at left) gets its softness and luster from smooth filling yarns that float across the surface. Medium-weight sateens are suitable for draperies and curtains, lighter weights for linings.

Antique satin (two at center), perhaps the most common formal drapery fabric, comes in a wide range of patterns. Usually a blend of rayon and acetate, this fabric may be slubbed or striped.

Shantung (at right), once made only of silk, is now made of synthetic fibers as well. Heavy slubs in the filling yarns create texture and luster.

Chintz (at left, above) is a closely woven, crisp fabric with a shiny glaze on the right side. It's widely available and comes in florals, stripes, and solids. All cotton or a cotton/polyester blend, chintz should be dry-cleaned only; washing removes the sheen.

Cotton and cotton/linen prints (at right, above) are popular with home sewers because they come in such a variety of colors and patterns. Their smooth, firm weave makes them suitable for treatments that require crisp, medium-weight fabrics.

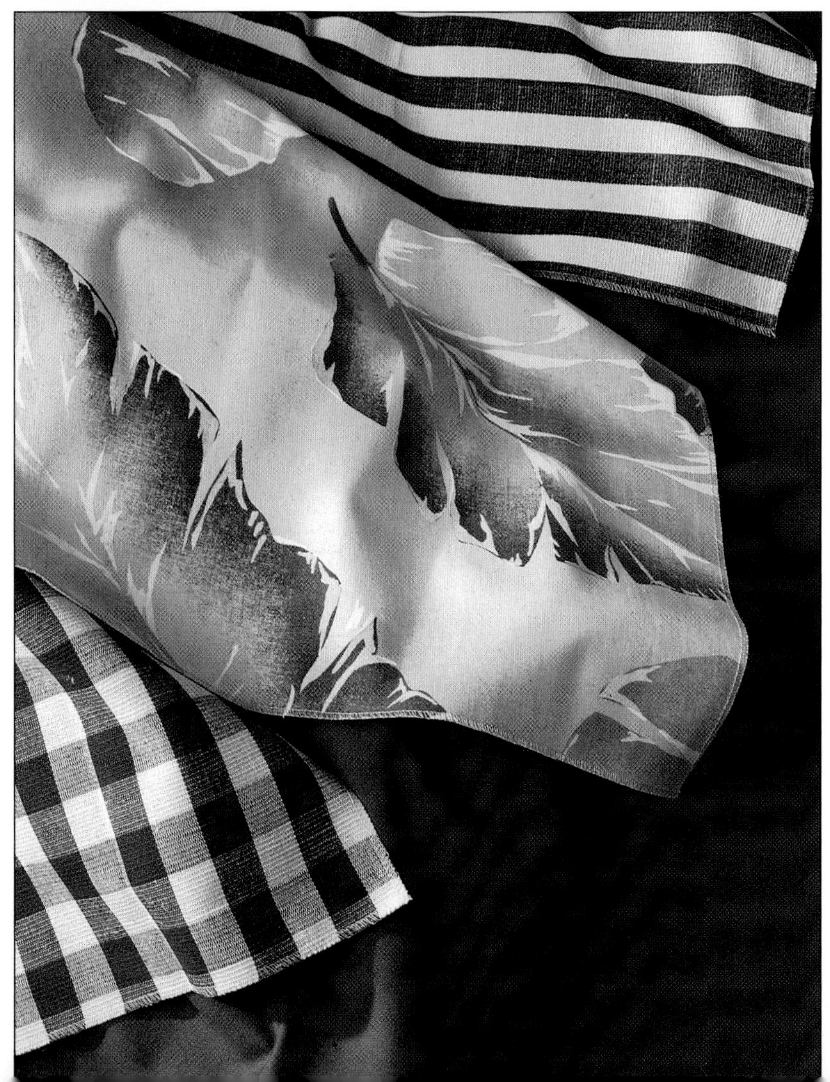

Canvas (at left, center, and top) is a durable, coarsely woven fabric made of cotton, linen, or blends. A heavy fabric, canvas can be used for shades as long as the fabric is pliable. Duck is a medium-weight version of canvas.

Sailcloth (at bottom), the lightest weight of these fabrics, has the same qualities as canvas and duck and is suitable for casual Roman and roller shades, tab curtains, pleated valances, and upholstered cornices.

Damask (three at left, above) is a type of jacquard, a fabric known for intricately woven, three-dimensional patterns. Damask combines two weaves, one lustrous and one matte, to create complex patterns. Made of silk, cotton, or rayon/acetate blends, damask is often reversible. One-color damasks are often described as tone-on-tone. Brocade (at far right), also a jacquard, has intricate raised patterns that resemble embroidery. Traditionally silk, brocade now comes in a variety of fibers.

Casement fabrics, with their uneven yarns and loose weaves, filter light and create interesting textures and patterns. Cotton, linen, and polyester are common fibers used in casement fabrics.

Lace (at left), available in a wide variety of patterns and weights, is ideal for romantic, airy treatments, such as tapered valances and one-way or café curtains. Used flat, laces display their patterns; gathered, they filter light and provide privacy.

Sheers (at center and right) include voile, batiste, organdy, and dotted Swiss. Usually made of polyester, sheers are often combined with other treatments for daytime privacy and light control. Many have one embroidered or finished selvage that's meant to be used as the hem.

Moiré (at left and center) displays a distinctive watermark pattern created by pressing rollers on taffeta or faille. Cotton/acetate moiré blends have that sought-after sheen, but they expand in humid conditions. Cotton moiré is less lustrous but more stable.

Faille (at right), a ribbed fabric, is soft and drapable. Made of silk, rayon, acetate, or blends, faille possesses a faint luster.

Sewing window treatments is about as simple as sewing can be. Here are a few tips to speed your work.

Using your machine. Guide the fabric as you sew, placing one hand behind the presser foot and the other in front. Without pulling, try to keep the fabric smooth and flat. Since you don't need an extremely strong seam, use relatively long stitches.

A tape trick. Masking tape can help keep seams and hems straight and parallel. For a seam guide, measure to the right of the needle a distance equal to the seam allowance. On the machine, place a strip of tape with the left edge at this point, parallel to the stitching line. As you sew, keep the seam allowance aligned with the tape's edge.

For a hem guide, measure ⅛ inch less than hem width; tape. This way, the stitches will run just inside the inner fold of the hem.

Trimming selvages. If your fabric is unpatterned, trim the selvages before joining widths. With some patterned fabrics, the pattern matches so close to the selvages that seam allowances will be reduced if you trim the selvages first. In this case, match the pattern and seam the widths (see below); then trim the seam allowances, cutting away part of the selvages.

On loosely woven fabrics, don't trim the selvages; clip them every 2 inches.

Joining and trimming fabric widths. For a neat appearance, full widths of fabric should hang at the leading edge of a treatment. Place partial widths on the sides. For draperies, a partial width must be at least half a width. On a single panel treatment, center a full width.

For unpatterned fabric, join widths with ½-inch seams. For a perfect match on patterned fabric, lay widths right sides together with selvages aligned. Fold back the top layer at the edge until the pattern matches exactly. Press the fold lightly.

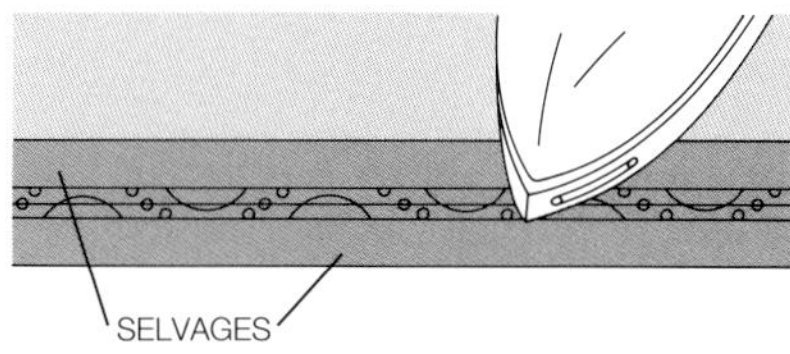

Unfold the top selvage, pin the layers, and stitch on the fold.

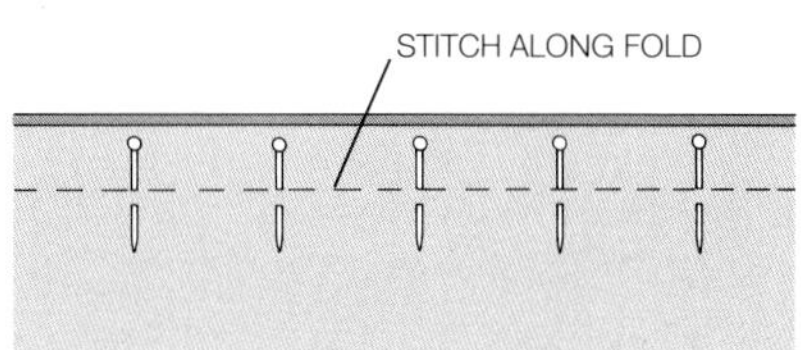

After seaming widths, trim the panel to the total width required.

Finishing seams. It's not necessary to finish the seams on a lined window treatment. Just press them open after stitching.

On unlined treatments or ravel-prone fabrics, finish the seams by zigzagging the edges together ⅛ inch from the stitching line. Trim the excess fabric close to the stitching and press the seam allowances to one side. If you serge the seams, press the seam allowances to one side.

Making hems. Both side and lower hems are doubled to make the treatment hang better. For most projects, the lower hem goes in before the side hems.

Weights sewn into the lower corners of each panel and at each seam make full-length panels hang straighter. Either purchase covered weights or enclose weights in small pockets of fabric.

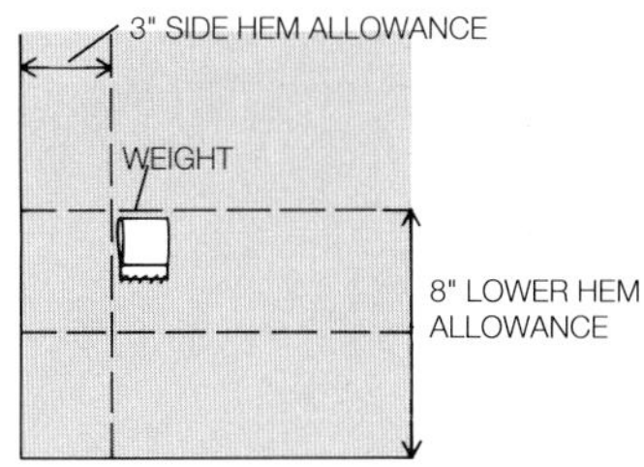

To make a double hem, turn up the lower edge of the hem allowance (8 inches for most treatments), wrong sides together, and press. Turn the raw edge in to meet the pressed fold and press again. Hem by hand or machine close to the second fold.

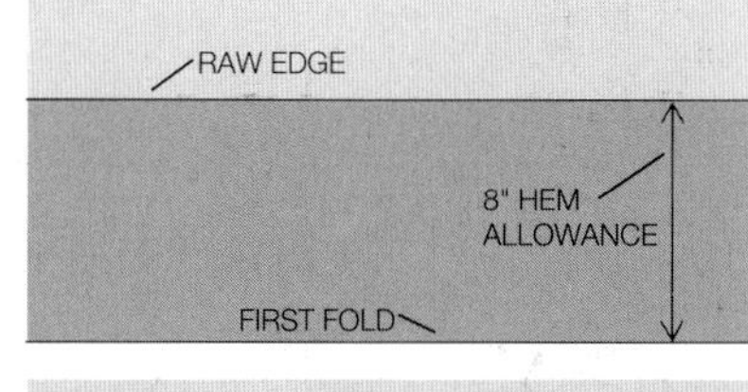

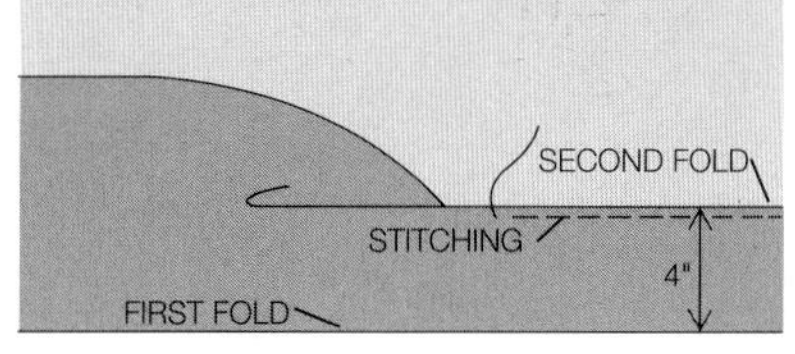

Repeat for the lining, if used, making the first fold 4 inches deep.

For 1½-inch doubled side hems, make the first fold 3 inches deep. Hand-stitch the 1½-inch opening closed at the lower edge.

If a fabric has a loose weave or is particularly heavy, it may stretch after hanging. Instead of stitching the hem, baste it and hang the treatment for a week or so. Then adjust the hem and stitch.

Window Treatment Projects

Whether your goal is to sew a pretty pair of curtains for the kitchen or fabricate sophisticated swags for the living room, the benefits of making your own window treatments are well worth the time and effort involved. Not only will you save money, but you'll also be able to create a truly original design.

Peruse the myriad of projects on the following pages. Once you've decided on one, make it your own with your choice of fabric, hardware, and trimmings. The result? A one-of-a-kind window treatment that suits your windows perfectly and reflects your style and creativity.

Making window treatments takes time and effort, but most projects aren't difficult. All you need are patience and some basic sewing skills.

Curtains

Taffeta rod-pocket curtains with a matching rod sleeve lend quiet sophistication to a formal scheme. On-the-edge banding and bow tiebacks accent the treatment. Elbows on the 3-inch pole allow the curtains to return at the sides.

DESIGN: GLENNA COOK INTERIORS

DESIGN: RUTH SOFORENKO ASSOCIATES

Canvas rod-pocket curtains are gathered on a wood pole. Cotton brush fringe trims the leading and lower edges. A simple rod sleeve visually unifies the panels.

DESIGNERS: CHARLOTTE TAYLOR AND STEPHANIE SMITH

The window coverings in this softly hued bedroom (above) are hung without rings or other hardware. Long tabs (left) are simply knotted onto the whitewashed wooden rod.

For a nursery, curtain panels in a vintage Peter Rabbit print tie back with colorful plaid bows that also form the cheerful valances. Roman shades fashioned of sheer dotted-swiss fabric add softness.

DESIGN: SANDY SHARP, COLOR WORKS. WINDOW TREATMENT: SIERRA CUSTOM DRAPERIES

Wide-rod valance with deep headings caps stationary rod-pocket curtains on flat curtain rods. The tiebacks, gathered sleeves of fabric stiffened with strips of crinoline, repeat the shirred effect.

Separate borders trim the leading edges of country French café curtains and the lower edges of matching pencil-pleated valances. The curtains hang from brass rings on café rods. The soft headings on the valances are achieved with shirring tape.

DESIGN AND WINDOW TREATMENT: SUSAN LIND CHASTAIN, FINE SEWING WORKSHOP

Patterned rod-pocket sheers—one hanging straight, the other held to the side by a twining ivy holdback—veil the view and echo the stylized wallpaper design.

Panels of scrim—a sheer woven fabric—make a gauzy backdrop for a fish-patterned valance in primary colors. The panels hang from the valance supports.

DESIGN AND WINDOW TREATMENT: MARTHA'S SEWING WORKROOM

French doors and sidelights are treated to sheer hourglass and sash curtains. Sash rods hold the treatments close to the frames. Rounded rosettes embellish the tailored tiebacks.

DESIGN: JUDITH APPEL, APPEL DECORATING DEN
WINDOW TREATMENT: DELTA PI DESIGN

Outside-mounted fan curtain decorates the small arched window in a wood door; the textured sheer fabric complements the door's warm tones. Pouf valances on either side balance the treatment.

HOW TO MAKE

Curtains

Rod-Pocket Curtains ■ Curtains on Rings ■ Unlined Rod-Pocket Curtains ■ Rod Sleeve ■ Bishop's Sleeve Curtains ■ Sash Curtain ■ Hourglass Curtain ■ Fan Curtain ■ Tab Curtains ■ Knotted & Bow-Tied Tabs

Today's curtains offer a myriad of style possibilities, from elegant full-length panels tied up in poufs to simple sash or tailored tab curtains. The projects offered here reflect the diversity of curtain styles and looks. Best of all, you'll discover that curtains are easy—and fun—to make.

Choose a fabric that's in keeping with the style of the curtain and the look you want to achieve. Crisp fabrics create a generous fullness on rod-pocket styles. For sash, hourglass, and fan curtains, sheers and lace are traditional. Tab curtains call for a fabric with enough body to hold its shape as tabs and panels.

A Look at Hardware

Your curtain hardware needs to complement the fabric you're planning to use, as well as the style of the curtains and room where they'll hang. Look for hardware in discount and department stores, home improvement centers, and large fabric stores that specialize in home decorating fabrics.

Don't be surprised if you see the same rods, poles, finials, and holdbacks again and again. Most curtain hardware available to the home sewer is manufactured by just two or three companies. For something more unusual, order through an interior decorator or look for shops specializing in decorative hardware.

For examples of curtain hardware, see below.

Rods & poles

Most rods are adjustable; most wood poles are not. Generally, both rods and poles rest in brackets attached to the wall or window frame.

Rounded *café rods,* available in a range of sizes, styles, and finishes, are designed for café or full-length curtains that are gathered on the rod or hung on rings.

Flat curtain rods hold lightweight rod-pocket curtains or valances that are either gathered on the rod or hung on oval rings or hooks. If you're using a sheer fabric for rod-pocket curtains, look for clear rods that won't show through the fabric. Flexible clear rods are used for fan curtains.

For corner or bay windows, choose adjustable hinged flat rods.

Double flat rods are designed for double curtain treatments, such as crisscross ruffled curtains or a curtain with a valance. Because the

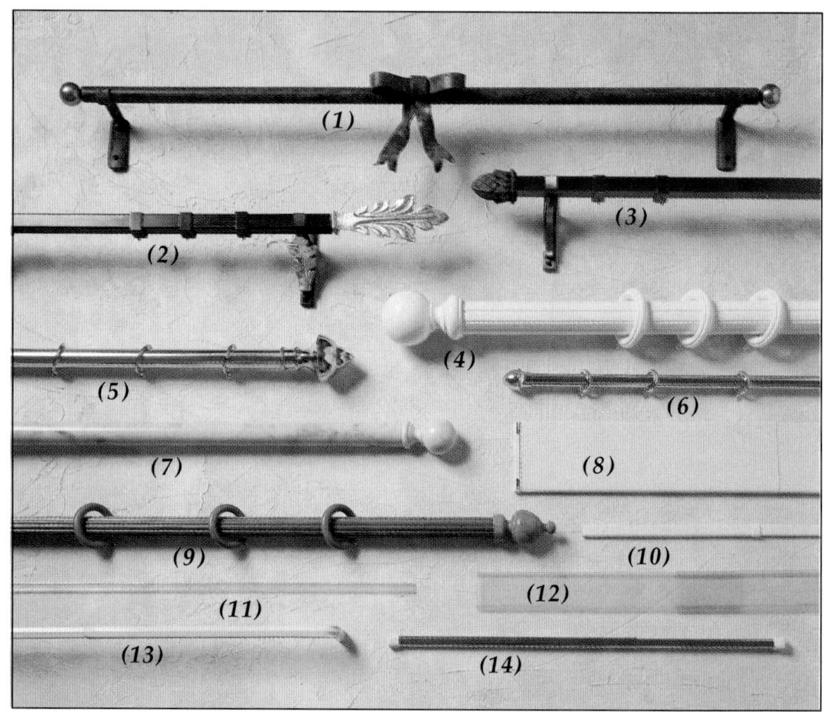

Collection of curtain hardware shows (1–3) decorative rods, (4) wood pole, (5) brass rod, (6) brass café rod, (7) marbleized pole, (8) wide rod, (9) wood pole, (10) sash rod, (11) flexible clear rod, (12) clear wide rod, (13) flat rod, and (14) tension rod.

return on the outside rod is longer than that on the inside rod, you can hang one curtain directly in front of the other.

Available in 2½- and 4½-inch widths, *wide rods* require an extra-wide rod pocket, adding visual depth and interest to traditional curtain styles. A gathered sleeve on a wide rod makes a simple valance.

You can also stack two wide rods or use a narrow decorative rod, which you leave uncovered, between two wide rods. These rods also come with corner connectors for use in bay windows.

Sash rods attach with shallow brackets to the top and bottom of the window frame. Flat or round, sash rods are commonly used on French doors and casement windows to hold sash or hourglass curtains.

Oval or round *tension rods* have a spring-tension mechanism to hold the plastic- or rubber-tipped rod within the window frame. Often, they're the only practical choice for recessed windows. Support a width greater than 36 inches with cup hooks.

Wood poles, used with decorative brackets and finials, lend distinction to rod-pocket or tab curtains. With the addition of matching wood rings, these poles are also suitable for flat curtain panels.

Accessories

Many of the following accessories can be found where curtain hardware is sold. Look for hooks, weights, and rings in the notions section of fabric stores.

Finials, decorative end pieces, attach to the ends of poles that aren't mitered or finished with elbows.

Small and unobtrusive, *wood sockets* hold wood poles in inside-mounted installations. The sockets are screwed into the frame.

To increase the length of the rod return, attach *extension plates* to ordinary brackets.

Concealed tieback holders project from the wall to prevent fabric tiebacks from crushing the curtains. They adjust to match the rod projection.

Decorative holdbacks, available in a wide variety of styles and finishes, act like fabric tiebacks, holding curtain panels back from the window.

Rope or *cord tiebacks* come in many different materials, colors, and lengths. They're often used to form poufs in bishop's sleeve treatments.

Use plain or stylized *cup hooks* to hold fabric tiebacks at the sides of the window. A plain cup hook is also used to anchor a fan curtain at its base or to support a sash curtain rod on a door.

Weights, inserted in a hem or tacked in the lower corners of a treatment, are designed to make the treatment hang straight and to prevent lightweight panels from billowing or drawing up at the seams.

Rings for curtains generally have little eyelets on the bottom. They can be sewn to the top edge of a curtain, but you'll have to remove them before dry-cleaning the treatment. If the eyelets are large enough, you can use them in combination with 1-inch *drapery hooks;* the hooks, which are pinned to the back of the curtain heading, slip through the eyelets.

Valance hooks, designed for stationary treatments, fit over rods.

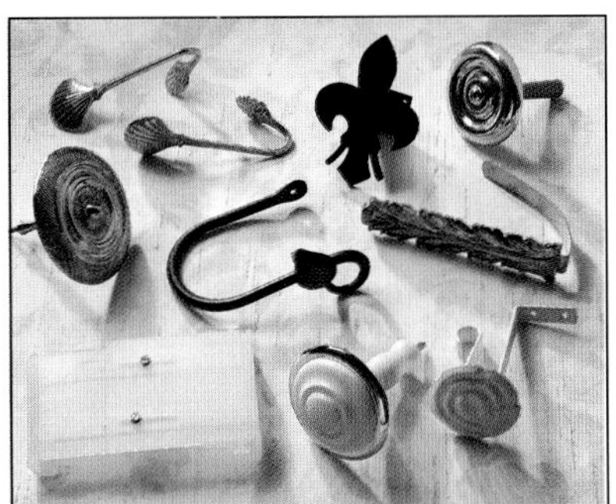

Curtain accessories include decorative holdbacks and concealed tieback holders (at lower left).

Hardware Installation

Mount your hardware only *after* you've completed your project. Follow the manufacturer's instructions for best results.

Where you'll install the hardware depends on the coverage you planned for when you calculated your yardage. Referring to your window treatment work sheet (see page 22), find the side extensions you allowed and mark those points at the window opening.

If your curtain has no heading, the top of the rod goes at the distance above the window opening noted on your work sheet. For a curtain with a heading, subtract the heading size from the distance the treatment extends above the opening. For example, if you planned to cover 5 inches above the window opening and your heading measures 2 inches, the top of the rod goes 3 inches above the opening.

To determine where to position the brackets, place the rod in a bracket and measure the distance from the top of the rod to the top screw hole in the bracket; add this distance to the previous figure and mark this point at the top of the window opening.

Install one bracket, attaching the top screw at the point you just marked. Place one end of the rod in the bracket and have a helper hold up the other end in its bracket. Before attaching the second bracket, check the rod with a carpenter's level. When the rod is level, mark the top screw hole for the second bracket and screw it to the wall.

If you're not able to screw into studs, use expansion bolts, also called molly bolts. Plastic anchors are good for lightweight treatments or when you're installing concealed tieback holders.

Rod-Pocket Curtains

Simple and speedy to sew, this basic curtain style can be shirred on a rod or pole or attached to rings or hooks. This project is good for beginners—calculations and stitching are as easy as can be.

You can make rod-pocket curtains with or without a heading; the instructions cover both. A heading above the pocket forms an instant ruffle as the rod is inserted. This curtain is lined; for an unlined version, see the facing page.

A simple trick for softening the top of a rod-pocket curtain is to sew a heading twice as wide as you would like it to appear at the window. Then, after slipping the rod or pole through the pocket, you pouf the heading by separating the two thicknesses.

Rod-pocket chart. The rod pocket must be large enough to accommodate the rod or pole comfortably and to allow the curtain to gather on the rod. Following are rod-pocket sizes for standard rods; use the appropriate pocket size when calculating yardage.

Rod type	*Rod diameter*	*Pocket size*
Sash or flat	Up to ¾"	1½"
Round	Up to 1" Up to 1½" Up to 2" Up to 3"	2¼" 3¼" 4¼" 5½"
Wide	2½" 4½"	3½" 5½"

Calculating yardage. Measure your window and fill in the window treatment work sheet (see pages 20–24). For most curtains, a fullness of 2½ times the finished width is best; if your fabric is a sheer, multiply finished width by 3. You'll need extra fabric for tiebacks (see pages 56–57).

Use the following allowances in your calculations:

	Fabric	*Lining*
Lower hems	8"	4"
Side hems	6" total	None
Top	2 x pocket + 2 x heading (if used)	None

Rod-pocket curtains step-by-step

1. ***Choose and prepare*** face fabric and lining, joining fabric widths as described (see pages 24–33). Press seams open.

2. ***Fold and stitch*** lower hems (see page 33).

3. ***On right side*** of face fabric, measure from lower edge a distance equal to finished length and mark with pins every 4 inches across panel.

4. ***With right sides together,*** lay lining on face fabric so lower edge of lining is 1 inch above lower edge of face fabric. Starting from leading edge, align first seam of face fabric with first seam of lining.

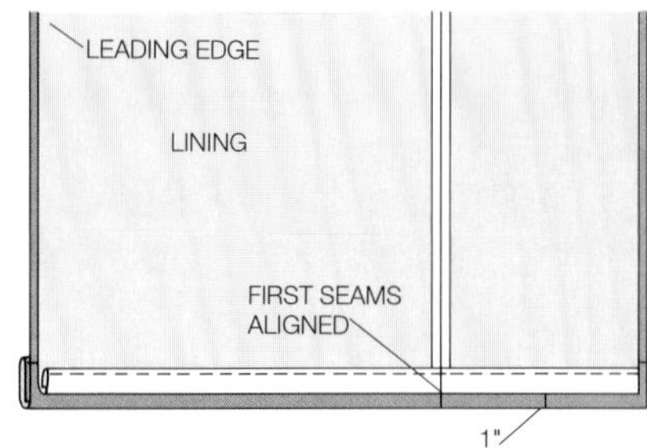

5. ***Trim face fabric*** or lining as necessary so lining is 3 inches narrower than face fabric at each side.

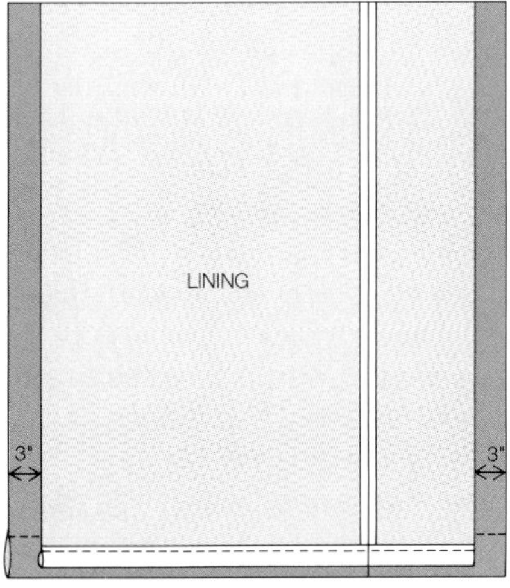

6. ***Trim lining*** so upper edge meets pin-marked finished length line on face fabric. Then, on face fabric, measure and mark proper top allowance (2 times pocket plus 2 times heading, if used) above finished length line. Trim ravel allowance.

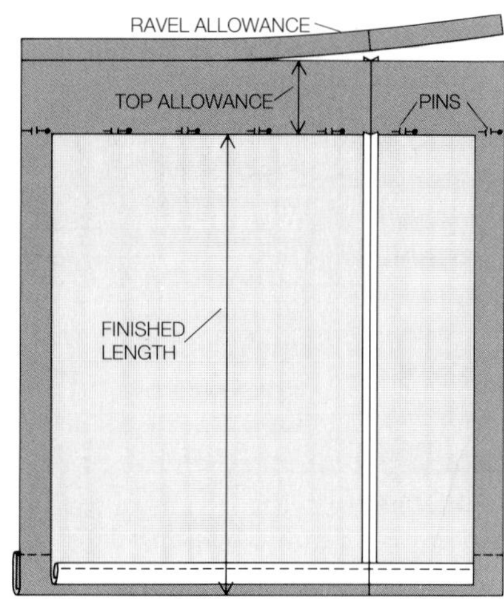

7. ***With right sides still together,*** pin lining to face fabric so edges are aligned at one side (lower edge of lining should still be 1 inch above lower edge of face fabric).

8. ***Beginning at lower edge*** of panel 1½ inches from side, stitch entire length of face fabric.

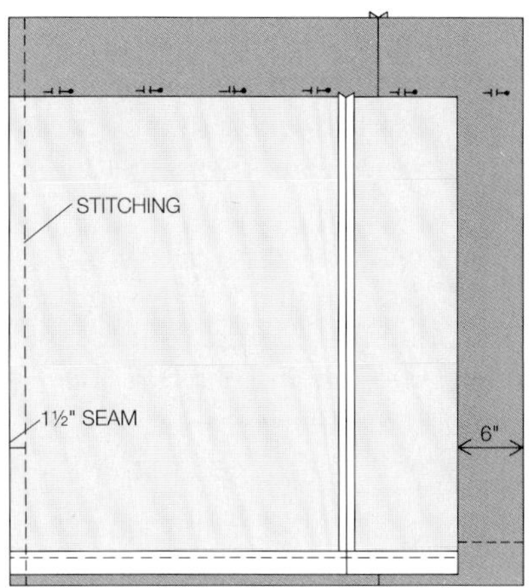

Repeat on other side. Press seam allowances toward face fabric.

9. ***Turn panel*** right side out, lining up, so an equal amount of face fabric shows at each side; press.

10. ***Fold top edge*** of fabric, wrong sides together, along finished length line; press. Remove pins. Turn raw edge in to meet pressed fold and press again. Stitch close to second fold. For heading, if used, stitch again from top fold a distance equal to heading depth; press.

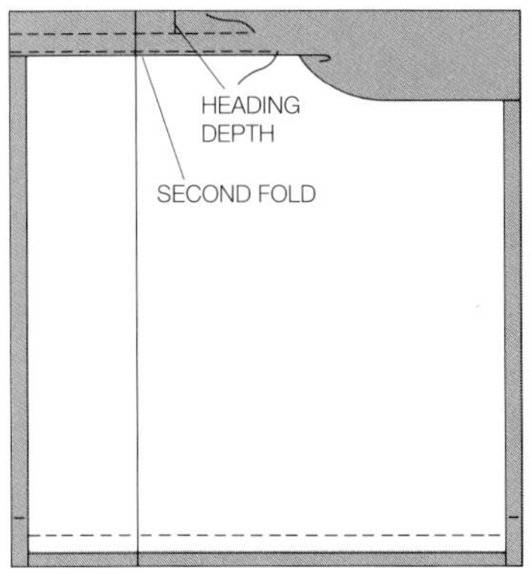

11. ***Slip rod through pocket*** between back two layers of fabric, gathering fabric evenly.

Curtains on Rings

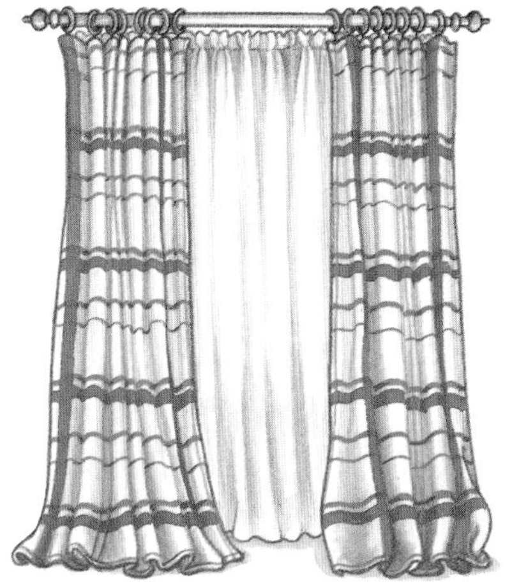

These simple curtains are made just like rod-pocket curtains without headings and pockets; leave a 3-inch top allowance. Sew rings to the top edge; or pin 1-inch drapery hooks along the edge and insert them into eyelet rings.

1. ***Follow steps 1–10,*** "Rod-pocket curtains," facing page. After stitching close to second fold, stitch again ½ inch from top edge to stabilize edge.

2. ***Divide width*** of each panel by 5 to find approximate number of spaces needed; round off to nearest whole number. Divide width by whole number of spaces for space size. To determine number of rings or hooks needed, add 1 to number of spaces.

3. ***At each end*** of panel, sew a ring to top edge; or insert point of a drapery hook just below lower row of stitching. Space additional rings or hooks according to your calculations.

4. ***Slip rings on rod;*** or insert hooks into eyelet rings and slip rings on rod.

Unlined Rod-Pocket Curtains

Unlined rod-pocket curtains are a simple, lightweight treatment.

1. ***Calculate yardage*** as for "Rod-pocket curtains," facing page, omitting lining.

2. ***Choose and prepare fabric,*** joining fabric widths as described (see pages 25–33). Finish seams and press to one side.

3. ***Fold and stitch*** lower hem (see page 33).

4. ***Fold and stitch*** side hems (see page 33).

5. ***On right side*** of fabric, measure from lower edge a distance equal to finished length; mark with pins every 4 inches across panel.

6. ***Measure and mark*** proper top allowance (2 times pocket plus 2 times heading, if used) above pin-marked finished length line. Trim ravel allowance.

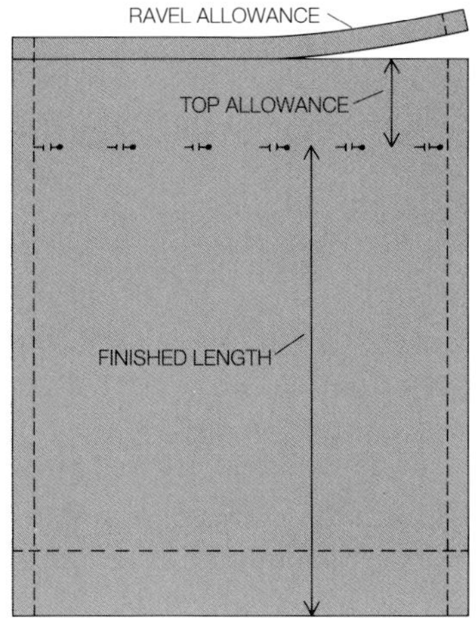

Continued on next page

7. *Follow steps 10–11,* "Rod-pocket curtains," page 45, to fold and stitch top and install on rod.

Rod Sleeve

When rod-pocket curtains don't meet in the center but just hang at the sides of the window, a simple sleeve that fits on the rod between the panels visually bridges the gap and completes the treatment.

If the panels on either side have a heading, give the rod sleeve the same heading. For a custom look, you can add another heading below the rod pocket.

Calculating yardage. The following method of determining yardage gives even fullness across the rod.

1. Multiply rod length by 2½ and subtract finished width (flat measurement) of side panels. Divide remainder by usable fabric width to arrive at number of widths needed for sleeve.

2. Cut length (up and down measurement) is equal to 2 times rod pocket plus 2 times heading depth for each heading, if used, plus 1 inch. For patterned fabric, calculate repeat cut length (see page 24). Try to match pattern horizontally on sleeve and curtain pockets.

3. Multiply cut length or repeat cut length by number of widths and divide by 36 for yards needed.

Rod sleeve step-by-step

1. *Join fabric widths* as described on page 33. Press seams open.

2. *Make a ½-inch hem* on each end. Fold fabric in half lengthwise, right sides together. Pin and stitch, making a ½-inch seam. Turn right side out. Center seam at back and press.

3. *For a single heading,* if used, stitch from top fold a distance equal to heading depth; for a double heading, if used, stitch upper and lower edges a distance equal to heading depth.

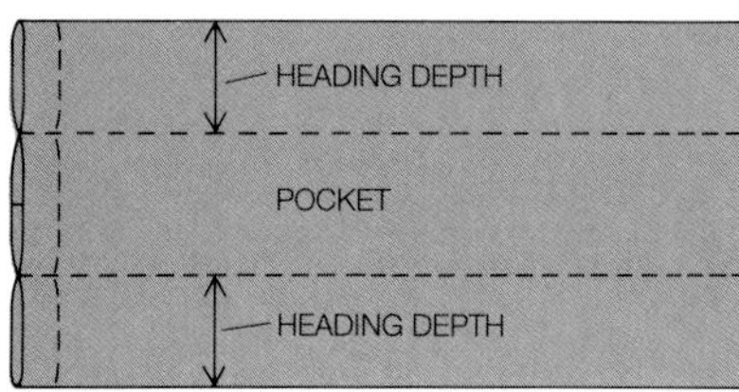

4. *Slip rod* through pocket, gathering fabric evenly.

Bishop's Sleeve Curtains

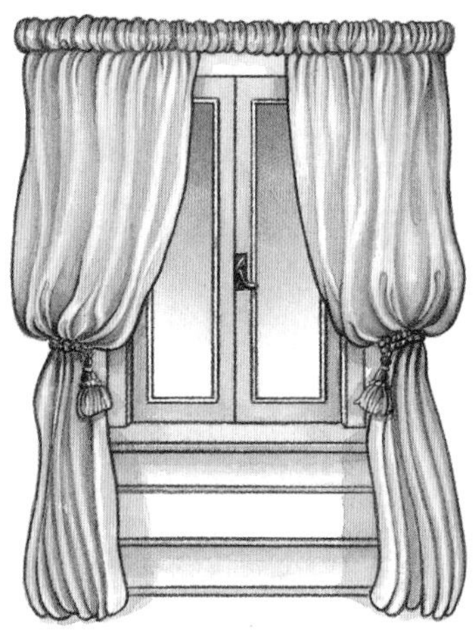

This elegant curtain style is achieved by adding extra length to curtain panels and tying them up in poufs. You can also blouse the fabric by attaching swag holders and drawing the fabric through, arranging and fanning it into a pouf.

You make this style just as you would rod-pocket curtains, but you need more fabric. To tie up each pouf with a decorative cord, add 8 inches to the length of each panel; to cover the cord, add 12 inches. If you want the panels to puddle on the floor, add another 8 to 12 inches to their length.

Once the panels are hung, lift each to determine where to place the pouf. Use enough cord to cinch the panel and attach to the rod support at the top.

Sash Curtain

Gathered and stretched on two rods, an unlined sash curtain is a good choice for a casement window or a French door—the lower rod keeps the curtain in place when the window or door is opened or closed. A sash curtain can be made with or without headings.

Calculating yardage. Measure your window and fill in the window treatment work sheet (see pages 20–24). For most sash curtains, a fullness of 2½ times the finished width is best. If your fabric is a sheer, multiply the finished width by 3.

Use the following allowances in your calculations. Remember that you need a pocket and a heading, if used, at both top and bottom. Refer to the chart on page 44 for pocket size.

Top and bottom	2 x pocket + 2 x heading (if used)
Side hems	6" total

Sash curtain step-by-step

1. ***Choose and prepare fabric,*** joining fabric widths and finishing seams as described (see pages 25–33).

2. ***Fold and stitch*** side hems (see page 33).

3. ***With wrong sides together,*** turn up lower edge a distance equal to bottom allowance; press. Turn raw edge in to meet pressed fold and press again. Stitch as you did side hems; press. For bottom heading, if used, stitch from lower fold a distance equal to heading depth.

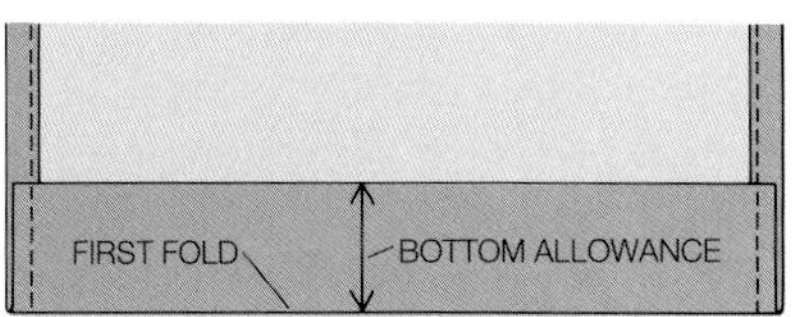

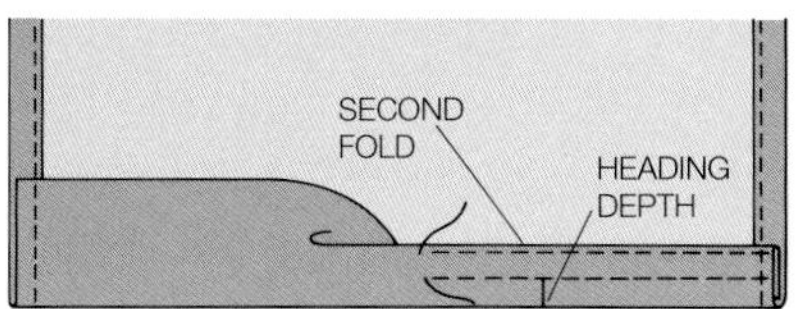

4. ***On right side*** of face fabric, measure from lower edge a distance equal to finished length and mark with pins every 4 inches across panel.

Continued on next page

All the Trimmings

When it comes to adding a trimming to a window treatment, the most difficult question is not "Should I?" but rather "Which one?" Described here are just a few of the countless possibilities.

Trimmings. When choosing trimmings, keep in mind the scale of the treatment. Always compare fabric and trimming samples to see how the colors and textures blend. Trimmings can be costly; carefully estimate the length you'll need.

Braid, a 1½- to 3-inch-wide flat border with two finished edges, is often used as mitered banding on the edges of treatments (see page 53).

Applied along the bottom of a valance or down the leading edge of a curtain, *fringe* imparts texture and interest. Bullion fringe is made of looped, twisted cords; brush fringe has a cut edge. Tassel and ball fringes create visual rhythm and emphasize a treatment's contours. Fringe can be sewn into the seam or, if you want to see the upper edge, topstitched to the fabric.

Tassel tiebacks, available in a variety of sizes, styles, and colors, lend grandeur to sophisticated curtains, draperies, or full-length cascades. A tassel's "skirt" can be made of cut or looped yarn or bullion fringe.

Sewn into seams, *welt* and *piping* define a treatment's shape and are especially effective on curved or angled edges, such as the lower edge of a scalloped valance or the inner edges of cascades. You make welt by encasing plain cord (¼ to 1¼ inches in diameter) in a continuous seamed bias strip of fabric. To determine the width of the strip, wrap a scrap of fabric around the cording and pin close to the cord. Trim fabric ½ inch from the pins, unpin, and measure the strip. Piping is like welt without the cord.

Shirred welt requires a strip twice the length of the cord. As you stitch, don't crowd the cord and stop every 12 inches or so to push the fabric strip toward the starting point, forming gathers.

Decorative cord or *rope,* with a sheen or matte finish, can be made into simple tiebacks or looped across the top of a treatment. To sew cord into a seam, choose the type that comes zigzagged to a seam allowance (often called lipped cord).

Gimp, a narrow braid with looped or scalloped edges, trims the edges of treatments and finishes the insides of cornices.

Attaching trimmings. Most trimmings can be stitched directly to fabric. If stitching would cause puckering, glue may be the best choice. Most glues are dry-cleanable; some are also washable. Test first to make sure the glue doesn't run or come through the trimming.

Some trimmings can be fused to fabric with plain or paper-backed fusible webbing. Use the plain type for fabric banding or flat trimmings; the paper-backed webbing works best with bulkier trimmings, such as gimp or braid. Follow the manufacturer's instructions carefully, cutting the webbing a bit narrower than the trimming so it won't melt onto your iron. To keep the webbing from shifting, pin it in its proper position, sticking pins straight down into your work surface every 4 inches.

5. *Measure and mark* proper top allowance (2 times pocket plus 2 times heading, if used) above pin-marked finished length line. Trim ravel allowance.

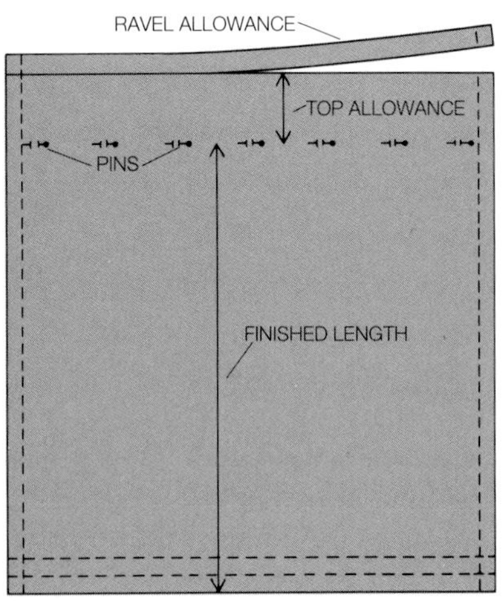

6. *Fold top,* wrong sides together, on finished length line and press; remove pins. Turn raw edge in to meet pressed fold and press again. Stitch close to second fold. For heading, if used, stitch again from top fold a distance equal to heading depth.

7. *Slip rods* through pockets between back two layers of fabric, gathering fabric evenly. Install top rod, then bottom rod so curtain is taut.

Hourglass Curtain

A cousin to the sash curtain, the hourglass style evokes a range of decorating moods. When made of fabric with a small, stylized print, the look is country classic. Choose a diaphanous sheer, and the mood is one of quiet elegance.

Because of the tension on the curtain, the curtain must be at least a third longer than the rod length. (If, for example, your rod is 24 inches, the curtain must be 32 inches or longer.) Any curtain closer to square than this won't stay in the hourglass configuration.

Calculating yardage. Measure your window and fill in the window treatment work sheet (see pages 20–24). For most hourglass curtains, a fullness of 2½ times the finished width is best; if your fabric is a sheer, multiply finished width by 3.

Use the following allowances in your calculations. Remember that you need a pocket and a heading, if used, at both top and bottom and additional fabric for a tieback and, if desired, a rosette. Refer to the chart on page 44 for pocket size.

Top and bottom	2 x pocket + 2x heading (if used)
Side hems	6" total
Stretch allowance	4"

Hourglass curtain step-by-step

1. *Choose and prepare fabric,* joining fabric widths and finishing seams as described (see pages 25–33).

2. *Fold and stitch* side hems (see page 33).

3. *Fold fabric panel* in half crosswise, lining up side hems, and press fold at center. Fold panel lengthwise and press again at center. Mark center point where folds intersect with a safety pin or a fabric marker.

4. *Measure from center point* toward top a distance equal to half finished length; measure and mark same distance from center point toward bottom. Mark with pins every 4 inches across panel.

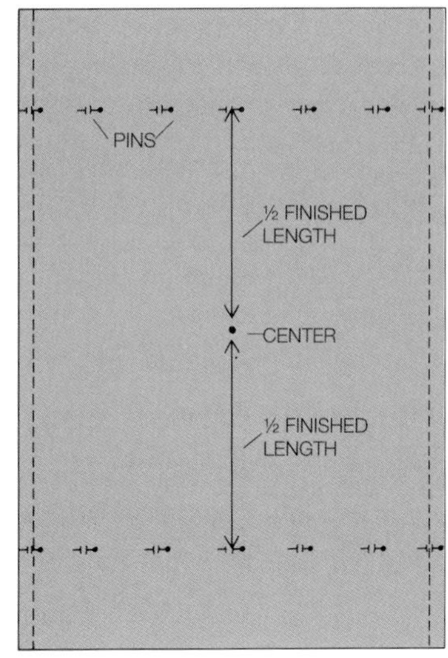

5. *At side hems,* add 2 inches to pinned lines at both top and bottom and mark these points. (Finished length of panel is now 4 inches more at edges than at center.) At top and bottom, strike a gentle curve from marks at side edges to center to mark new finished length line.

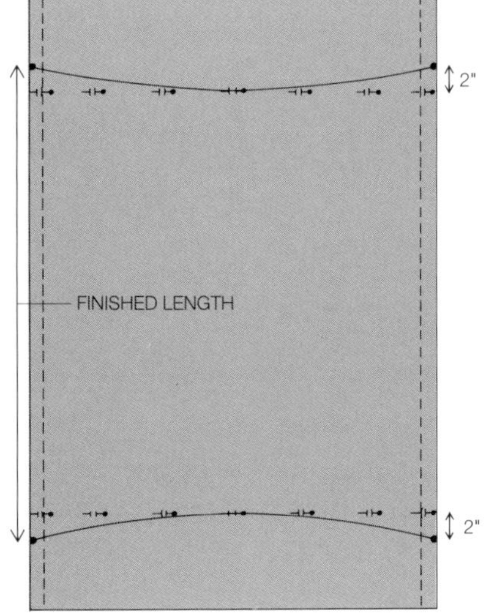

6. *Using first curve* as a reference, strike another curve at top and bottom a distance equal to top and bottom allowance (two times pocket plus two times heading, if used). Cut on second curved lines.

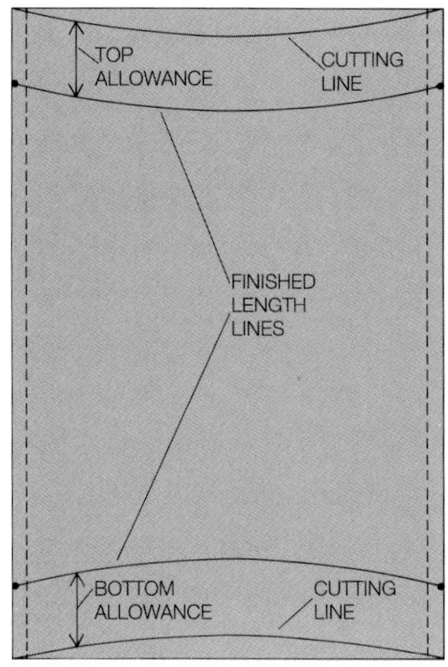

7. *Fold top,* wrong sides together, on finished length line and press; remove pins. Turn raw edge in to meet pressed fold and press again. Stitch close to second fold. For heading, if used, stitch again from top fold a distance equal to heading depth. Repeat for lower pocket.

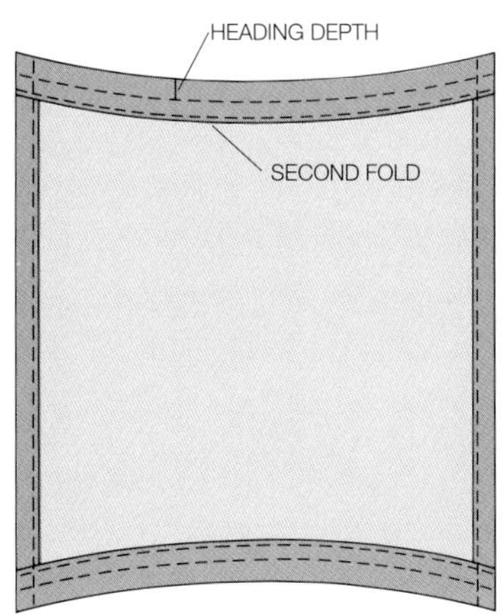

8. *Slip sash rods* into rod pockets between back two layers of fabric, gathering fabric evenly. Mount curtain, installing top rod first and then bottom rod so curtain is taut in center.

9. *To determine size* of tieback, pull panel into hourglass shape at center and tie with string or scrap fabric (make sure side hems are straight and ends of rods are covered). Add 2 inches for overlap to arrive at finished length of tieback and add 1 inch for seam allowances. For finished width, choose either 2 or 3 inches; double that figure and add 1 inch for seam allowances.

10. *Cut a rectangle* to those dimensions; also cut a strip of crinoline equal to finished width less ¼ inch and to finished length.

11. *With right sides together,* pin and stitch tieback lengthwise, making a ½-inch seam. Turn right side out and center seam on back; press. Slip in crinoline. Turn ends inside and hand-stitch closed. Wrap tieback around curtain and pin or stitch in place on back.

12. *To make rounded rosette,* see page 126.

Sheers & Laces

For generations, sheer and lace fabrics have quietly graced windows, subduing bright light, protecting furnishings, and ensuring daytime privacy. The following pointers will help you shop wisely and attain professional results when sewing sheers and laces.

- *Many sheers and laces* come 118 inches wide. Because they're meant to be railroaded, that is, fabricated with selvages running parallel to the floor, they don't require seams to join widths. Some also come prefinished on one side, which is used as the bottom hem. Otherwise, remove the lower selvage.

- *With narrower sheers and laces,* you'll need to join widths. To finish seams, see page 33.

- *Hemming lace* is challenging, especially if the lace is loosely woven, so hand-baste hems. To keep the presser foot from catching the lace, put masking tape across the prongs.

- *Make all your cuts* absolutely straight. On a sheer, pull a thread as a guide (see page 27); on a patterned sheer or lace, use the pattern as a guide. When cut edges are folded into a hem, be certain they're flush with the crease.

- *Because sheer fabrics* are usually finely woven, they pucker more easily than other fabrics. When you sew, use a slightly longer stitch than usual.

- *If a lace fabric* is fairly heavy, it may sag near the selvages, which tend to be tightly woven. Cutting off ⅛ or ¼ inch from each selvage will allow it to relax. Or notch the selvage every few inches.

Fan Curtain

A fan curtain is actually a type of sash curtain, but on a fan curtain the lower hem is gathered and pulled through a ring. Choose a lightweight or sheer fabric; when possible, railroad the fabric.

Don't attempt this style if your window's radius is greater than 36 inches—you'll have too much fabric at the center. Also, because a fan curtain relies on equal tension from the center out to the curve, you'll get the best results on half-circle windows. Don't use a fan curtain on an elliptical window if the difference between the window's height and the radius at the base is greater than 6 inches.

Hang the curtain on a flexible clear rod supported with brackets. You'll also need a drapery ring with an eyelet to form the rosette and a cup hook to secure the ring.

Calculating yardage. Refer to the drawing below as you measure.

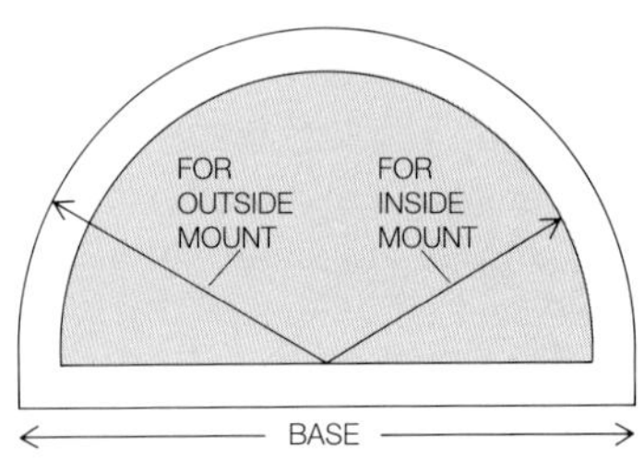

1. For number of fabric widths, measure window's finished width, or curve, and multiply by 2 for fullness; add 6 inches for side hems. For fabric that runs vertically, divide figure by usable fabric width. If railroading fabric, divide figure by 36 for yards needed.

2. To find finished length, divide base of window by 2 and add 3 inches to allow for rosette; for an outside mount, add coverage beyond opening. For top allowance on an inside or outside mount, add 5 inches total for a 1½-inch pocket and a 1-inch heading (a heading is recommended even on an inside mount to ensure a snug fit). Add 6 inches for hem at base.

3. For fabric that runs vertically, multiply cut length by number of widths and divide by 36 for yards needed.

Fan curtain step-by-step

1. ***Choose and prepare*** fabric, joining fabric widths and finishing seams as described (see pages 25–33).

2. ***Fold and stitch*** side hems (see page 33).

3. ***With wrong sides together,*** turn up lower hem 6 inches and press. Turn raw edge in to meet pressed fold and press again. Stitch close to second fold.

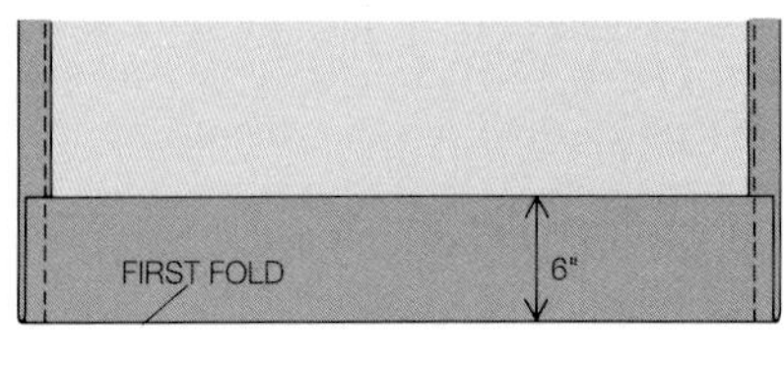

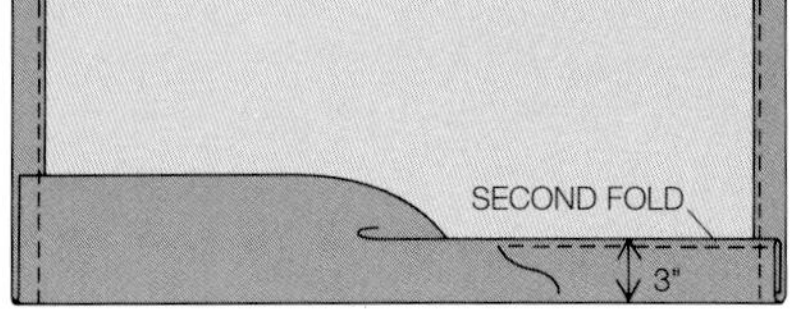

4. ***On right side of fabric,*** measure from lower hem a distance equal to finished length plus 3 inches for finished length line; mark with pins every 4 inches across panel. Measure and mark 5 inches beyond pin-marked line. Trim ravel allowance.

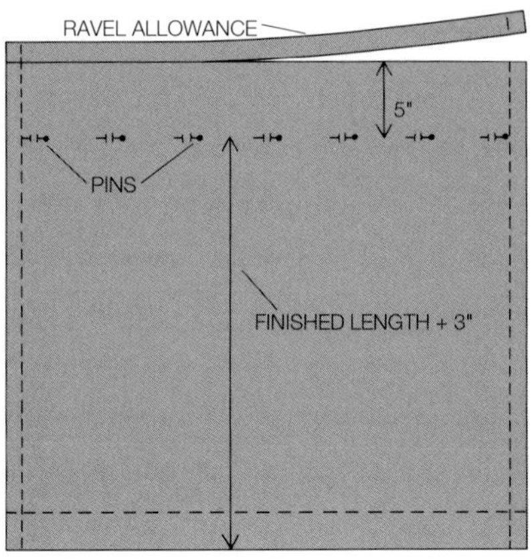

5. ***Fold top,*** wrong sides together, on finished length line and press; remove pins. Turn raw edge in to meet pressed fold and press again. Stitch close to second fold. For heading, stitch again 1 inch from top fold.

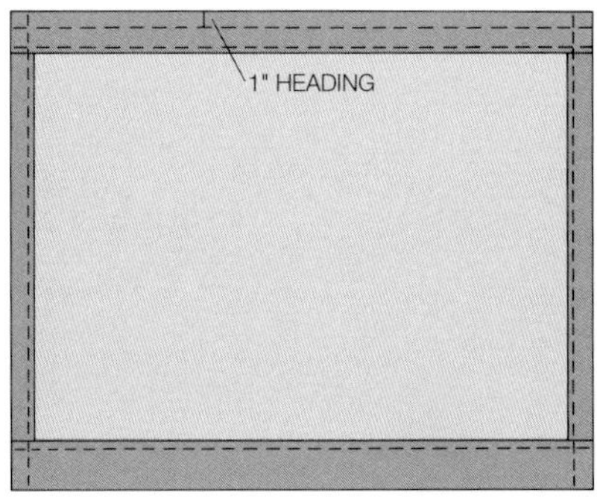

6. ***Slip rod through pocket,*** adjusting gathers evenly, and mount. To make rosette, gather lower hem and pull through ring.

7. ***For an outside mount,*** screw in a cup hook below center point of window. Turn hook sideways, slip eyelet over, and turn hook down. For an inside mount, screw hook into sill; slip eyelet over hook.

Decorative Edgings

Custom finishes, such as ruffles and banding, lend sophistication and style to ordinary window treatments.

Ruffles

Along the bottom of a shaped valance or down a curtain's leading edge, ruffles provide texture and interest.

Measuring and calculating yardage. Cutting ruffle strips crosswise on the fabric is the most economical method, though some patterns call for lengthwise strips. When you're working with a plaid or stripe, consider bias-cut ruffles.

1. Taking into account scale of treatment and fabric, determine finished width of ruffle (most are 1½ to 3 inches wide). *For a single-thickness hemmed ruffle,* add 1 inch (½ inch for seam allowance and ½ inch for a narrow hem) to finished width to arrive at cut width. *For a folded ruffle,* a more common style, double finished width and add 1 inch for two ½-inch seam allowances.

2. Measure edges for ruffle and multiply by 2 or 2½ for total length. Subtract half the cut width of a strip from usable fabric width and divide length by this figure to arrive at number of crosswise strips needed.

3. Multiply cut width of each strip by number of strips and divide by 36 for yards needed.

Making ruffles. You'll need to piece fabric strips to make ruffles.

1. ***Cut strips as needed.*** To join, arrange strips, right sides together, at a right angle and seam on bias. Trim seam allowance; press open.

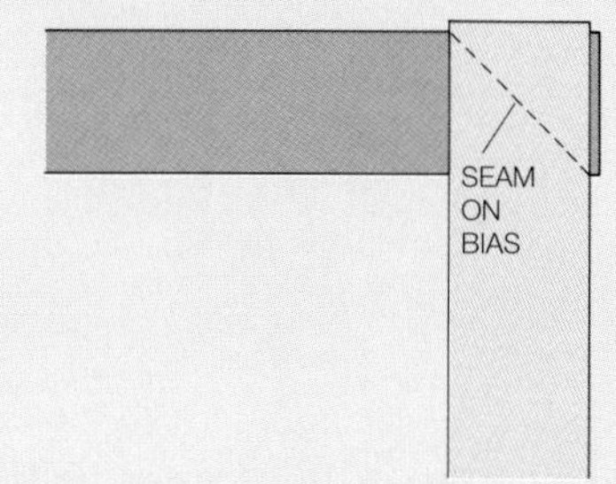

2. ***For a hemmed ruffle,*** fold each end in ½ inch, wrong sides together, and press; turn raw edge in to meet pressed fold and press again. Machine-stitch ends. Repeat along one long edge.

For a folded ruffle, fold pieced strip in half lengthwise, right sides together, and stitch across ends, making ¼-inch seams. Turn right side out and press in half lengthwise.

3. ***Zigzag*** (use wide stitch) over a cord (buttonhole twist or crochet cotton) about ⅜ inch from raw edge. Back-stitch over cord at one end to secure.

Attaching ruffles. If you're using a hemmed ruffle on an unlined treatment, you serge the ruffle and panel together or attach the ruffle using a mock French seam.

To attach a folded ruffle to the leading edge of a lined rod-pocket curtain, you'll need to trim the face fabric side hem allowances even with the edges of the lining.

1. ***To make lower hems,*** to measure and mark finished length line, and to trim top edge of face fabric and lining, follow steps 2–4 and step 6, "Rod-pocket curtains," page 44.

2. ***Divide ruffle strip*** and edge to be ruffled into fourths, marking off each section with a pin. (Note that on a rod-pocket curtain, ruffle extends over top and to *bottom of pocket* on wrong side, so be sure to include allowance for pocket plus heading when dividing edge into fourths.)

3. ***With raw edges aligned*** and ruffle fold pointing in, match pins on ruffle and curtain edge; pin. Gather ruffle strip to fit edge. Baste strip to face fabric, making a ½-inch seam and stitching just inside zigzag stitches.

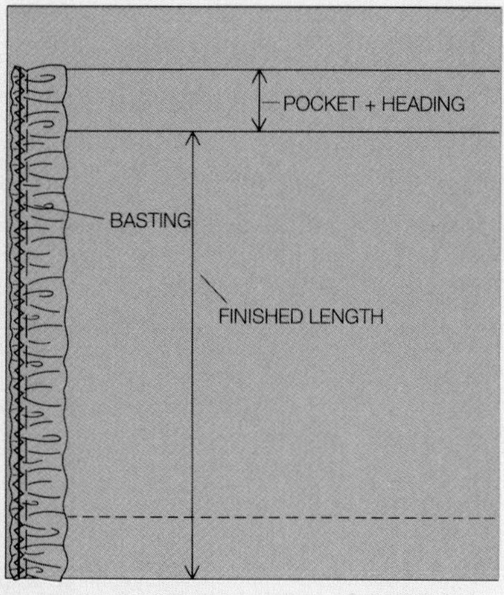

Continued on next page

4. *With right sides together,* pin lining to face fabric along ruffled edge so edges are aligned (lower edge of lining should be 1 inch above lower edge of face fabric). Beginning at lower edge of panel, stitch face fabric and lining, using basting as a guide. Remove gathering cord. Pin and stitch return side hem, making a ½-inch seam. Turn panel right sides out and press edges.

5. *Press face fabric seam allowance* on each side to top edge.

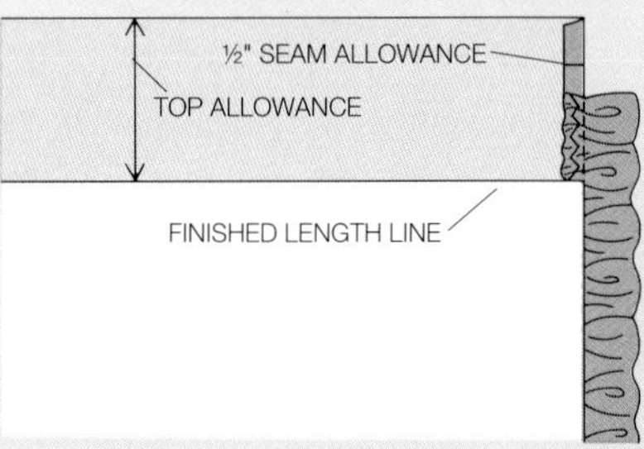

6. *Fold face fabric* on finished length line and press, without pressing ruffle. Turn in raw edge to meet pressed fold and press again. Stitch pocket and heading, if used, as instructed in step 10, "Rod-pocket curtains," page 45, stopping stitching at ruffle.

7. *On wrong side of curtain* at bottom of leading edge, zigzag (by hand) raw edges of ruffle to back of hem; or cover with a small facing made of face fabric.

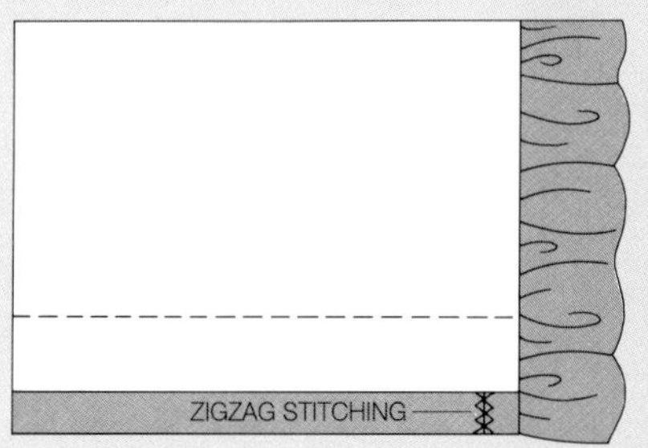

Contrast banding

On curtains or draperies (lined treatments only), bands of fabric on or near leading edges create a visual border. You have two options: on-the-edge banding or set-in banding. Banding is attached after the lower hems are stitched but before the lining goes in.

On-the-edge banding. This simple trimming goes along the leading edge and wraps around to the wrong side.

1. *Cut a contrast strip* two times desired finished width as seen from front plus 3 inches. Cut length of band is equal to distance from top cut edge of face fabric to 2 inches beyond lower hem fold.

2. *Press and stitch* lower hems on face fabric and lining. With right sides together and raw edges aligned at top and sides, pin and stitch band to leading edge of face fabric, making a seam equal to width of finished band. Stitch to end of band.

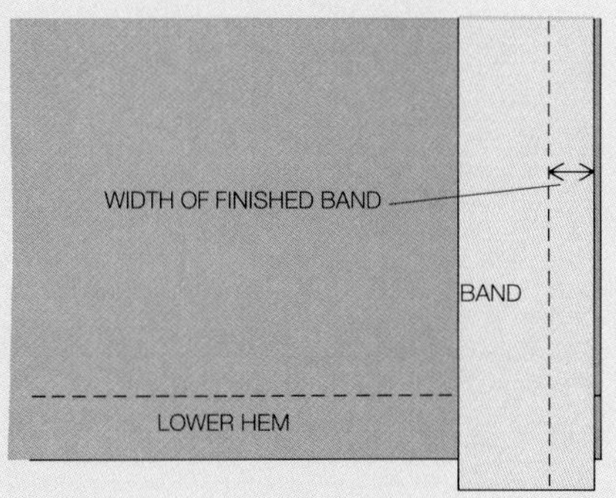

3. *Turn panel* wrong side up, open up band, and press seam allowances toward band. Fold band over raw edges and press (pressed fold will be leading edge).

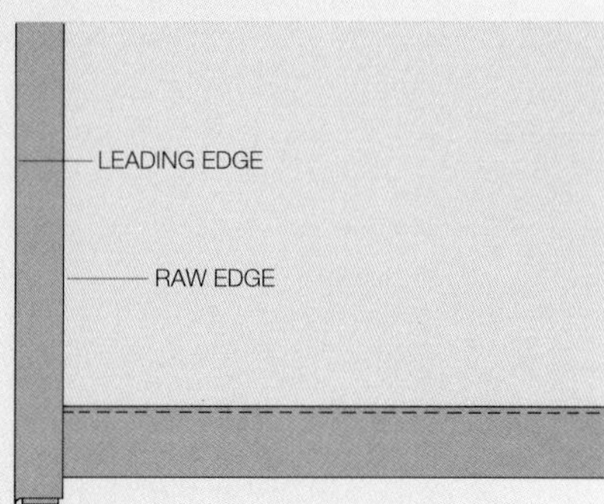

4. *Flip panel* right side up and open up band. Pin lining to band, right sides together and raw edges aligned, positioning lower edge of lining 1 inch above lower edge of face fabric. Stitch to end of band, making a 1½-inch seam.

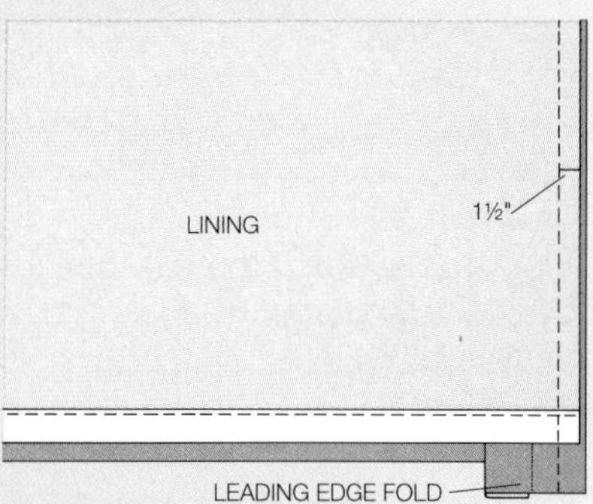

5. *Press seam allowances* toward band. (On back of panel, 1½ inches of band will show.)

6. At lower edge, open lining, turn up band even with lower hem, and hand-stitch to hem.

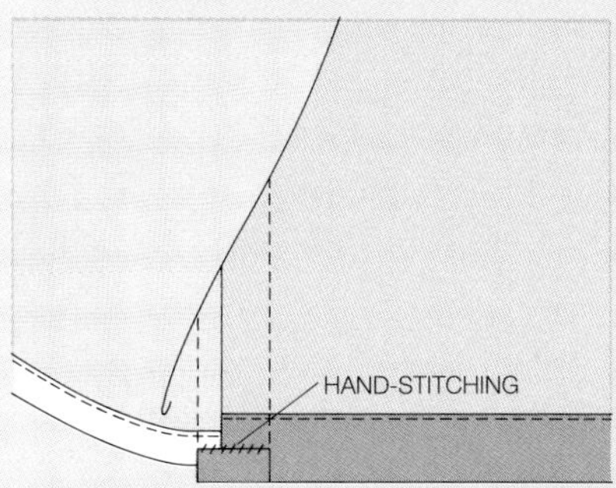

Set-in banding. Because this trimming is applied 1½ inches from the edge of the face fabric, it allows the face fabric to show at the edge.

Banding that ends at the lower edge of the fabric:

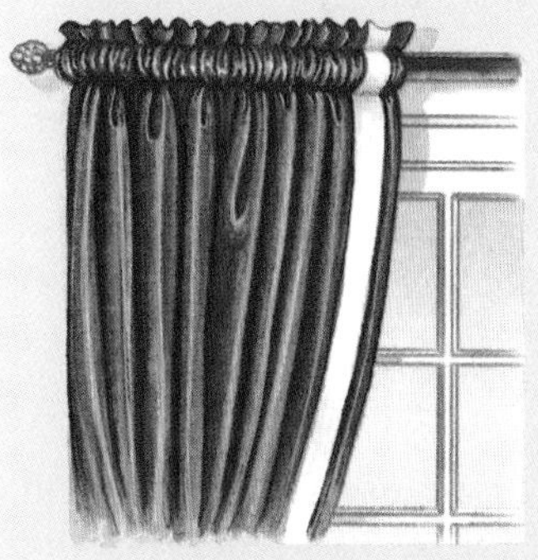

1. *Cut a contrast strip* twice desired finished width plus 1 inch. (For example, for a 2-inch band—a good standard width—cut a 5-inch strip.) Cut length is equal to distance from top cut edge of face fabric to 2 inches beyond lower hem fold.

2. *With wrong sides together,* fold one long edge along finished width measure; press. Fold and press 1 inch on other edge, overlapping first edge.

3. *Make lower hems* on face fabric and lining. Mark a line on face fabric 4½ inches from leading edge. With raw edges aligned at top, pin folded band so leading edge of band aligns with marked line; band should extend 2 inches below lower hem. Topstitch to face fabric, stitching in same direction on each edge and extending stitching to end of band.

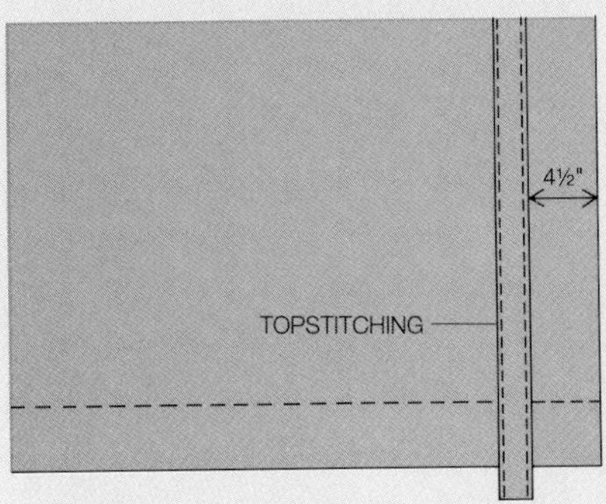

4. *Attach lining* as directed in project. Press seam allowances toward face fabric. At lower edge, open lining, turn up band even with lower hem, and hand-stitch to hem.

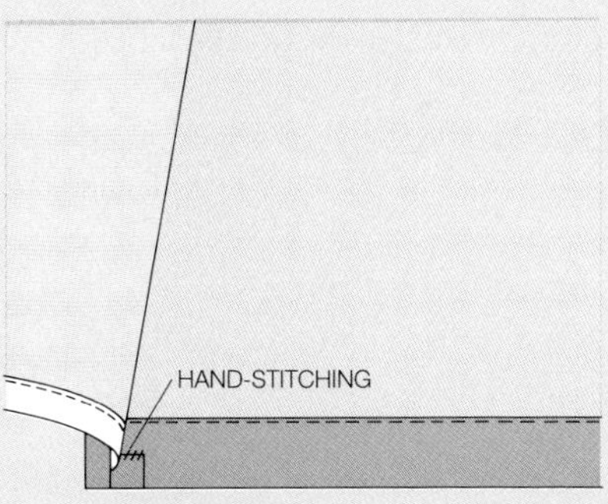

Mitered banding that continues above hem:

1. *Determine finished width* of trim and how far from edge to place it. (A 2-inch-wide band set 1½ inches from leading edge and 4¼ inches from bottom—so you don't stitch through lower hem fold—is typical.)

Follow steps 1–2, "Set-in banding," at left, to cut, fold, and press contrast strip.

2. *Mark a line* on face fabric 4½ inches from leading edge and 4¼ inches from lower hem. Starting at top edge of left panel or lower return edge of right panel, pin band to face fabric so leading edge of band aligns with marked line.

Topstitch band, stopping at marked line just above hem stitching. Keep needle in fabric, raise presser foot, and pivot work; fold to form a mitered corner.

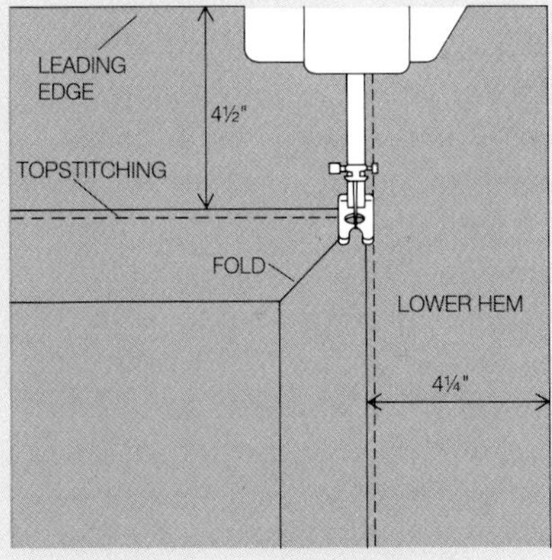

Continue topstitching band, keeping edge parallel to lower hem. Press band. Pin and topstitch inner edge of band, stitching in same direction and pivoting carefully at corners; press.

Tab Curtains

A tailored alternative to rod-pocket curtains, tab curtains have a distinctly crisp, casual look.

Calculating yardage. Measure your window and fill in the window treatment work sheet (see pages 20–24). Tab curtains don't have returns. For fullness, allow only 1½ to 2 times the finished width, rather than the usual 2½.

How much fabric you'll need for looped tabs depends on their size and number. Read steps 10–11 on the facing page to determine the cut size of each tab and the number of tabs. Buy extra fabric for the facing (see step 7, at right) and, if desired, for tiebacks (see pages 56–57).

Use the following allowances in your calculations:

	Fabric	*Lining*
Lower hem	8"	4"
Side hems	3" total	2½" total
Top seam	1½"	None

Tab curtains step-by-step

1. ***Choose and prepare*** face fabric and lining, joining fabric widths as described (see pages 24–33). Press seams open.

2. ***Fold and stitch*** lower hems (see page 33).

3. ***On right side*** of face fabric, measure from lower edge a distance equal to finished length and mark with pins every 4 inches across panel.

4. ***With right sides together,*** lay lining on face fabric so lower edge of lining is 1 inch above lower edge of face fabric. Starting from leading edge of treatment, align first seam of face fabric with first seam of lining.

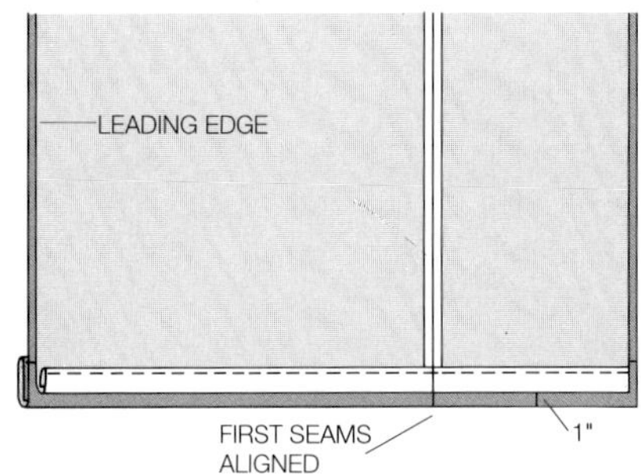

5. ***Trim face fabric*** or lining as necessary so lining is ¼ inch narrower than face fabric at each side.

6. ***Trim lining*** so upper edge meets pin-marked finished length line on face fabric. Then, on face fabric, measure and mark 1½ inches above finished length line. Trim ravel allowance.

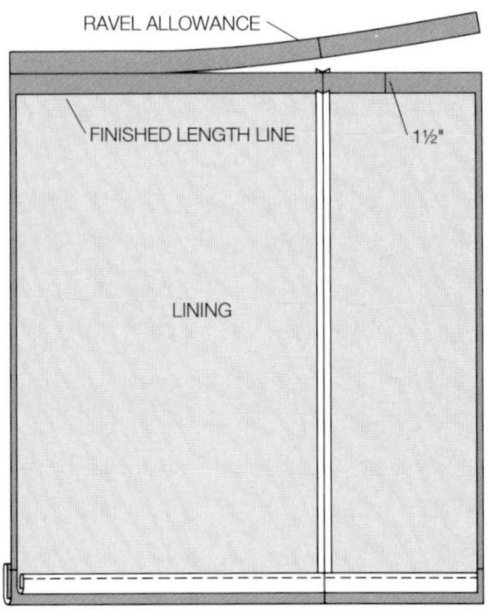

7. ***Remove lining.*** To face upper edge of lining so it doesn't show from front, cut a 4½-inch strip of face fabric equal in length to cut width of lining. With right sides together and raw edges aligned, pin and stitch facing to top edge of lining, making a 1½-inch seam.

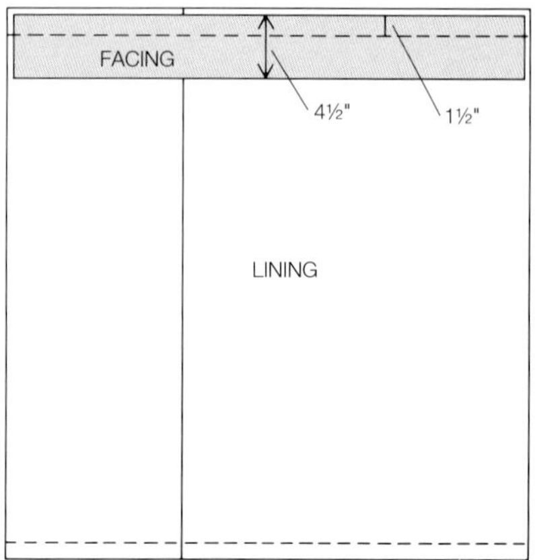

Press seam allowances up.

8. ***Place lining*** on face fabric, right sides together, with lower edge of lining 1 inch above lower edge of face fabric and side edges aligned (lining is slightly narrower); pin along sides. Starting at bottom of lining, stitch, making 1½-inch seams.

9. ***Turn panel*** right side out, lining facing up, so an equal amount of face fabric shows at each side. With seam allowances toward center, press.

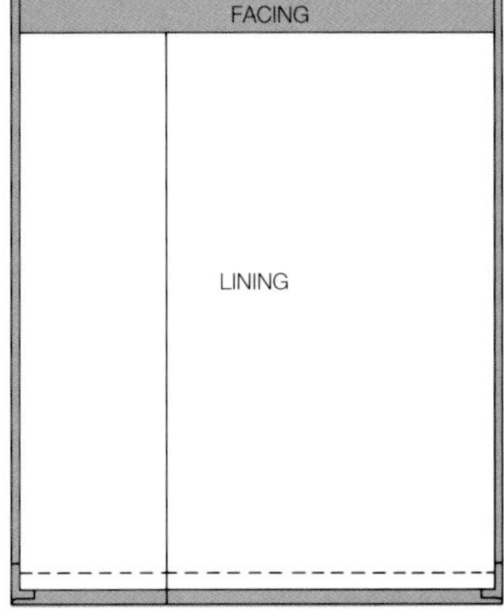

10. ***For tabs,*** drape a strip of fabric over rod. Pin and measure desired length; add 3 inches for two 1½-inch seam allowances to arrive at cut length (10 inches minimum). Finished width of tabs can vary (1½ to 2 inches is standard); add 1 inch for two ½-inch seam allowances to arrive at cut width.

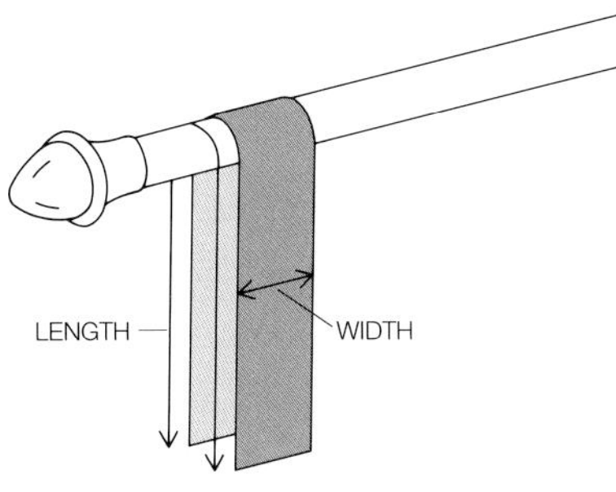

11. ***To figure number*** of spaces, subtract finished width of one tab from finished width of panel; divide by 6 and round up to next whole number. (For example, for a 60-inch-wide finished panel with 2-inch-wide finished tabs, subtract 2 from 60 to get 58; divide by 6. Round result, 9.67, up to 10 for number of spaces.)

To get actual space size, again subtract finished tab width from finished panel width and divide by number of spaces. (In example, divide 58 by 10 for a space size of 5.8, or 5¾ inches.)

Mark off spaces at top edge of face fabric, right side up, starting with a mark at half a tab width from each end of panel.

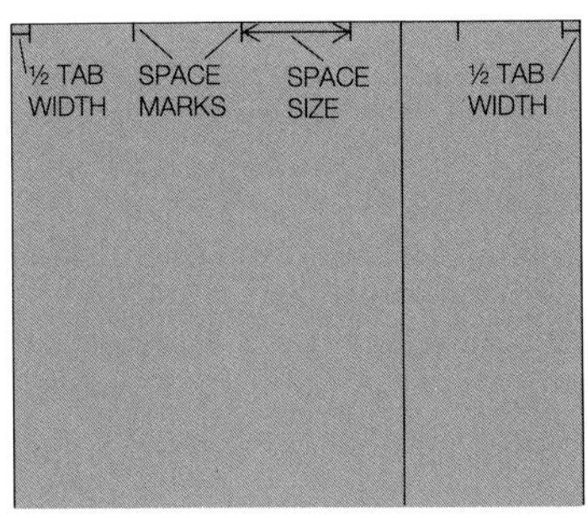

Number of tabs needed is equal to number of spaces plus 1.

12. ***Cut lengthwise strips*** long enough so you can cut several tabs from each strip (this is easier and faster than stitching and turning each tab).

Fold each strip in half lengthwise, right sides together, and stitch length of strip, making a ½-inch seam. Turn right side out and press so seam is at center. Cut tabs and, placing seam inside, fold each in half crosswise.

13. ***Turn curtain*** wrong side out. Sandwich folded tabs, raw edges even with top edges of curtain and folds pointing down, between face fabric and facing, placing a tab against each side fold and centering remaining tabs over space marks.

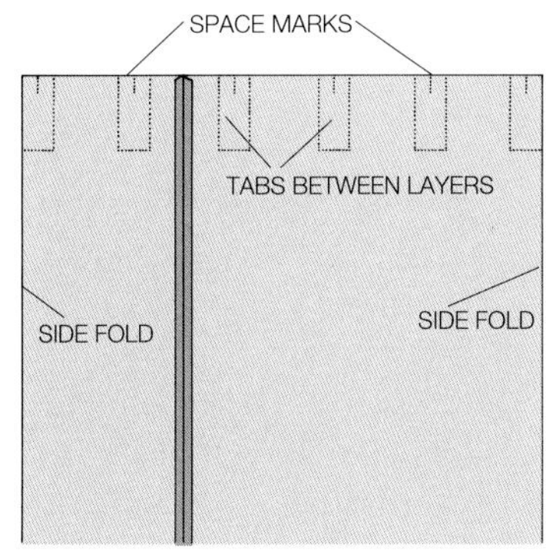

Pin all layers together. Stitch top edge, making a 1½-inch seam. Trim corners.

14. ***Turn curtain*** right side out and press. For added stability, topstitch again 1¼ inches from top edge through all layers.

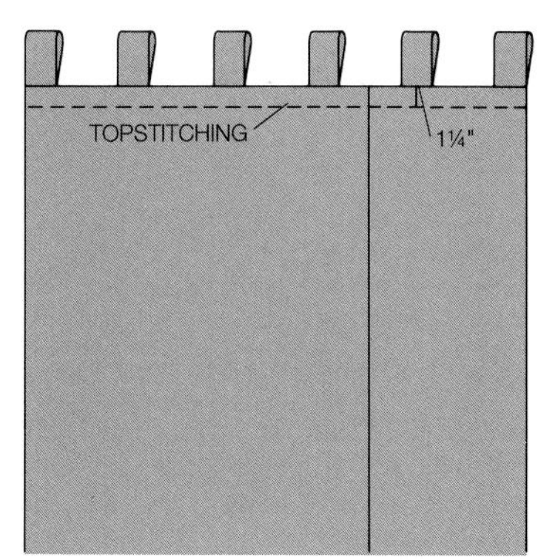

Knotted & Bow-Tied Tabs

For tabs that are tied in knots or bows, experiment with strips of fabric tied and placed over the rod or pole, as in step 10, "Tab curtains," at left, to determine the length and width you'll need.

Instead of one looped tab, you'll need pairs of tabs; on each tab, turn the raw edges inside on one end and slip-stitch closed. For tabs that are tied in bows in the front, make the back tabs longer than the front.

Stitch pairs of tabs to the top edge as you would for looped tabs. For a different look, separate and angle the tabs slightly; this attachment is especially pretty if the tabs are different colors.

Curtain & Drapery Tiebacks

Tiebacks hold treatments back from the window, shaping the treatment and letting in light. For a pair of tiebacks you'll need fabric, four ½-inch-diameter rings, and a pair of concealed tieback holders or cup hooks.

Tailored & bow tiebacks

For tailored tiebacks only, you'll need two strips of crinoline.

1. ***To determine finished size*** of tailored tiebacks, cut a strip of scrap fabric 4 to 6 inches wide and as long as finished width of panel. Wrap strip around panel and experiment until effect is pleasing. Mark finished length and width.

For bow tieback, tie a long strip of scrap fabric into a bow; leave a loop to slip over panel. Experiment with bow position and loop size. Cut loop at desired point; untie and measure finished length.

2. ***Install concealed tieback holders*** or screw in cup hooks.

3. ***For cut size*** of each tailored tieback or each piece of bow tieback, add 1 inch to finished length; double finished width and add 1 inch. Measure and cut two strips of fabric on lengthwise grain. *For tailored tieback,* measure and cut two strips of crinoline to finished length and width.

4. ***Fold each strip*** in half lengthwise, right sides together. Stitch across one end and down one long edge, making a ½-inch seam.

5. ***Turn tieback*** right side out so lengthwise seam is face up and centered and stitched end forms two points. Running your finger along seam toward points, push one point into other, forming a flat point.

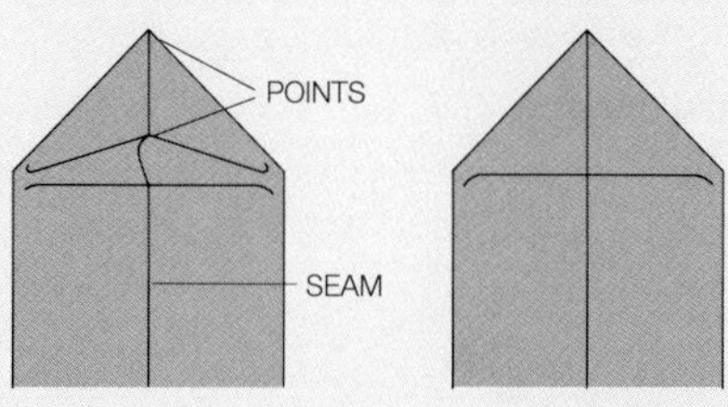

6. ***Trim one long edge*** of crinoline ¼ inch. Cut one end to match pointed end of tieback. Slip in crinoline. Turn under ½ inch on open end and slip-stitch closed.

7. ***Stitch a ring*** to flat end of each piece. For tailored tieback, stitch another ring to pointed end, catching fabric underneath but not stitching through front.

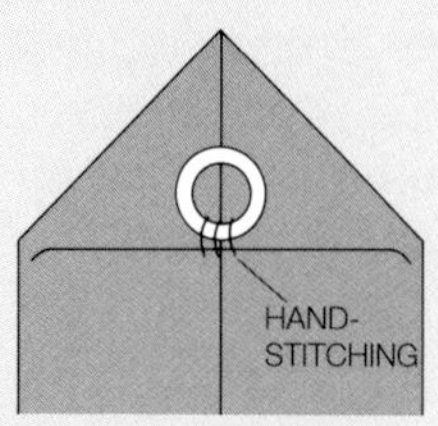

Banded tiebacks

Cut the tieback out of contrast fabric and then topstitch a band to it that matches the curtain fabric.

1. ***Follow steps 1–3*** for tailored tiebacks, at left, using contrast fabric for tieback.

2. ***From matching fabric*** cut a band 2½ times finished width and same length as cut length of tieback.

3. ***With wrong sides together,*** turn and press one raw edge of band a distance equal to finished width. Turn and press other edge so first raw edge is encased next to fold and other raw edge is centered on back.

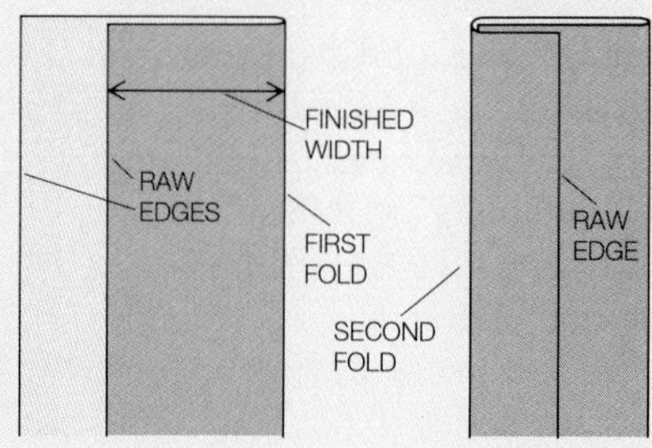

4. ***Center band*** over contrast tieback; pin and topstitch in same direction along each edge.

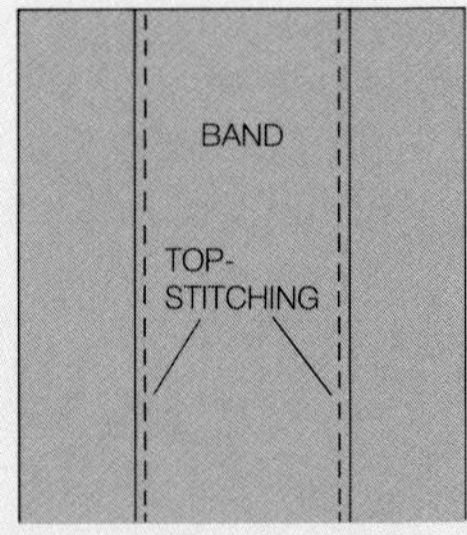

5. ***Follow steps 4–7*** for tailored tiebacks, at left, to finish.

Shirred tiebacks

In addition to face fabric, you'll need lining, crinoline or stiff interfacing, and contrast welt (see page 47).

1. Follow steps 1–2 for tailored tiebacks, facing page.

2. For cut size of each tieback, multiply finished length by 2 and add 2 inches; add 1 inch to finished width. Cut two strips of fabric on lengthwise grain. For lining, add 2 inches to finished length and 1 inch to finished width; cut two strips. Cut two strips of crinoline equal to finished length and width.

3. To gather edges, zigzag over a cord (buttonhole twist or crochet cotton) or make rows of gathering stitches ½ inch from each edge. Gather to finished length plus 2 inches. With raw edges aligned, baste welt to right side of tieback (don't crowd welt).

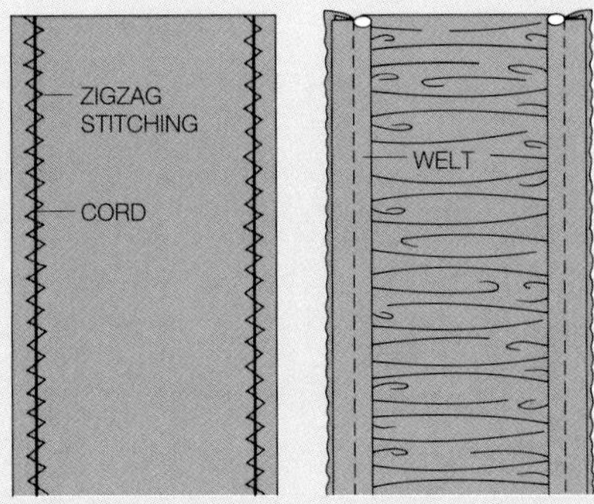

4. Pin lining to tieback, right sides together, and stitch close to welt, just inside previous stitching. Turn right side out.

5. Round corners on one end of crinoline and trim one long edge ¼ inch; slip crinoline inside each tieback. Turn under 1 inch on each open end and slip-stitch closed.

6. Sew rings to wrong side of tiebacks, placing ring on tieback end that shows 1 to 1½ inches from end to hide ring.

Knotted jumbo welt tiebacks

Plump cord ¾ inch or more in diameter gives jumbo welt tiebacks their soft, oversize look. Choose a cord size appropriate to the scale of the treatment. With this method, you'll have leftover cord.

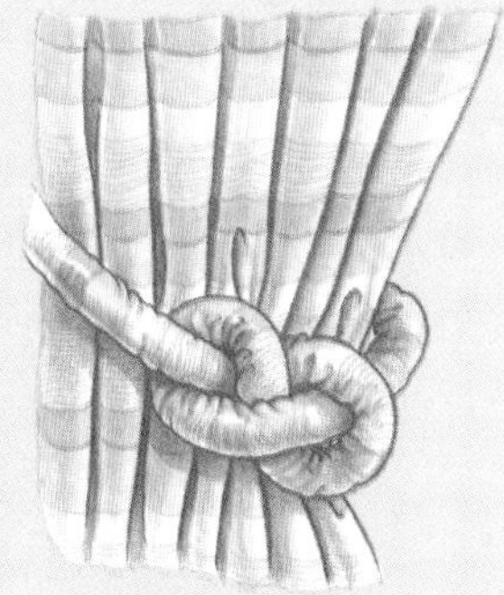

1. To determine finished length of one tieback, tie a knot in a length of cord and tie back a panel, adjusting length and height, until effect is pleasing. Mark desired finished length on cord; remove, untie, and measure length.

2. Cut a length of cord equal to four times finished length of one tieback plus 4 inches. Cut a strip of fabric equal to twice finished length of one tieback plus 2 inches, and 1 inch wider than circumference of cord. (If you must piece strip, try to do it at midpoint.)

3. Starting at midpoint of cord, wrap strip of fabric around cord, right side in, aligning raw edges. Using a zipper foot, stitch down long edge of fabric close to cord (don't crowd cord). Where fabric strip begins at midpoint, hand-stitch securely to cord to hold.

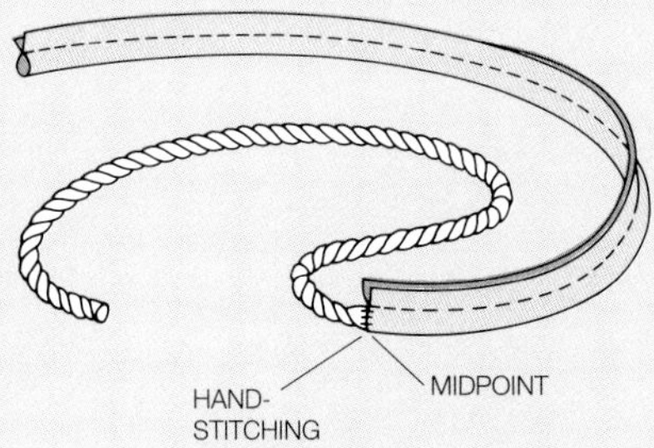

4. Pull end of encased cord free from casing. Holding this end of cord, slide fabric over itself toward uncovered cord until all fabric is right side out.

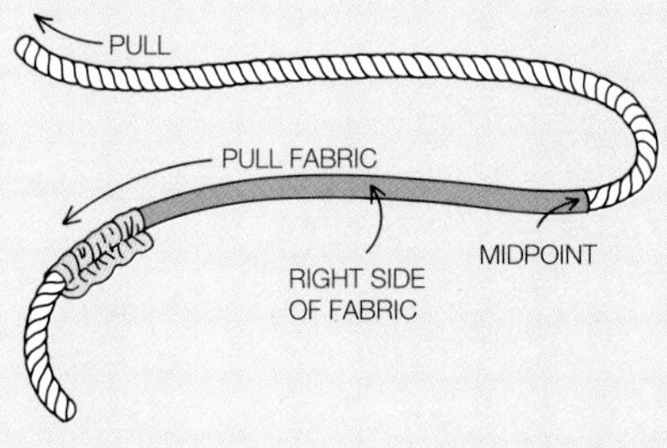

Cut cord at midpoint. Also cut fabric-covered portion of cord at midpoint.

5. To finish ends, trim ½ inch of cord from ends; turn casing to inside and slip-stitch closed. Knot.

6. To attach rings, follow step 6, "Shirred tiebacks," at left.

Draperies

Handsome Palladian windows (below) wear creamy cotton draperies with elegant goblet pleats. Contrast fabric is railroaded at the top and used again for the revealed linings and twisted welt tiebacks. When goblet pleats are linked with knotted cord, the style is referred to as a Flemish heading (detail at right).

DESIGN: SHARON LEGALLET AND BEBE TRINKNER, ISID, LEGALLET-TRINKNER DESIGN ASSOCIATES

DESIGN: TRISHA'S INTERIORS

Hand-drawn pinch-pleated draperies hang from a white lacquer pole with brass fittings. Drapery hooks slip through eyelets at the base of the rings; one ring goes beyond the bracket at each end.

DESIGN: DIANNE VAN VOORHIS, LOS GATOS PORCH
WINDOW TREATMENT: DELTA PI DESIGN

Understated pinch-pleated draperies on a standard traverse rod play a supporting role, allowing attention to focus on the view. Cotton sateen lends itself to this neat, timeless treatment.

HOW TO MAKE

Pinch Pleats ■ Unlined Pinch Pleats ■ Goblet Pleats ■ Reverse Pinch Pleats ■ Butterfly Pleats

What was once the mainstay of window fashions—the pinch-pleated drapery—has evolved into a collection of appealing pleated styles. The ever-popular pinch pleats and three variations are offered here. Once you decide on a style, look at your hardware options to select an appropriate rod.

Drapery hardware

Rods and accessories (shown on the facing page) range from conventional traverse rods to high-end designer rods with decorative finials.

Most of the hardware you'll see in department stores, home improvement centers, and large fabric stores comes from just a handful of manufacturers. For other choices, consult a decorator or visit a design center. Make sure your hardware is in keeping with the treatment style and fabric.

Rods and brackets. Standard for draperies is the traverse rod, which allows you to open and close the panels by pulling a cord that moves small slides along a track.

An adjustable *conventional traverse rod* is designed to be concealed when the treatment is closed. The first two drapery hooks on the leading edge of each panel fit into a master slide; the two master slides overlap at the center of the rod.

For sliding glass doors and corner windows, look for a rod with a one-way draw. On a bay window, try placing a one-way rod at each side and a two-way rod at the center.

Decorative traverse rods, which range in style from contemporary to traditional, are exposed whether the drapery is open or closed. These rods come with half-round ring-slide combinations and with finials that attach to the ends.

End brackets can be plain or decorative. The plain ones, which are adjustable, are placed at the ends of a conventional traverse rod and are hidden from view by the draperies. Most decorative brackets are adjustable and visible; they support the rod from underneath.

Support brackets, also adjustable, ease some of the strain on long drapery rods. As a rule, you'll need one support bracket for every 40 inches of rod length.

Notions and accessories. You'll find these items in the notions section of fabric stores.

Four-inch-wide *crinoline* (sometimes called buckram) stiffens the headings on pleated draperies. Crinoline comes in woven and nonwoven types; some nonwoven crinoline has a slightly sticky side that adheres to the face fabric when you press the heading, preventing the crinoline from slipping.

Drapery hooks, available 1 and 1¼ inches long, are designed to sit in the slides of a traverse rod without shifting under the weight of the fabric.

For most draperies, 1-inch hooks are best—they make small holes and are easy to insert. For draperies made of heavy fabric or lined with a blackout or heavy lining, you may want 1¼-inch hooks; note, however, that they leave larger holes and may catch threads when inserted.

Drapery weights sewn into the corners of the lower hem assure that panels will hang straight (see page 33 for details).

Concealed tieback holders and *decorative holdbacks* are sometimes used with draperies. For more information, see page 43.

Hardware & drapery installation

Installing a drapery rod and adjusting it for smooth operation can be demanding. Carefully read the manufacturer's instructions before you begin.

Rod placement. You must install the rod where it will give you the coverage you determined when you measured your window and calculated the amount of fabric you needed (see pages 20–24).

Find the distance the drapery goes above the window opening. For a conventional traverse rod, mount the brackets so the top of the rod is at that point. (Because the top of each pleat will be ⅛ inch above the rod, the drapery will actually be ⅝ inch from the floor—that extra ⅛ inch is of no consequence.)

For a decorative rod, see the manufacturer's instructions to determine the distance from the top of the drapery heading to the top screw hole on the brackets.

Fasteners. Attach brackets to the window frame or to studs with wood screws. For lightweight treatments, use the screws that come with the rod; substitute number 6 or 8 screws for heavier treatments. To avoid splitting the wood, drill a starter hole (the drill bit should be slightly smaller than the diameter of the screw).

Plastic anchors and expansion bolts are the proper fasteners for installation in wallboard or plaster. For a lightweight treatment or concealed tieback holders, use plastic anchors; for heavier treatments, use expansion bolts.

How to mount rods. Most rods are installed in the following sequence:

1. Mount the end brackets and support brackets, if used, in the positions you determined when you measured for rod placement. Don't simply follow the lines of the window frame: if the frame isn't square, the rod will be crooked and the draperies won't hang properly. Instead, use a carpenter's level to position the brackets; mark the wall through the screw holes.

2. Mount a conventional rod by slipping it over the end brackets. For a decorative rod, arrange the rings before you tighten the brackets. For either rod, adjust the clips on any support brackets so they fit snugly over the rod.

3. Adjust the cord, mount the tension pulley, and center the master slide. Add or remove the slides or ring-slides (move them through an opening at the end of the rod) so you have a sufficient number for the number of hooks in your treatment. Cut the cord only after you're sure you've allowed enough length to pull the panels shut.

Hanging draperies. Because draperies are heavy and awkward, it's best to have help hanging them.

With the master slides near the center but not overlapping, start hanging one panel by inserting the first two hooks on the return edge into the holes on the bracket. Insert the remaining hooks into the slides, ending with the master slide. Repeat for the other panel.

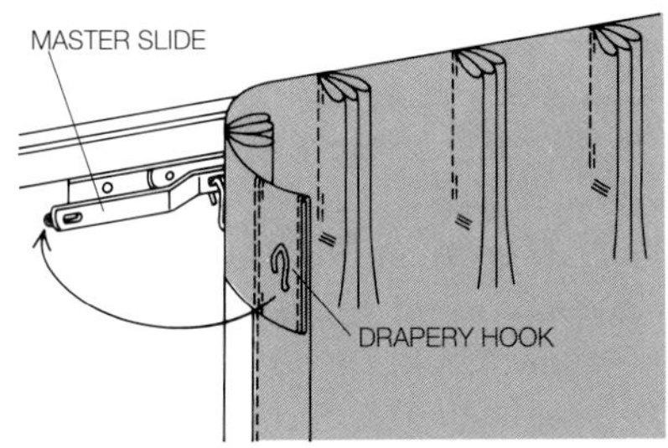

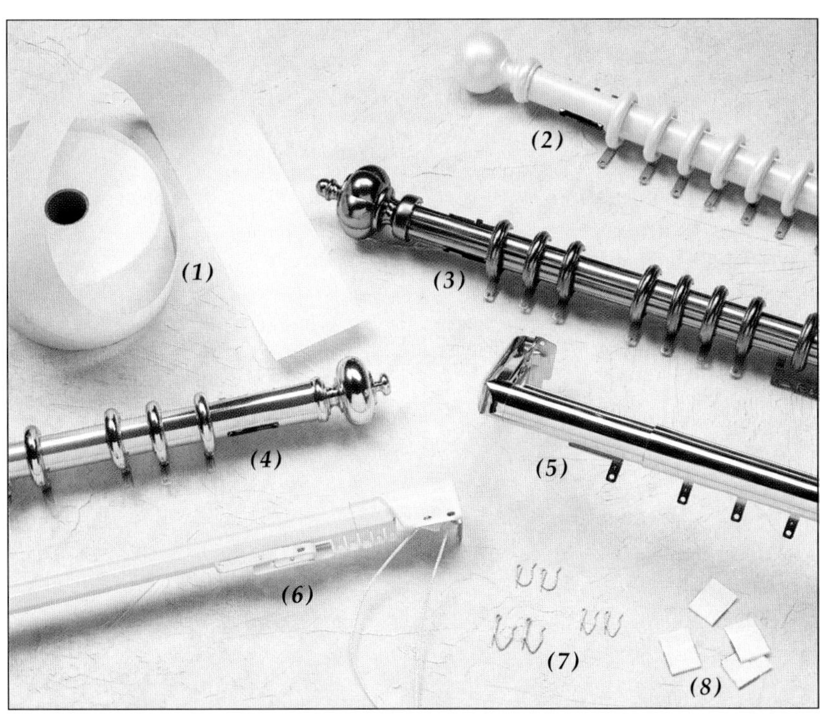

Hardware for draperies includes the following: (1) crinoline, (2) China white traverse rod, (3) fluted antique brass traverse rod, (4) brass traverse rod, (5) contemporary brass traverse rod, (6) conventional traverse rod, (7) drapery hooks, and (8) drapery weights.

"Training" draperies. After they're hung, train draperies so their pleats and folds are uniform.

Open the panels to the stackback position. Then "comb" and smooth them with your fingers, pulling pleat folds forward and pushing back the folds in between. Gently tie the bundle near the top and bottom with fabric strips or soft cord. Leave the ties on for several days to set the folds.

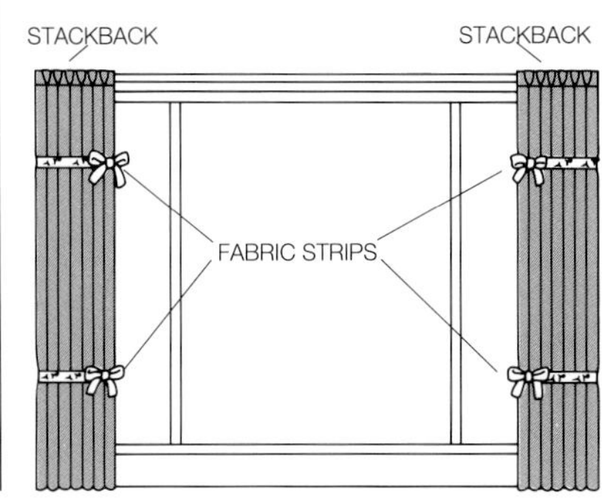

Pinch Pleats

Pinch-pleated draperies and their close relatives (see the variations on page 65) are versatile treatments that offer a range of looks, from strictly utilitarian to ultrasophisticated.

At each end of the panel and at every pleat, you'll need a pin-on drapery hook. For stiffener, use 4-inch-wide crinoline; you'll need about 1½ yards per fabric width.

The directions that follow are for a single lined panel (for an unlined version, see page 64). If you're making two panels for a window, remember that they must be mirror images of each other.

Calculating yardage. Measure your window and fill in the window treatment work sheet (see pages 20–24). Draperies have returns and overlaps; fullness is usually 2½ times finished width. Most draperies begin 5 inches above the window opening and end ½ inch above floor level.

Use the following allowances in your calculations:

	Fabric	*Lining*
Lower hem	8"	4"
Side hems	6" total	None
Top	8"	None

Pinch pleats step-by-step

1. ***Choose and prepare*** face fabric and lining, joining fabric widths as described (see pages 24–33). Press seams open.

2. ***Fold and stitch*** lower hems (see page 33).

3. ***On wrong side*** of face fabric, measure from lower hem a distance equal to finished length and mark with pins every 4 inches across panel.

4. ***With right sides together,*** lay lining on face fabric so lower edge of lining is 1 inch above lower edge of face fabric. Starting from leading edge, align first seam of face fabric with first seam of lining.

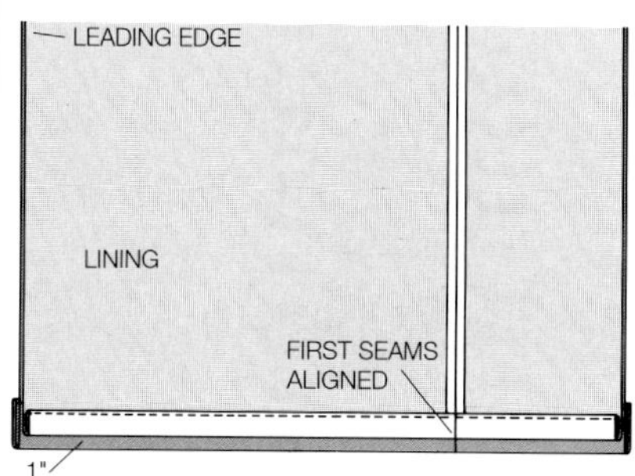

5. ***Trim face fabric*** or lining as necessary so lining is 3 inches narrower than face fabric on each side.

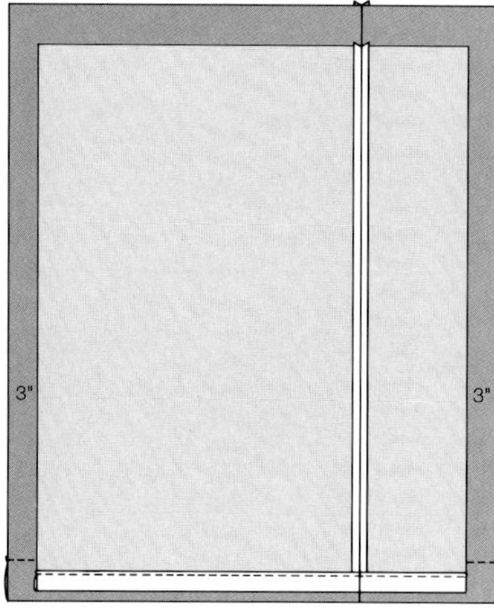

6. ***Trim lining*** so upper edge meets pin-marked finished length line on face fabric. Then, on face fabric, measure and mark 8-inch top allowance above finished length line. Trim ravel allowance.

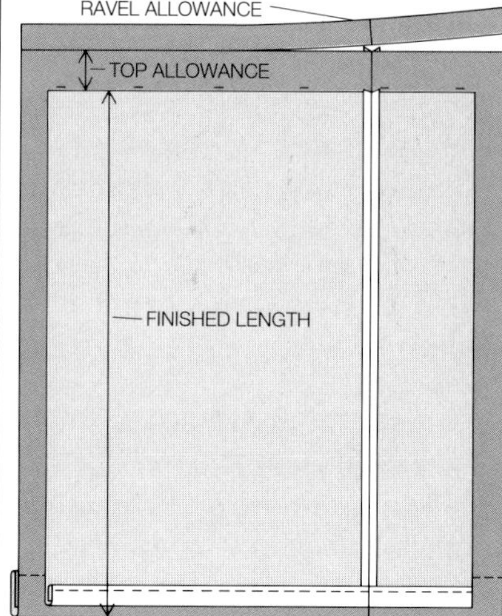

7. ***With right sides still together,*** pin lining to face fabric so leading edge of lining is aligned with leading edge of face fabric (lining hem should still be 1 inch above face fabric hem). Starting at lower edge and continuing to top, stitch, making a 1½-inch seam.

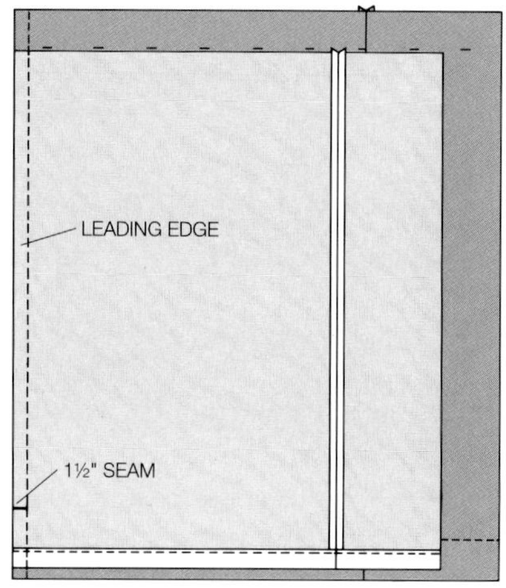

8. ***Separate face fabric*** from lining, laying both right sides down. Press seam allowance toward face fabric.

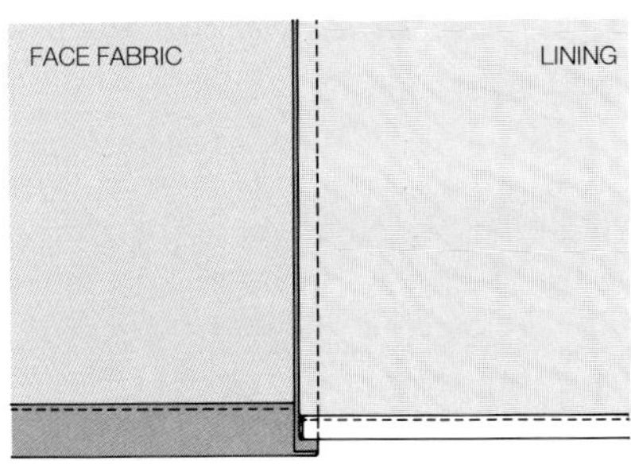

Bring lining over, wrong sides together, so 1½ inches of face fabric show on back and seam allowance is tucked into fold; press.

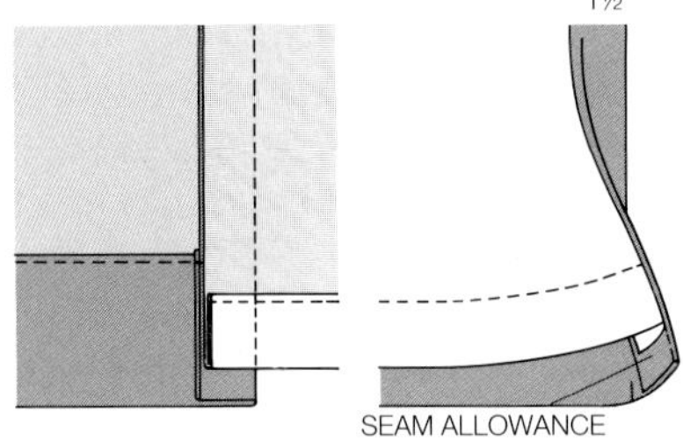

9. *Fold back lining* so only 1 inch rests on face fabric. Inserting needle into lining 10 inches from lower edge of panel, catch-stitch leading edge of face fabric about 6 inches up (use heavy-duty thread). Take a second stitch in lining 6 inches above, keeping stitches loose. Continue to top edge of lining, securing thread to lining.

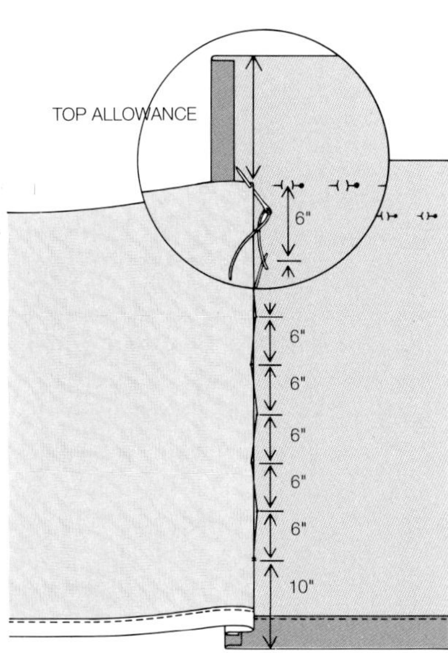

10. *With right sides together,* align other side edges of lining and face fabric (be careful not to pull out catch-stitching). Pin and stitch as in step 7 (facing page). Turn panel right side out. Fold seam toward return edge as in step 8 (facing page) so 1½ inches of face fabric show at each side; press.

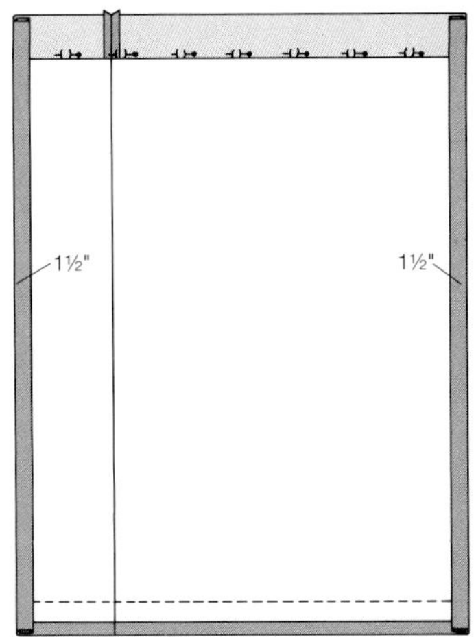

11. *Fold one end of crinoline* under 1 inch; place fold ¼ inch from edge of panel, aligning lower edge of crinoline with finished length line; pin. Smooth and pin crinoline across panel to opposite side. Trim and fold under 1 inch, positioning fold ¼ inch from edge. Remove pins from finished length line.

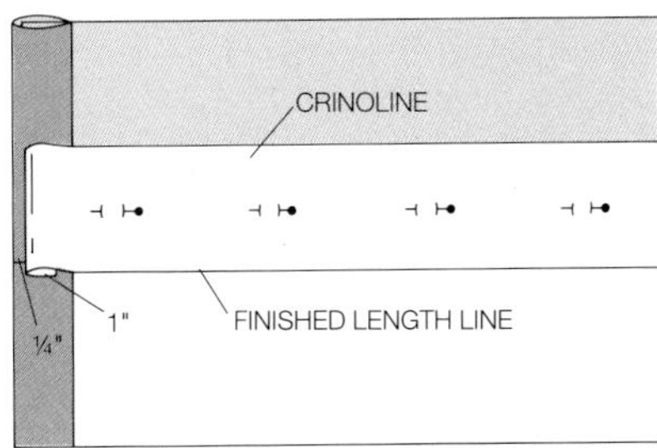

12. *Fold 4-inch allowance* over crinoline, press along edge, and remove pins. Fold and press again; pin in place.

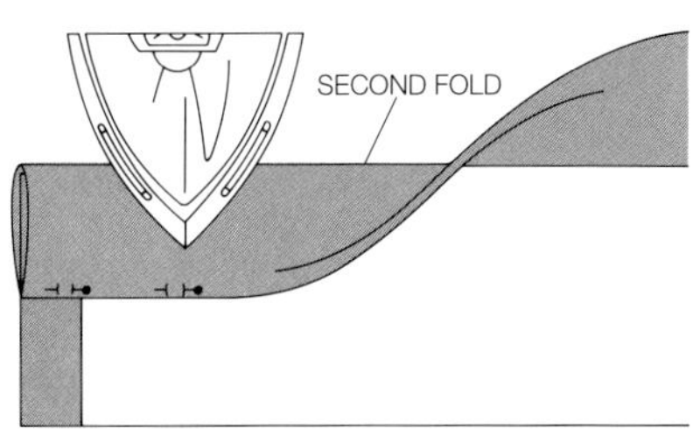

13. *Stitch side of heading closed,* ⅛ inch from edge; backstitch. Stitch again parallel to first row, 1⅜ inches from edge.

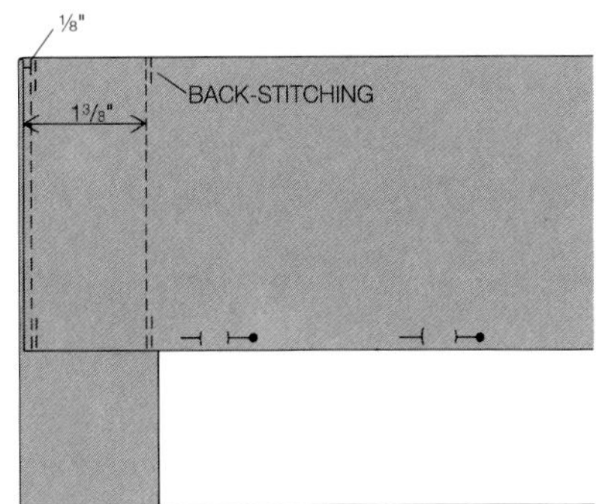

14. *For a single-panel treatment,* subtract finished width from width of flat panel. *For each panel of a two-panel treatment,* subtract half of finished width from width of flat panel. Record result to use in step 16.

15. *Multiply number* of full fabric widths used in each panel by 5 and half-widths by 2 to find number of pleats per panel. Number of spaces between pleats will be one less than number of pleats.

16. *To determine pleat size,* divide result from step 14 by number of pleats (step 15) to arrive at fabric allowance for each pleat. Round off to nearest ¼ inch.

17. *To determine amount of space* between pleats, subtract return (determined previously) and 3½ inches for overlap from finished width. Divide by number of spaces between pleats (step 15) to arrive at fabric allowance for each space. Round off to nearest ¼ inch.

Continued on next page

18. ***Starting at leading edge,*** measure in 3½ inches and pin to indicate start of first pleat (heads of pins should project ¼ to ½ inch above top of panel). Measure and pin end of pleat and space to next pleat.

Continue across panel until all pleats and spaces are marked; end with a pleat. Remaining portion should equal return measurement. Adjust pins slightly, if necessary, so last pleat ends where return begins.

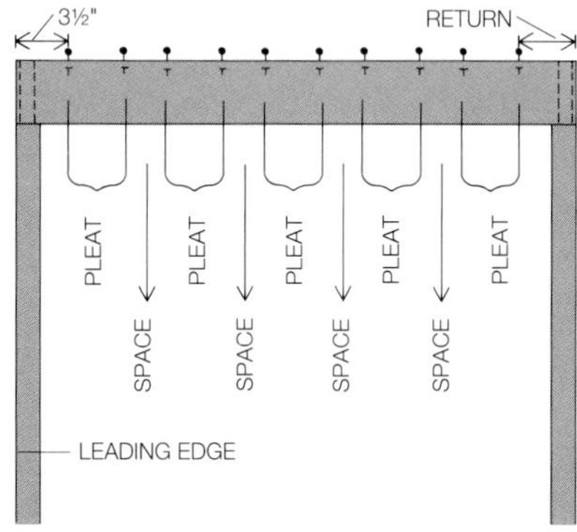

If fabric widths have been joined to make panel, readjust pins so seams fall close to edges of pleats. Don't alter size of space; make adjustments in pleats only.

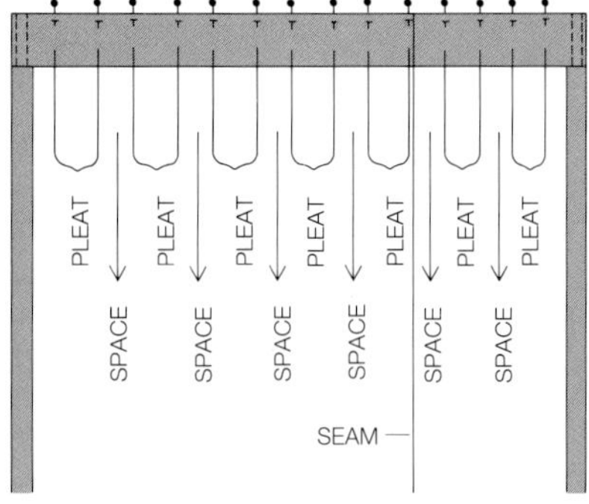

19. ***On wrong side of heading,*** bring together pins at sides of pleats. Lightly finger-press folds.

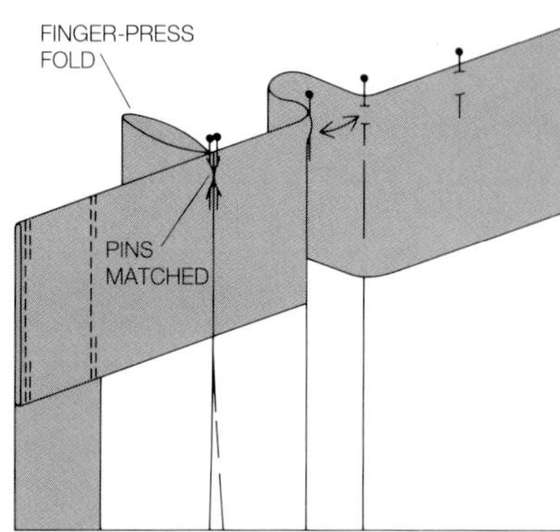

Stitch pleats from bottom of crinoline to top of panel at point where pins meet; back-stitch at each end. Push down on each side of each crease to form two more loops, making sure all three are even.

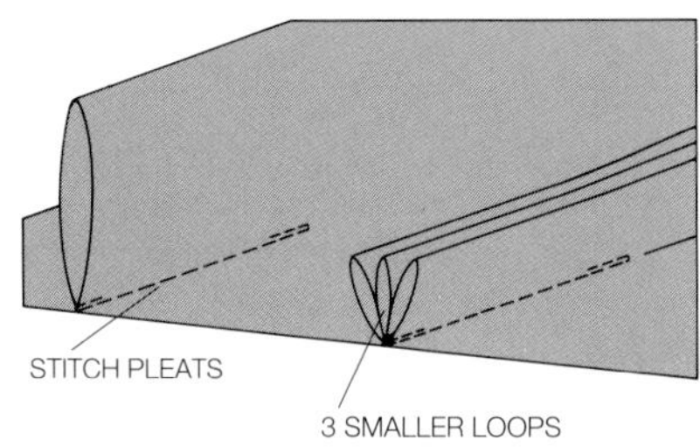

20. ***Insert machine needle*** ¼ inch from fold and ¼ inch above bottom of crinoline. Stitch across each pleat to vertical stitching; back-stitch at each end. (Or use button attachment feature of a machine to tack pleat at center; or tack by hand, using a sturdy needle and a thimble.)

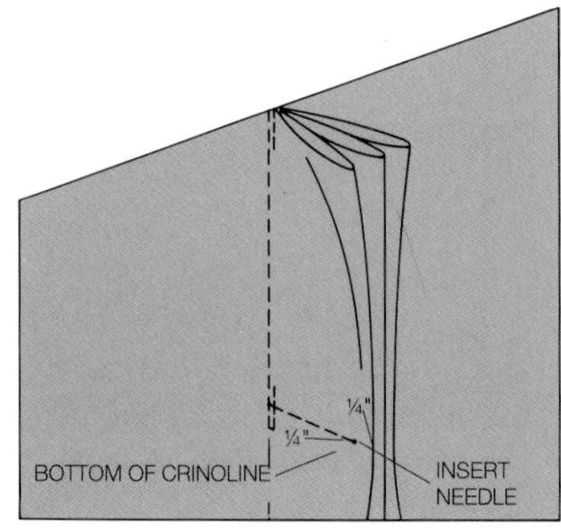

Finger-press folds above tacking.

21. ***To determine insertion point*** for drapery hooks, see chart below. Decorative rods may vary; check manufacturer's instructions.

Type of rod	*Insertion point* 1" hook	1¼" hook
Conventional		
wall mount	2⅝"	2⅞"
ceiling mount or underdrapery	2⅜"	2⅝"
Decorative	1⅜"* 1¾"**	1⅝"* 2"**

* Use this figure if distance from hole in slide to bottom of ring is ⅜".
** Use this figure if distance from hole in slide to bottom of rod is ¾".

Pin a drapery hook to back of each pleat, to end of return, and ¾ inch from leading edge so it pierces crinoline but not face fabric.

22. ***To give crinoline*** a pleat "memory," crease vertically at midpoint between pleats, creasing crinoline forward for a conventional rod, back for a decorative rod.

Unlined Pinch Pleats

Draperies made from sheer and casement fabrics are unlined. You can also make casual unlined draperies from firmly woven fabrics. You'll need the same amount of face fabric as you would for lined draperies.

1. ***Follow steps 1–3,*** "Pinch pleats," page 62, disregarding reference to lining.

2. ***Measure and mark*** 8-inch top allowance above finished length line. Trim ravel allowance.

3. ***Make side hems*** (see page 33).

4. ***Follow steps 11–22,*** "Pinch pleats," pages 63–64, to complete project.

Goblet Pleats

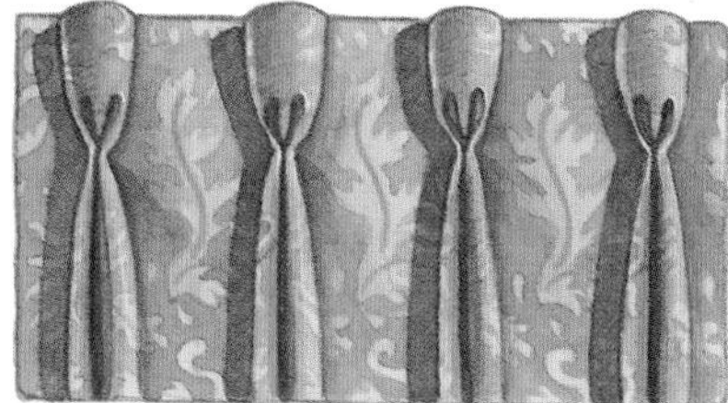

This formal pleat style lends sophistication and softness to a decorating scheme. Goblet pleats don't stack compactly; use them only for a stationary treatment.

1. *Follow steps 1–18,* "Pinch pleats," pages 62–64.

2. *On wrong side of heading,* bring together pins at sides of pleat. Stitch pleat from bottom of crinoline to top of panel at point where pins meet. Back-stitch at each end.

3. *At base of each pleat,* make three tucks and hand-tack just above lower edge of crinoline.

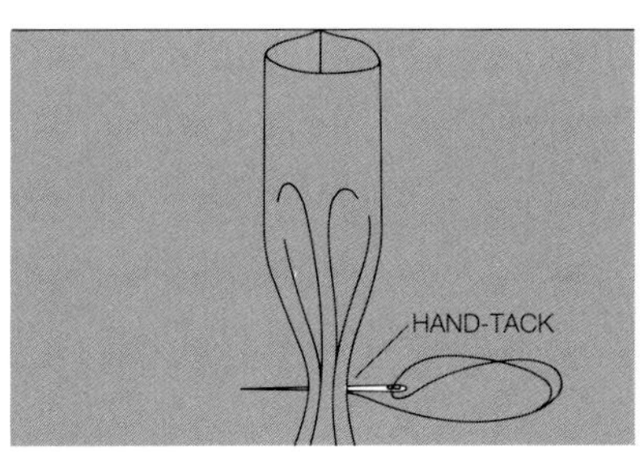

4. *Round each pleat* into a goblet shape. Hand-tack back of each goblet to top of panel on either side of vertical stitching.

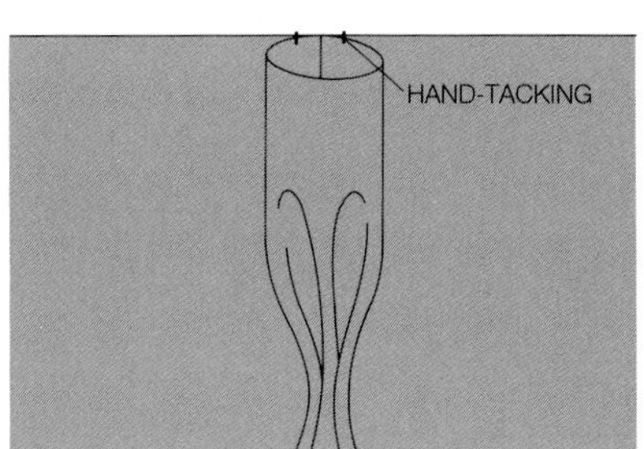

5. *Follow step 21,* "Pinch pleats," facing page.

6. *Slip a roll* of crinoline into each goblet to maintain shape.

Reverse Pinch Pleats

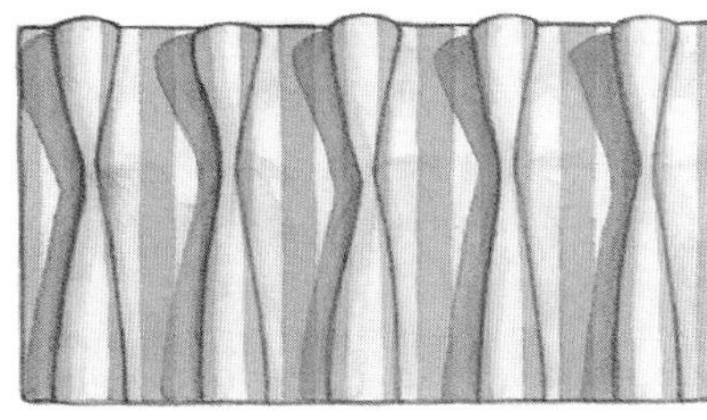

Sleek reverse pinch pleats are folded to the back.

1. *Follow steps 1–18,* "Pinch pleats," pages 62–64.

2. *Follow step 2,* "Goblet pleats," at left, to stitch pleats.

3. *Center each pleat* over vertical stitching and gently flatten.

4. *Roll folded edges* around to touch stitching.

5. *Hand-tack pleats* just above lower edge of crinoline, placing stitches at back of each pleat and just catching folded edges.

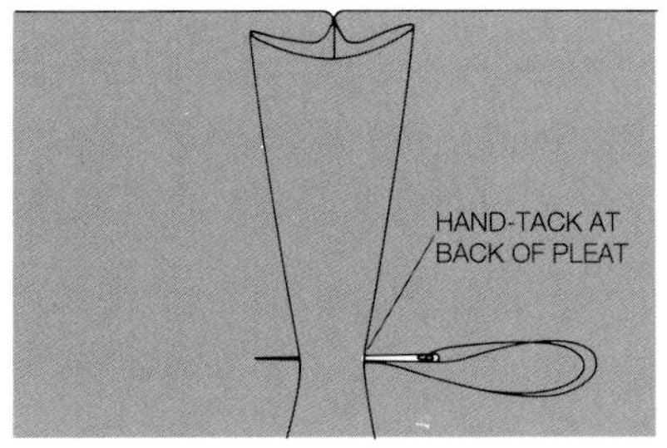

6. *Follow steps 21–22,* "Pinch pleats," facing page.

Butterfly Pleats

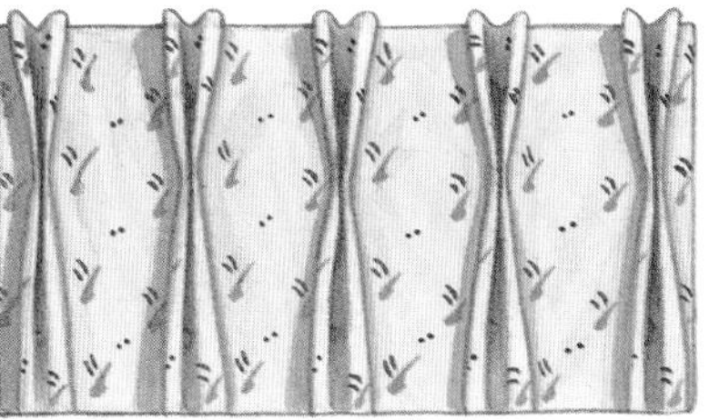

Two rather than three folds in each pleat distinguish the butterfly pleat from the basic pinch pleat.

1. *Follow steps 1–18,* "Pinch pleats," pages 62–64.

2. *Follow step 2,* "Goblet pleats," at left, to stitch pleats.

3. *Center each pleat* over vertical stitching and flatten.

4. *Bring folded edges together* and, making sure they're even, finger-press two pleats.

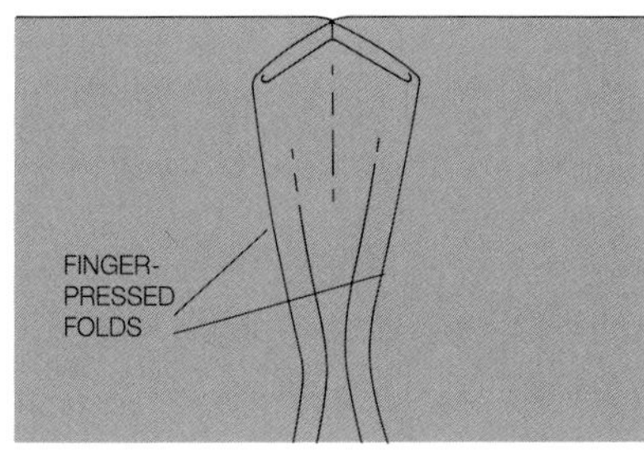

5. *Follow steps 20–22,* "Pinch pleats," facing page.

Shades

Tailored, translucent Roman shades filter light in a remodeled New Orleans cottage. They not only suit the living room's understated contemporary scheme, but also add softness to its angles.

DESIGNER: MARTY SEARS

In a Tampa family room, outside Roman shades in a colorful plaid provide privacy as well as relief from the afternoon sun.

A simple shade with a bright red, boldly scaled rickrack trim turns an upstairs alcove into a focal point.

Subtly striped cloud shade softens the room's hard lines. The shade's contrast banding and bows were made of folded strips of chintz glued together and attached to the shade after the shirring tape was stitched to the back.

WINDOW TREATMENT: ROSSETTI & CORRIEA DRAPERIES INC.

DESIGN: TRISHA'S INTERIORS

Tucks only on the front folds allow the stitched Roman shades to lie flat against the French doors and sidelights. When drawn up, the shades, which allow easy passage through the doors, look like valances. A balloon shade maintains the tailored mood.

DESIGN AND WINDOW TREATMENT: SUSAN LIND CHASTAIN, FINE SEWING WORKSHOP

Attic window seat gets treated to a simple roller shade made of a cotton toile fabric. A rod-pocket valance with a deep heading and welt trim finishes the shade and hides the roller.

The window treatment in this family room is simple, yet dramatic. The flat Roman shade is finished with harlequin points. The pocket-rod curtains are set off with a simple dark-green fringe.

DESIGNER: CANDY LLOYD, CANDLER LLOYD INTERIORS INC.

Four-cord shirring tape creates the softly gathered heading and voluminous poufs on this cloud shade. Unifying the look are the matching fabric on the sofa and the companion pattern on the walls.

In a contemporary variation on a French provincial theme, windows are dressed in colorful cloud shades made of striped cotton chintz and mounted at the ceiling. Transparent pleated shades underneath filter bright light.

DESIGN: RUTH LIVINGSTON INTERIOR DESIGN

HOW TO MAKE

Flat Roman Shade ▪ Soft-fold Roman Shade ▪ Stitched Roman Shade ▪ Balloon Shade ▪ Cloud Shade ▪ Ruffled Cloud Shade ▪ Roller Shade

Shades are as practical as they are good-looking—they control light, provide insulation, and ensure privacy. Use them alone or team them with curtains, draperies, valances, or cornices.

Careful fabric selection is a must when making shades (for specific suggestions, see the individual projects). Be sure the fabric's grain is straight (see page 25); if it's not, the shade may not move smoothly.

It's best to line Roman, balloon, and cloud shades; they hang better and the lining protects the face fabric from deterioration. And, as with other treatments, a lining provides added insulation.

Inside or outside mount?

An inside-mounted shade fits between the frame on either side of the window and ends at the sill. For Roman, balloon, and cloud shades, the finished width of the shade is the width of the window opening (measure at the top, middle, and bottom and use the smallest figure) less ¼ inch.

An outside-mounted shade's finished width will be the width of the area you decide to cover (see pages 20–21 for guidelines). The lower rod comes to the sill, with the skirt or permanent pouf, if used, covering the apron or extending below the window opening.

For an inside- or outside-mounted roller shade, the finished width of the shade will be the same as the length of the roller.

Hardware & notions

Roman, balloon, and cloud shades use the same basic materials; roller shades require their own hardware. For a look at shade hardware, see below.

Hardware for Roman, balloon, and cloud shades. To make any of these shades, you'll need specialized notions from shops that carry shade and drapery supplies, as well as some general hardware store items.

Supplies for rigging the shade include ¼- or ½-inch rings, Roman shade cord or lightweight traverse cord, a shade pull, screw eyes, a small awning or shade cleat, and a

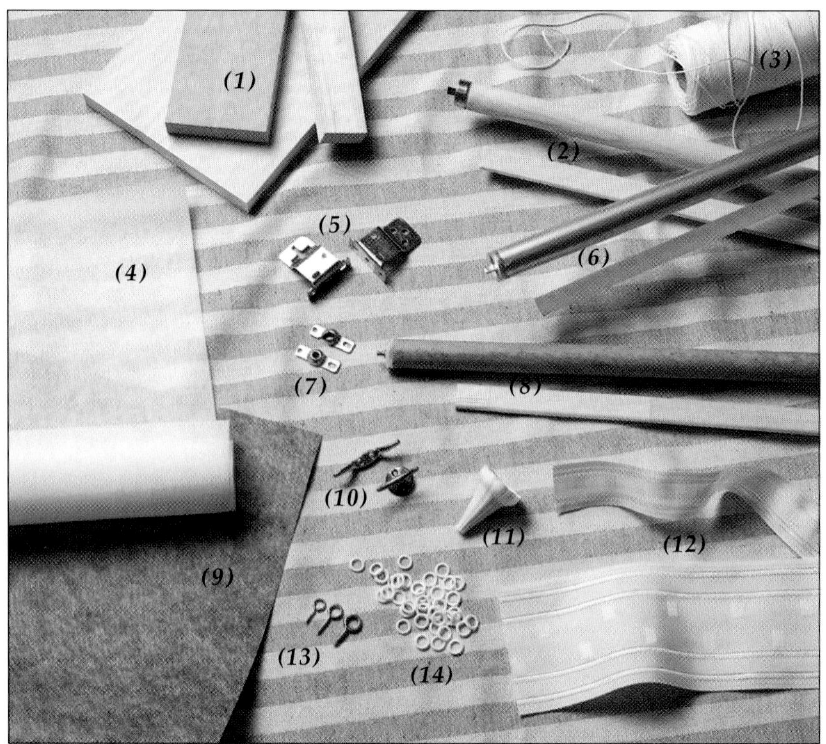

Typical hardware for shades includes (1) mounting boards, (2) wood roller and slat, (3) shade cord, (4) fusible backing, (5) outside-mount brackets, (6) metal roller and slat, (7) inside-mount brackets, (8) cardboard roller and slat, (9) blackout fusible backing, (10) cleats, (11) shade pull, (12) shirring tape, (13) screw eyes, and (14) shade rings.

⅜-inch-diameter sash curtain rod ½ inch shorter than the finished width of your shade (adjust it to that length and tape it in that position).

To mount and hang the shade, you'll need a board (typically a 1 by 2) ¼ inch shorter than the finished width of the shade, a staple gun, and, to attach the board to the window header, screws (for an inside mount or a flat mount on a door) or angle irons (for an outside mount).

For a cloud shade, buy shirring tape (see page 80).

Roller shade hardware. If you're replacing an existing shade, you can simply cut new fabric to fit the roller you already have. Otherwise, you'll need to buy a roller (see page 83 for information on types of rolls and mountings). Rollers can be made of wood, cardboard, or steel.

If you can't find a roller that's the exact length you need, look for an adjustable model or order one from a custom shade shop.

Another alternative is to buy a wood roller and cut it to size. Before you cut, note the difference in the ends: the pin end is the one to cut off; the blade end contains the spring mechanism that makes the shade roll up.

With pliers, remove the pin and end cap. Cut the roller with a saw, making sure you don't cut through the spring. Replace the end cap and pound in the pin with a hammer.

Longer wood rollers are larger in diameter than shorter ones. Buying a longer wood roller and cutting it to size is a good way to get a stronger shade.

The placement of your shade determines the type of brackets you'll need. One type serves an inside-mounted shade; another type is for an outside mount. Both work with either a conventional-roll or a reverse-roll shade.

Flat Roman Shade

Though nearly flat when unfurled, this basic Roman shade draws up into graceful, horizontal folds. The accordion effect is accomplished by cords that run through rings attached to the back of the shade.

The success of a Roman shade depends, in part, on square corners and parallel sides, so measure and cut carefully.

Because it hugs the window, a flat Roman shade insulates well. For even more protection, you can interline your shade if it won't require seaming the interlining (the seams will show). Cut the interlining to the finished width and length, with the allowance at the top for going over the board. Slip the interlining under the pressed side and lower hems, and treat the panel as one.

Planning. Decide on an inside or outside mount and note the hardware you'll need (see facing page).

Typical vertical spacing between rings is 6 to 8 inches—you determine the exact vertical spacing as you make the shade. Typical horizontal spacing of rings is from 9 to 14 inches, depending on the width of the shade and where any seams fall. Typical skirt length is 6 inches.

If you need to join fabric widths, center a full width, adding partial widths to the sides (to match pattern repeats when seaming widths, see page 33). Also, when determining where to seam your fabric, keep in mind that you should have a row of rings at each seam; you may need to adjust the horizontal spacing slightly.

Choosing fabric. What characterizes a flat Roman shade is its series of crisp, horizontal folds. Consider firmly woven natural-fiber fabrics, such as chintz, cotton/linen blends, sailcloth, duck, or canvas (if it's pliable). As a test, crease the fabric with your hand—if it leaves a crisp fold, the material is suitable.

Calculating yardage. Measure your window and fill in the window treatment work sheet (see pages 20–24). A Roman shade has no fullness or returns. For each seam, add a 1-inch allowance to your finished width figure.

Finished length for an inside-mounted shade equals the length of the opening; for an outside mount, finished length is the length of the opening, plus the distance above, plus the shade's skirt.

For a patterned fabric with a repeat, plan to place a full repeat at the bottom of the skirt.

Use the following allowances in your calculations (assuming a 6-inch skirt):

	Fabric	*Lining*
Top	3"	3"
Side hems	3" total	1" total
Skirt hem	6"	5½"
Lower hem (if no skirt)	1½"	1"

Flat Roman shade step-by-step

1. ***Choose and prepare*** face fabric and lining, joining fabric widths as described (see pages 24–33). Press seams open.

2. *With face fabric* wrong side up, fold over each side edge 1½ inches, wrong sides together; press. On lining, press under 1 inch on each side edge. With wrong sides together, fold up lower skirt hem on face fabric 6 inches (if no skirt, fold up hem 1½ inches); press. Repeat on lining, folding up 5½ inches (1 inch if no skirt).

3. *Lay face fabric,* wrong side up, on work surface. Unfold skirt and make a small horizontal tuck in each side hem near lower hem fold, causing side hems to widen and angle in about ½ inch.

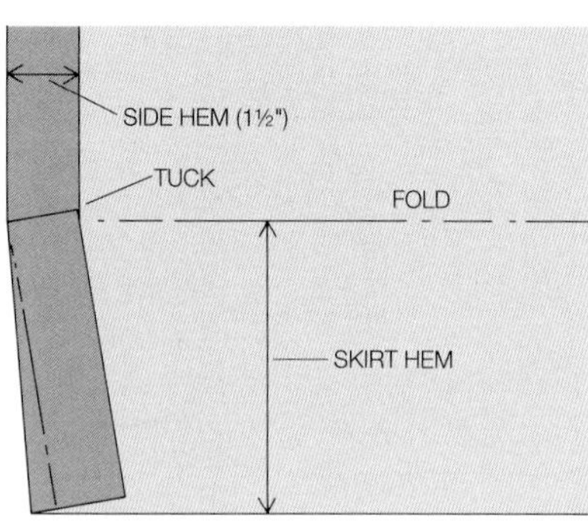

4. *Fold hem up again.* Place lining, right side up, on face fabric so top edges are aligned and lining is ½ inch from side and lower edges. Raw edges of face fabric and lining hems should be aligned.

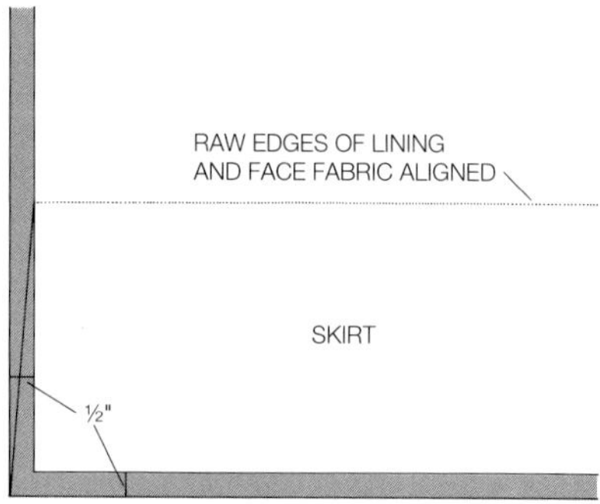

5. *Carefully fold back lining* to expose raw edges of both hems. Without shifting layers, pin together hems only; stitch 1½ inches from raw edges.

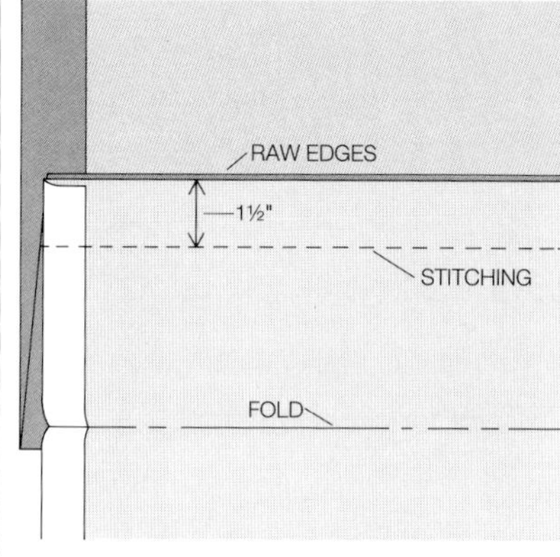

6. *Bring lining back* over face fabric; pin layers together along sides and across top of skirt. Stitch through all layers, ¼ inch below enclosed raw edges of face fabric and lining skirts (you can usually see raw edges through lining), creating a 1¼-inch hidden rod pocket (match top thread to lining and bobbin thread to face fabric).

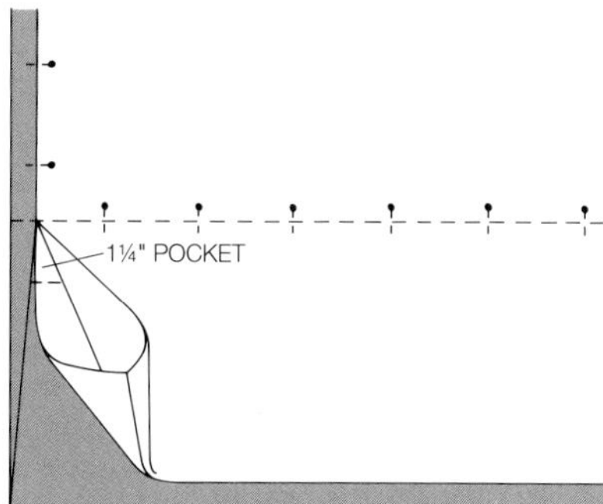

7. *With layers* still pinned together and lining facing up, stitch down right side, beginning at top right edge and making a ¾-inch seam. Stop stitching at pocket stitching. Repeat on other side, beginning stitching at pocket stitching.

8. *On right side* of shade, measure finished length from bottom of hem and mark with pins every 4 inches across width. Measure and trim top allowance to 1¼ inches. Fold top, lining sides together, along pin-marked finished length line and press. Remove pins.

9. *To join lining* and face fabric, overcast top edge with a wide zigzag stitch, or serge.

10. *To determine positions* for rings, measure width from side hem to side hem and divide by desired spacing (9 to 14 inches); round off to nearest whole number to get number of spaces. Divide width by number of spaces to arrive at exact space size. If fabric is seamed, adjust so a row of rings falls on each seam.

With lining side up, use space size to mark vertical lines, starting at rod-pocket stitching and extending to top. Pin lining to face fabric along marked lines, placing pins perpendicular to lines.

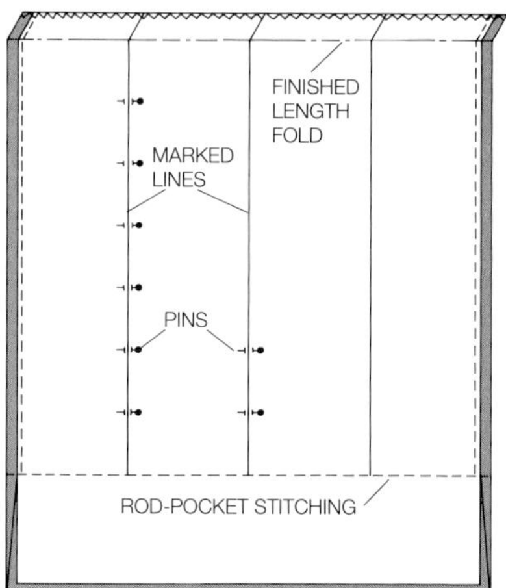

11. *Sew a straight seam* over each marked line.

12. *To find vertical space* between rings, divide distance from top of pocket to top fold by desired vertical spacing (6 to 8 inches) and round off to nearest whole number to get number of spaces. Divide same distance by number of spaces to arrive at exact space size.

Mark ring positions with pins, aligning marks horizontally.

13. Using doubled heavy-duty thread to match lining, sew bottom rings over stitching at top of pocket and other rings at marked positions, directing needle through lining and under stitching without catching face fabric (a buttonhole stitch is strongest).

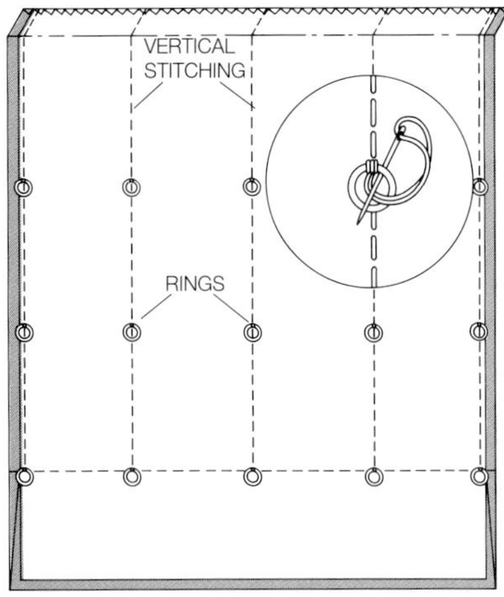

14. Insert rod in pocket and slip-stitch pocket closed, continuing down edge of lining on each side. Also slip-stitch angled face fabric fold to each side.

15. To cover mounting board, cut a piece of fabric 1 inch wider than distance around board and 5 inches longer on each end. Fold and staple fabric to board.

Position shade right side up over board so finished length fold aligns with top front edge of board (for an inside or outside mount, face of board is up; for a flat mount on a door, face is against door). Staple top allowance to board.

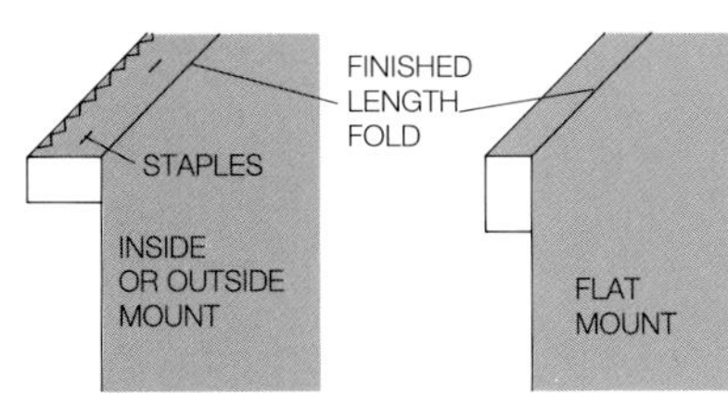

16. Turn shade and board wrong side up. Insert screw eyes in board ¾ inch from front edge (⅜ inch on a flat-mounted shade) and above each row of rings.

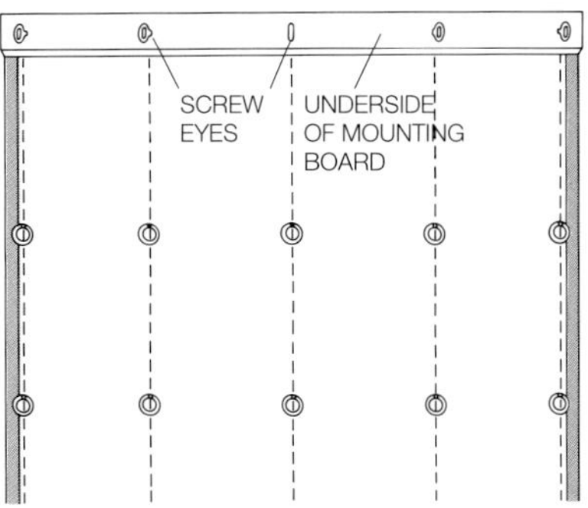

17. For each row of rings, cut a separate length of cord long enough to go through a row of rings, across top of shade to left, and halfway down side (instructions are for a shade with cords on right; to place cords on left, run cords to right).

18. With shade still wrong side up, tie one end of cord to bottom left ring and thread cord up through all rings in row; pass cord from right to left through screw eye at top and let remainder of cord hang down left side. Repeat for all rows of rings.

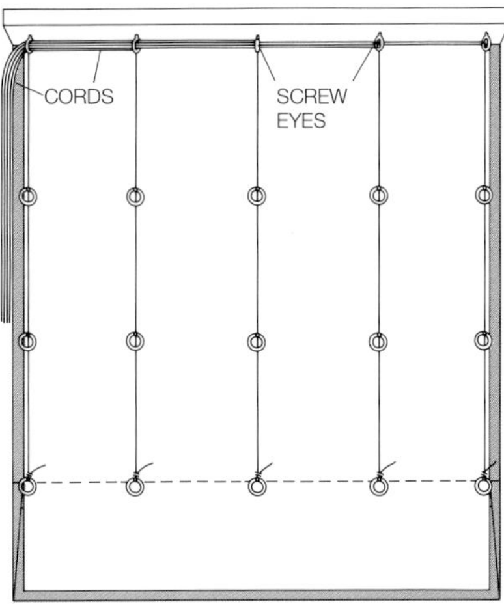

19. Before hanging, lay shade flat, pull cords to draw shade up to board, and secure cords. Straighten horizontal folds and lightly crease with your hands. When folds are arranged, tie fabric strips around shade every 6 to 8 inches; keep tied for 3 or 4 days.

20. With shade unfurled, adjust tension of cords so shade draws up in even horizontal folds when cords are pulled. Lower shade and knot cords together just below right-hand screw eye.

Divide cords; braid to within 2 inches of end of shortest cord. Put cords through shade pull, knot, and trim ends. Slide pull over knot. To secure cords, mount a cleat.

21. For an inside mount, screw board directly into window frame (narrow edge faces out).

For an outside mount, measure from ceiling to angle iron position (¾ inch lower than top of board) on one side; also measure proper distance to side of opening. Install angle iron. Lay one end of board over angle iron. Place a carpenter's level on top of board at other end; adjust board until level. Mark position of other angle iron; install.

For a flat mount on a door, lift up shade and screw board into door, checking level with a carpenter's level.

Soft-fold Roman Shade

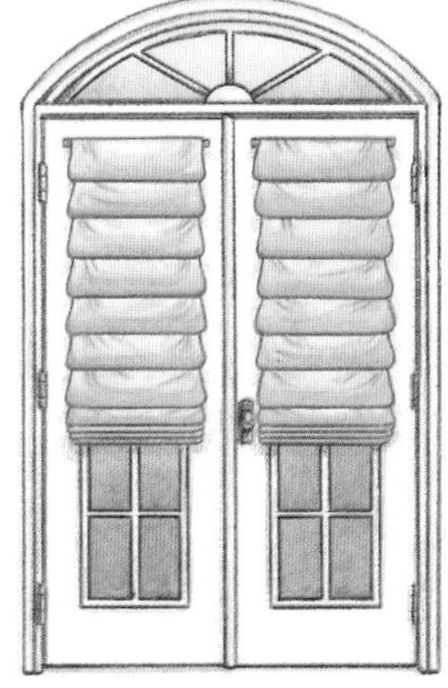

Continued on next page

Rounded folds of fabric flow down the face of this shade, even when it's lowered. This version takes more time to make and requires more fabric than a flat Roman shade, but you'll like its custom look.

Planning. Follow the planning guidelines for "Flat Roman shade," page 73, with these additional typical dimensions: Vertical spacing between rings is 5 inches, the distance between folds (seen from the front) is 5 inches, each loop of fabric that becomes a soft fold takes 9 inches, and skirt length is equal to the distance between rings, plus 2 inches (7 inches in example below).

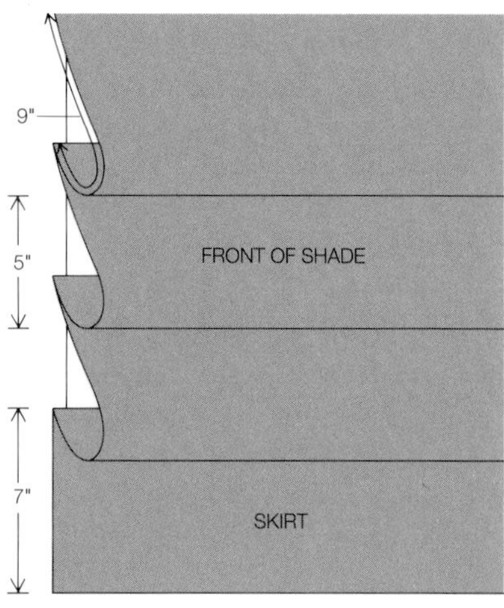

To determine the exact vertical space between rings, subtract the skirt length from the finished length and divide by the desired spacing between rings to arrive at the number of spaces; round off to the nearest whole number. Divide the finished length less the skirt length by the number of spaces for the exact space size. Each loop will be 4 inches more.

You'll space rings 9 to 14 inches apart horizontally, depending on the width of the shade and where any seams fall.

Choosing fabric. Many fabrics suitable for flat Roman shades will also work for this shade. The fabric must be supple enough to form the soft loops but not so soft that the loops flatten.

Calculating yardage. Measure your window and fill in the window treatment work sheet (see pages 20–24). A soft-fold Roman shade has no fullness or returns. For each seam, add a 1-inch allowance to your finished width figure.

To determine the cut length of the face fabric, one easy method is simply to double the finished length of the shade. This allows for plenty of fabric to go over the board and create the soft folds and skirt. Calculate lining fabric separately, adding the top allowance and skirt to the finished length.

Use the following allowances in your calculations (assuming a 7-inch skirt):

	Fabric	*Lining*
Top	3"	3"
Side hems	6" total	3" total
Skirt hem	7"	6½"

Soft-fold Roman shade step-by-step

1. *Choose and prepare* face fabric and lining, joining fabric widths as described (see pages 24–33). Press seams open.

2. *With face fabric* wrong side up, fold over each side edge 3 inches, wrong sides together; press. Turn in raw edge to meet pressed fold and press again. Repeat on lining, folding over each side edge 2 inches.

3. *Fold up lower skirt hem* on face fabric 7 inches, wrong sides together; press. Repeat on lining, pressing up 6½ inches.

4. *Follow steps 3–6,* "Flat Roman shade," page 74, to make tucks and stitch rod pocket.

5. *Lay shade,* right side up, on work surface. From stitching at top of pocket, measure up 2 inches on face fabric and mark with pins across width, pinning through face fabric *only*.

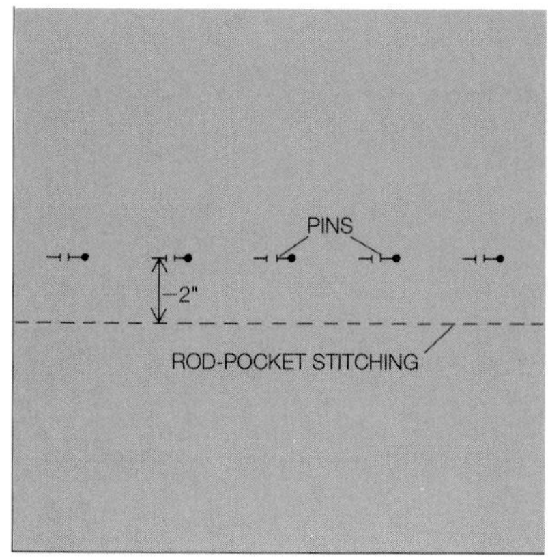

Fold on pin-marked line and pull down "flap" of fabric to create first fold.

6. *From pin-marked line,* measure up distance to be seen between folds plus 2 inches (7 inches in example). Pin across width through face fabric *and* lining; place masking tape across width so lower edge of tape is on pin-marked line.

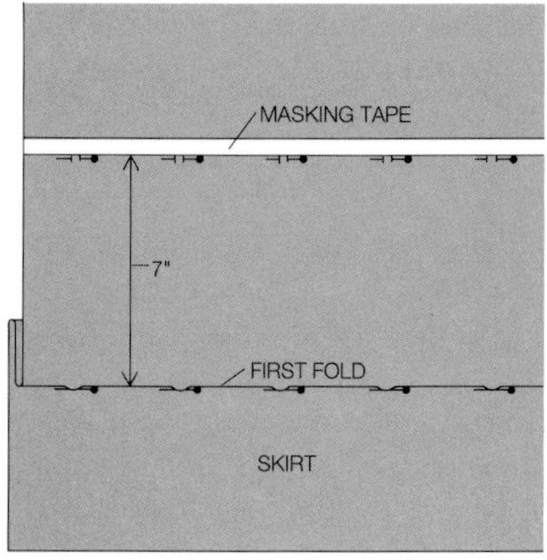

7. *Measure up* 2 more inches from pin-marked line on face fabric and pin across width through face fabric *only*.

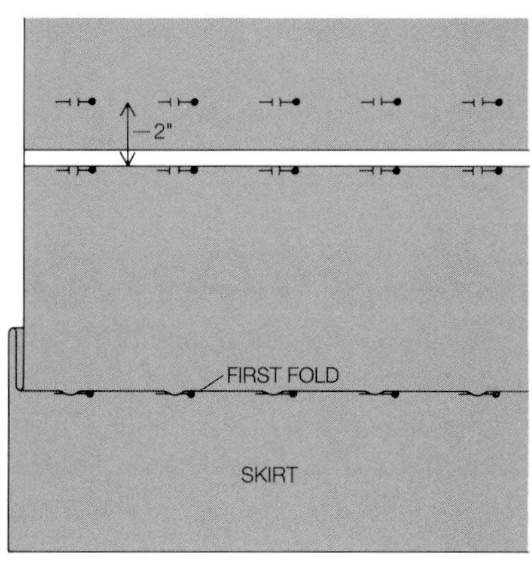

Fold on upper pin-marked line and pull down flap for second fold.

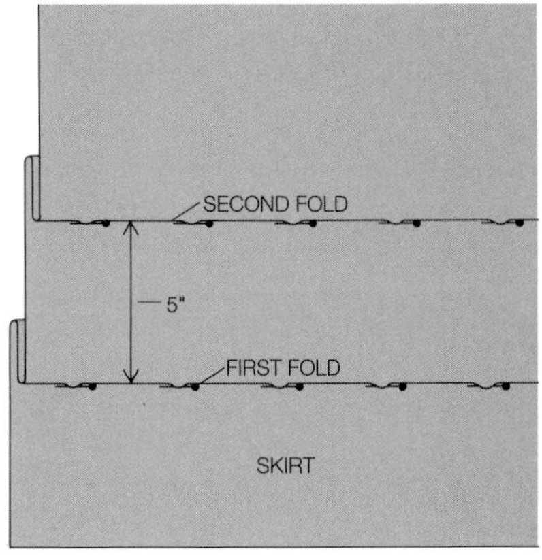

8. ***Repeat steps 6 and 7*** (facing page), ending with step 7 and forming required number of folds.

9. ***At second flap*** from bottom, lift and stitch through face fabric and lining along lower edge of tape, removing pins as you go. Repeat up face of shade. Remove tape.

10. ***Follow steps 8–9,*** "Flat Roman shade," page 74, to measure finished length and finish top edge.

11. ***Follow first part*** of step 10, "Flat Roman shade," page 74, to mark positions for rings with pins, making sure rings align vertically (bottom rings go on rod-pocket stitching, remaining rings on horizontal rows of stitching).

12. ***Using doubled heavy-duty thread*** to match lining, sew rings to lining only (a buttonhole stitch is strongest).

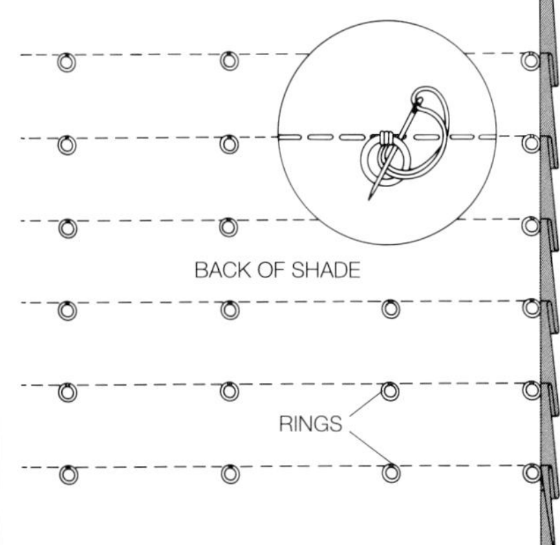

13. ***Follow steps 14–18*** and 20–21, "Flat Roman shade," page 75, to finish shade.

Stitched Roman Shade

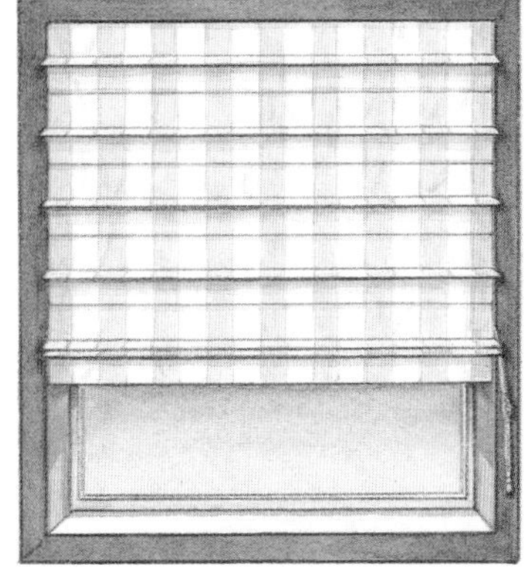

Stitching along the edge of each fold creates neat horizontal tucks in this tailored Roman shade. Take your time—accuracy is essential.

Planning. See "Flat Roman shade," page 73, for general planning guidelines. Because of the stack, it's best to mount this shade outside the window frame.

Choosing fabric. Fabrics that form a crisp fold are best.

Calculating yardage. Calculate yardage as you would for a flat Roman shade, except that you must add extra fabric for the tucks.

1. Determine finished length; subtract skirt length.

2. Divide result by 7 (trial space size) to arrive at number of spaces; round off to nearest whole number. Divide same distance by number of spaces for exact space size.

3. Multiply number of spaces by 2 inches (1 inch for each front and back tuck) and add to finished length. Add 1 inch for natural take-up of tucks.

Stitched Roman shade step-by-step

1. ***Follow steps 1–7,*** "Flat Roman shade," pages 73–74, to make hems and rod pocket.

2. ***On back of shade,*** measure ½ inch from rod-pocket stitching. Pin across width every 4 inches, pinning through both layers. From pin-marked line, measure space size plus 2 inches and pin across width. Repeat up shade one less time than number of spaces.

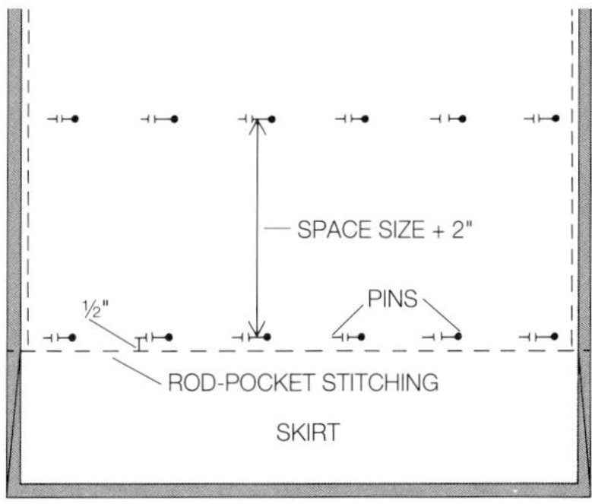

Remaining distance should equal space size plus 1½ inches.

Continued on next page

3. *Make first fold,* face fabric together, along bottom row of pins. Remove pins and press fold. Repin, placing pins perpendicular to fold.

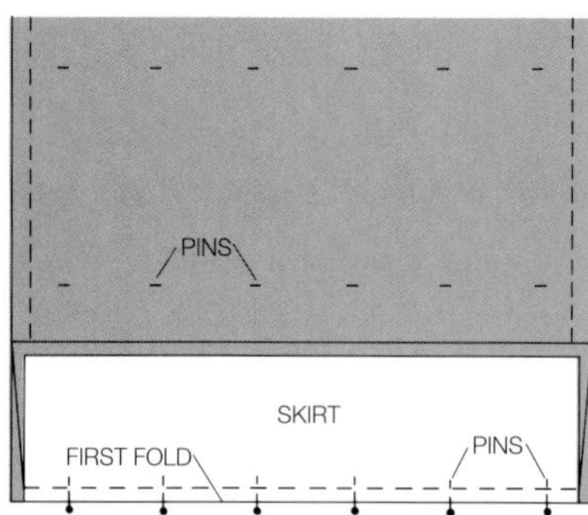

4. *Make next fold* on next row of pins. Repeat for all rows up back of shade.

5. *Stitch each fold* ½ inch from folded edge, using thread to match lining; on bottom fold, stitch just to left of rod-pocket stitching.

6. *Starting at bottom,* bring bottom two tucks together. Crease loop on front and pin perpendicular to fold. Repeat for remaining front tucks. Stitch as for back tucks, using thread to match face fabric.

7. *Follow steps 8–9,* "Flat Roman shade," page 74, to measure finished length and finish top edge.

8. *Follow first part* of step 10, "Flat Roman shade," page 74, to determine spacing for rings. Mark positions for rings with pins on back tucks.

9. *Using doubled heavy-duty thread* to match lining, sew rings through tucks on back at pin marks.

10. *Follow steps 14–21,* "Flat Roman shade," page 75, to finish shade.

Balloon Shade

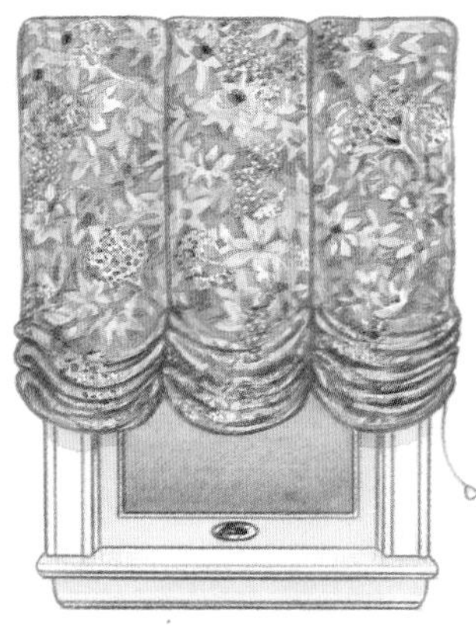

True to its name, a balloon shade is airy and rounded, with deep inverted pleats that fall into poufs at the bottom. You draw the shade up using cords threaded through rings. Some balloon shades have a bottom pouf that remains even when the shade is lowered, an effect achieved by adding to the length and tying the lower rings together.

Planning. This project is for an outside-mounted balloon shade. Note the hardware and notions you'll need (see page 72).

On a balloon shade, each fabric width will make a half-pleat, a space, a full pleat, a space, and another half-pleat (sizes depend on board size and usable fabric width).

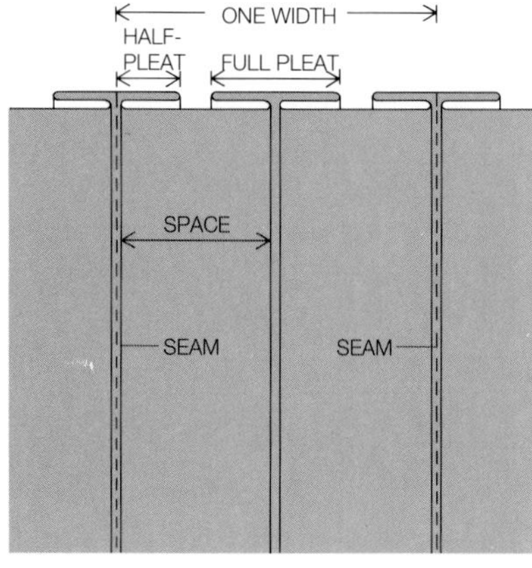

For unpatterned fabric or fabric with an allover pattern, you'll start with a trial space size of 10 inches. If your fabric has large motifs, analyze the design and choose space and pleat sizes that will place the desired part of the pattern in each space. (This takes careful planning; if you're at all unsure, choose a pattern that doesn't have large motifs.)

You'll add returns to cover the ends of the board once you've seamed widths. A half-pleat extends to each end of the face board; the return and side hem are beyond.

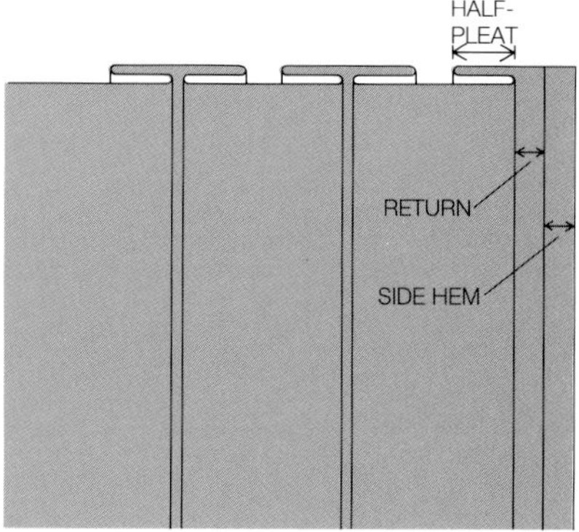

Vertical spacing of rings can range from 6 to 10 inches, depending on how deep you want the folds.

Choosing fabric. Select a fabric that's firm enough to hold pleats and soft enough to form poufs.

Calculating yardage. Follow these steps to arrive at pleat and space sizes and yards needed. In the following example, the board is 1½ inches wide and 48 inches long and the fabric 54 inches wide.

1. Measure your window and fill in window treatment work sheet (pages 20–24) to arrive at board size. Return size is equal to depth of board.

2. Divide board size by 10 (trial space size) to arrive at number of spaces ($48 \div 10 = 4.8$); round off to nearest whole number (4.8 rounds to 5). Divide board size by number of spaces for exact space size (48 ÷ 5 = 9.6 rounded to 9⅝ inches).

3. Subtract exact space size from half the usable fabric width (26 inches for fabric with 52 inches usable width) for pleat loop size (26 – 9⅝ = 16⅜, rounded to 16¼ inches). When flattened, each full pleat will be half the loop size (about 8⅛ inches).

4. To determine number of fabric widths needed, divide number of spaces (from step 2) by 2. If result is a whole number, add a width; if result contains a half-width, round up to next whole number of widths. Continue to fill in second row of work sheet.

Also use the following allowances in your calculations:

	Fabric	*Lining*
Top	3"	3"
Lower hems		
with pouf	21"	18"
without pouf	3"	None

Balloon shade step-by-step

1. *Choose and prepare* face fabric and lining (see pages 24–32).

2. *Align seams* on face fabric and lining when joining widths.

If you have an odd number of spaces, join fabric widths as described on page 33; press seams open. Lay face fabric right side up; measure, mark, and trim a quarter-width from far right width. Pin and stitch piece to far left width.

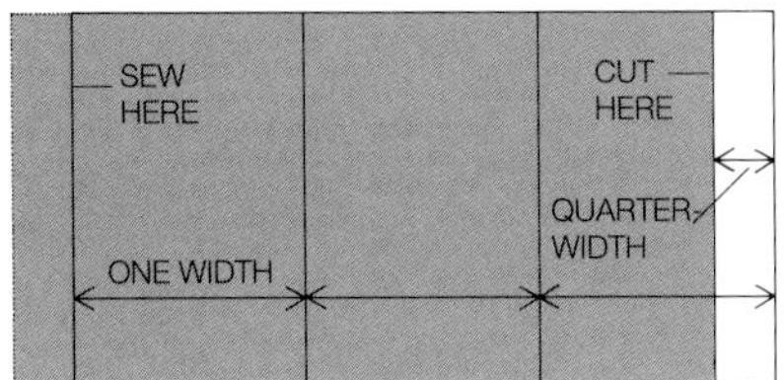

Press seam open. From this seam, measure, mark, and trim fabric a distance equal to return plus 1½ inches. From right seam, measure a distance equal to a half-width; from this point, measure, mark, and cut fabric a distance equal to return plus 1½ inches. Repeat on lining; trim 1 inch on each side.

If you have an even number of spaces, join all widths except one. Split this width and sew half to one side and half to other side; press seams open. From each end seam, measure and mark toward edge a distance equal to return plus 1½ inches; cut fabric. Repeat on lining; trim 1 inch on each side.

3. *With face fabric* wrong side up, fold over each side edge 1½ inches, wrong sides together; press. Repeat on lining, folding over each side edge 1 inch.

4. *Lay face fabric,* wrong side up, on work surface. Place lining, right side up, on face fabric ½ inch in from side edges; lower edge of lining should be 3 inches above lower edge of face fabric. Pin together at side edges and stitch, making a ¾-inch seam and continuing stitching to lower edge of face fabric (match top thread to lining and bobbin to face fabric).

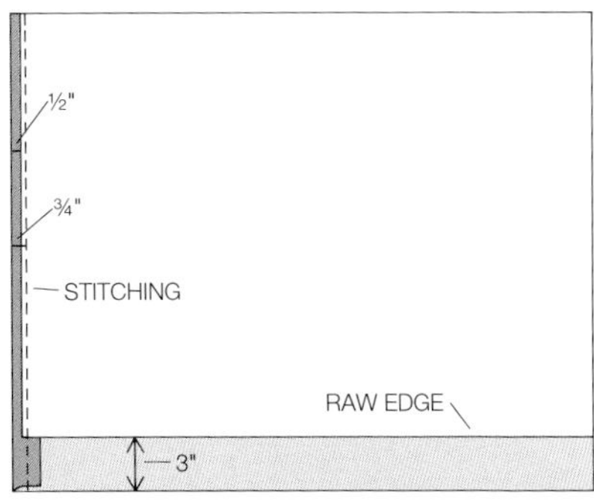

5. *With lining* still right side up, measure and mark vertical lines for rows of stitching and rings at midpoint of each full width. For a shade with an odd number of spaces, also measure and mark a line where return begins on unseamed side edge. Pin all seams and marked lines.

6. *Beginning at raw edge* of lining at lower hem, stitch over marked lines and seams.

7. *Turn shade* right side up and, on right edge, measure from line of return stitching toward center a distance equal to a half-pleat loop; pin vertically down length of shade.

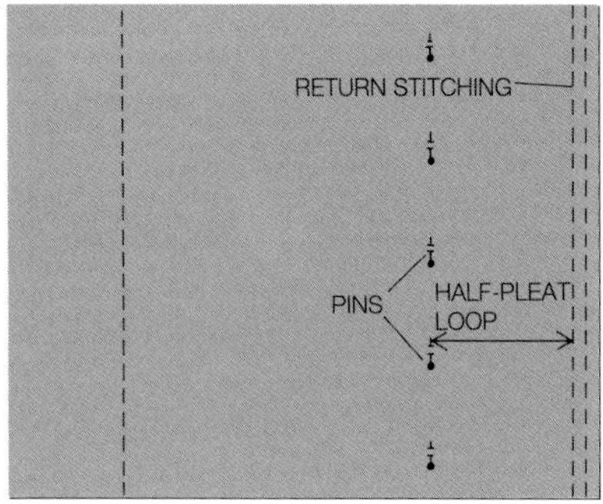

To form half-pleat, bring pin-marked line to return stitching. Pin layers together close to front and back folds.

Repeat on other edge.

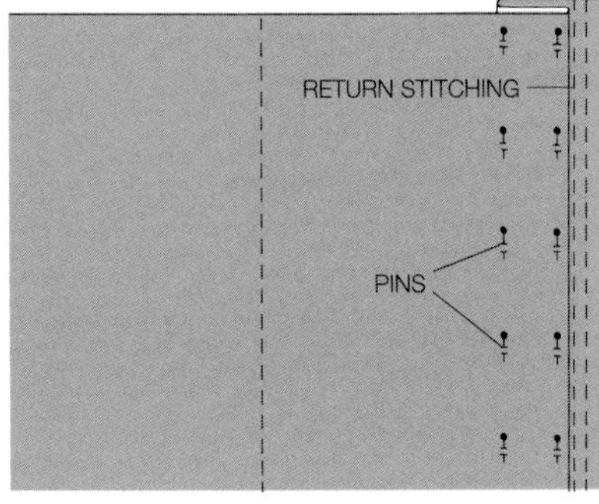

8. *Measure and mark* same distance on either side of each row of vertical stitching. To form a full pleat, bring each pin-marked line to row of stitching; pin in place vertically near front folds so pleats "kiss." Space size must be as determined earlier; adjust pleats if necessary.

Continued on next page

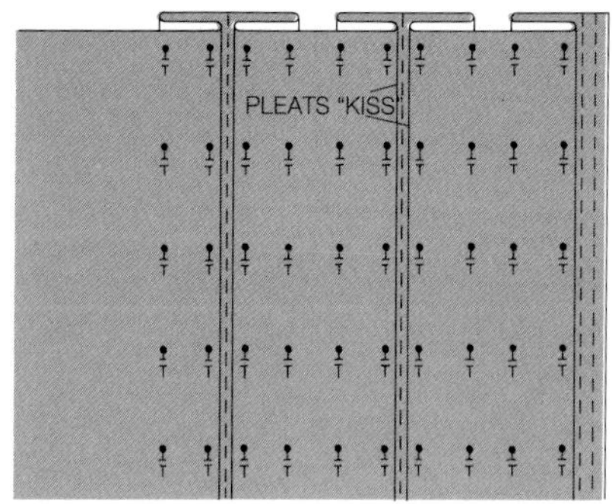

Pin through all layers where pleats form folds on back.

9. *Turn shade* lining side up. To hold pleats in place, stitch all folds from edge of lining to lower edge of face fabric, back-stitching at beginning and end.

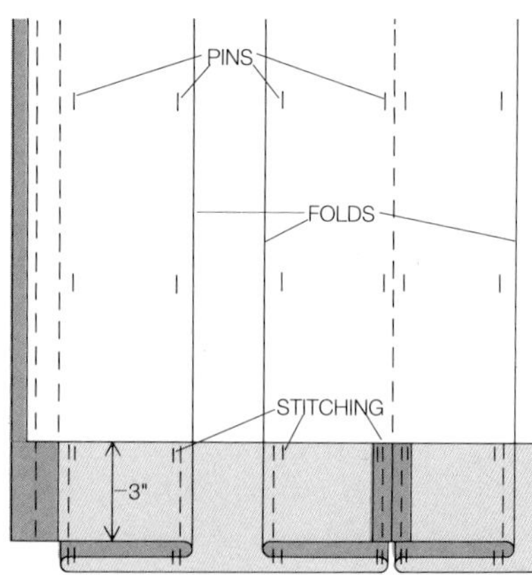

10. *At bottom edge,* turn up face fabric 3 inches; press. Turn raw edge in to meet pressed fold and press again. Stitch lower hem close to second fold to form rod pocket.

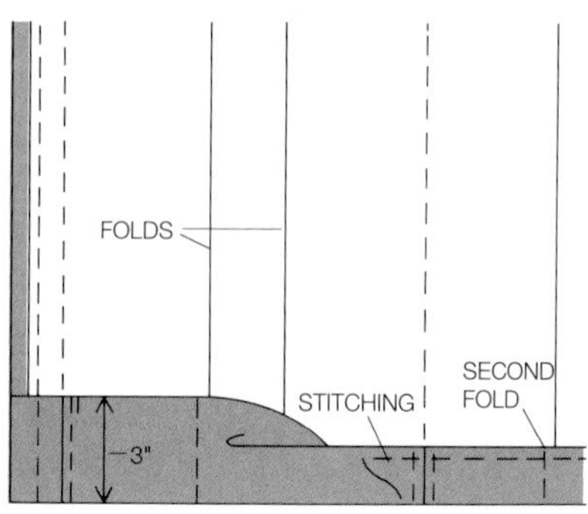

11. *Turn shade* right side up. On one edge, fold back return along return stitching. Then, fold edge of shade forward to meet return stitching, forming a ¾-inch pleat. Hand-stitch pleat to lower edge of pocket.

12. *On right side* of shade, measure finished length from bottom of hem and mark with pins every 4 inches across width. Measure and trim top allowance ¼ inch narrower than board. Fold top allowance, lining sides together, along pin-marked finished length line; press. Remove pins. Press pleats in place above finished length line.

To join face fabric and lining, overcast top edge with a wide zigzag stitch, or serge.

13. *With pins,* mark each ring position, aligning rings horizontally (rings will be sewn to side hem stitching and vertical stitching but not return stitching). Place bottom rings at top of rod pocket and other rings 6 to 10 inches apart.

14. *Follow step 13,* "Flat Roman shade," page 75, to sew on rings, being careful not to catch sides of pleats.

15. *Cover one end* of rod with masking tape and insert in pocket; slip-stitch closed. Form ¾-inch pleat as on other end; hand-stitch pleat to lower hem.

16. *Follow steps 15–18* and 20–21, "Flat Roman shade," page 75, with these changes or additions: In step 15, fold and staple return portion of top allowance to each board end; in step 18, tie together lower four rings in each row to create pouf; and in step 20, disregard reference to folds.

Cloud Shade

Soft shirring across the top differentiates the cloud shade from the balloon shade. The tape used to achieve this look comes in a variety of patterns, from simple gathers to pencil pleats and smocking. Rings are attached to the back of the shade; when the shade is drawn up, gentle scallops form.

Planning. This project is for an outside-mounted cloud shade. Note the hardware and notions you'll need (see page 72). Buy shirring tape equal in length to total shade width. Two-cord tape, the narrowest, creates about an inch of shirring; four-cord tape creates about 4 inches.

For the heading (the ruffle above the shirring), choose a size according to the width of the tape. With two-cord tape, a 2- to 3-inch heading is appropriate. With three- or four-cord tape, the heading is usually ½ inch.

Vertical spacing of the rings can range from 6 to 10 inches, depending on the depth of the folds.

To create a base for the rings on an unlined sheer shade, take ¼-inch vertical tucks midway between seams joining widths. Press the tucks to one side and stitch them down. Sew the rings to the tucks, keeping vertical spacing equal.

Choosing fabric. A cloud shade made from a crisp fabric will hold its shape and provide good light control and privacy. One made from batiste, voile, or lace will hang in soft folds and filter light (if such a shade is unlined, the cord, rings, and window frame will show through).

Calculating yardage. The following project assumes a 1½-inch-wide board.

1. Measure your window and fill in window treatment work sheet (see pages 20–24) to arrive at board size. Add 3 inches for two 1½-inch returns. (If, for example, your board is 60 inches long, adjusted board size would be 63 inches.)

2. Divide adjusted board size by 10 for number of spaces (in example, 63 ÷ 10 = 6.3); round off to nearest whole number (6.3 rounds to 6).

3. To determine number of widths, divide number of spaces by 2 (each width of fabric will make two spaces, or scallops); if result contains a half-width, round up to next whole number.

Continue to fill in second row of work sheet, using number of widths just determined.

Use following allowances in your calculations:

	Fabric	*Lining*
Top	Heading size + ½"	None
Lower hems	21"	18"

Cloud shade step-by-step

1. ***Choose and prepare*** face fabric and lining, joining fabric widths as described (see pages 24–33) and aligning seams on face fabric and lining. Press seams open.

2. ***For an odd number of spaces,*** measure and cut a half-width from right or left width on face fabric. Trim lining 1 inch narrower than face fabric on each side.

3. ***Follow steps 3–4,*** "Balloon shade," page 79, to make side hems.

4. ***With lining*** right side up, measure and mark vertical lines for rows of stitching at midpoint of each full width. Pin marked lines and seams.

5. ***Follow step 6,*** "Balloon shade," page 79, to stitch lines and seams.

6. ***At bottom edge,*** turn up face fabric 3 inches; press. Turn raw edge in to meet pressed fold and press again. Stitch lower hem close to second fold to form rod pocket.

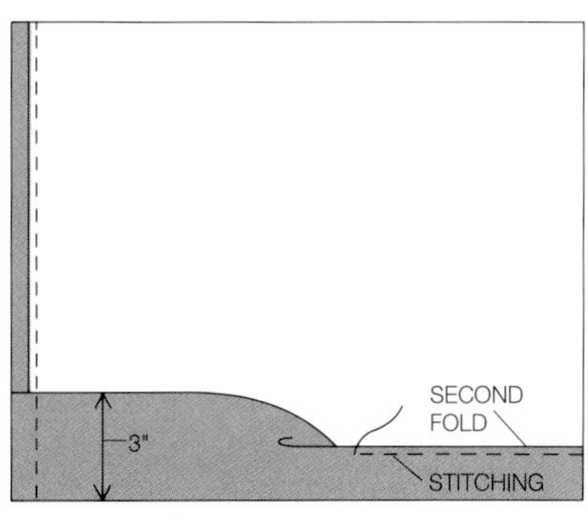

7. ***Follow step 13,*** "Balloon shade," facing page, to mark ring positions (disregard reference to return stitching).

8. ***On right side*** of shade, measure finished length from bottom of hem and mark with pins every 4 inches across width. Measure proper top allowance beyond finished length line; trim. Remove stitching at top of each side hem to finished length line. Trim lining so upper edge meets pin-marked line.

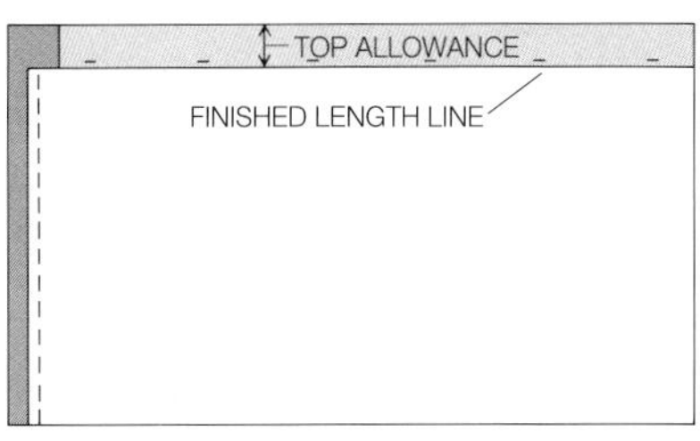

9. ***Fold top allowance,*** wrong sides together, on finished length line; press. Remove pins. Position shirring tape, right side up, on back of shade, turning under ends and placing top edge ¾ inch above raw edge.

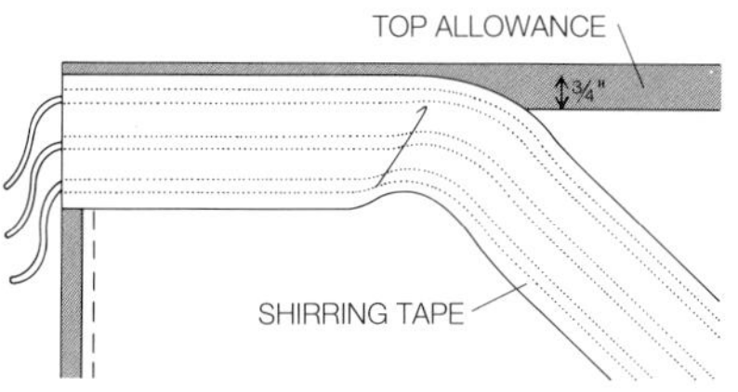

Pin, stitch, and gather tape, following manufacturer's instructions (shirred heading should equal adjusted board size).

10. ***Follow step 13,*** "Flat Roman shade," page 75, to sew on rings.

11. ***Follow first part*** of step 15, "Flat Roman shade," page 75, to cover mounting board.

12. ***Staple shade*** to face and ends of mounting board, placing staples vertically 2 inches apart and concealing them between gathers. Insert rod in pocket and slip-stitch closed.

13. ***Follow steps 16–18,*** "Flat Roman shade," page 75; in step 18, tie together lower four rings in each row to create pouf.

14. ***Follow steps 20–21,*** "Flat Roman shade," page 75, to finish shade (disregard reference to folds in step 20).

Ruffled Cloud Shade

A ruffled bottom adds a frilly detail to a cloud shade. Plan your shade and calculate yardage as for a plain cloud shade (see page 80), except that you'll need extra fabric for the ruffle; also, lower hem allowances for both face fabric and lining are 18½ inches. A fabric-covered rod is sewn to the shade's back.

Ruffled cloud shade step-by-step

1. *Choose and prepare* face fabric and lining, joining fabric widths as described (see pages 24–33) and aligning seams on face fabric and lining. Press seams open.

2. *For an odd number of spaces,* measure and cut a half-width from right or left width on face fabric. Trim lining 1 inch narrower than face fabric on each side.

3. *On face fabric,* turn under and press 1½-inch side hems. Repeat on lining, turning under 1 inch.

4. *Make folded ruffle* (see page 51). With raw edges aligned, pin to right side of lower edge of face fabric. Baste, making a ½-inch seam.

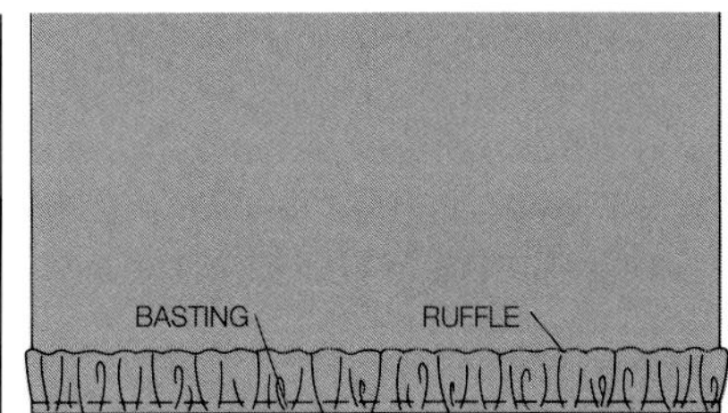

5. *With right sides together* and lower raw edges aligned, center lining over face fabric and ruffle (side edges of lining should be ½ inch from face fabric edges). Pin lower edge; stitch, making a ½-inch seam.

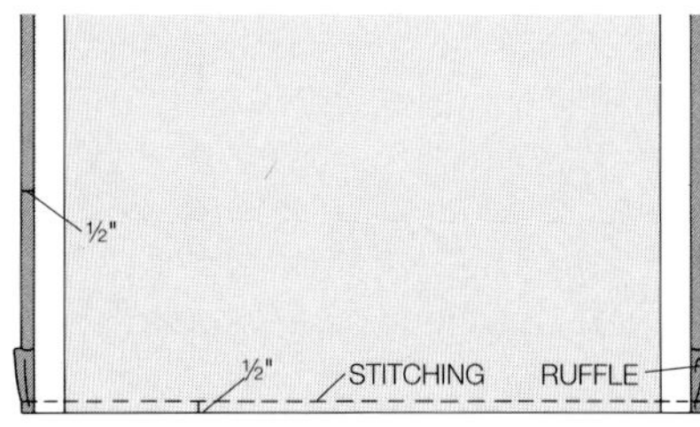

6. *Turn face fabric* and lining right sides out; press lightly just above ruffle. With lining side up, pin side and lower edges together. Starting at upper right and making a ¾-inch seam, stitch side edge, across bottom, and up other side, pivoting at corners.

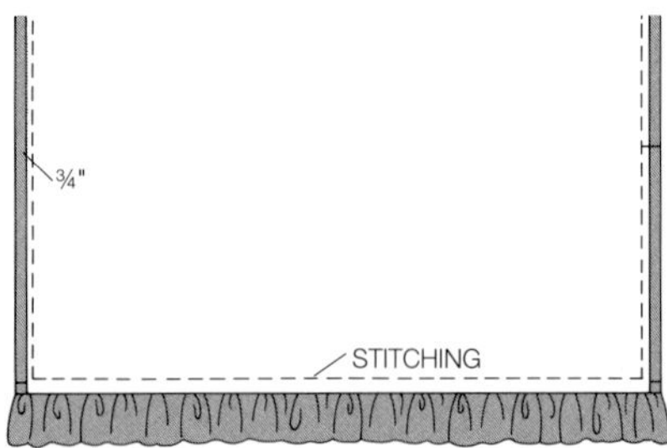

7. *With lining side up,* measure and mark vertical lines for rows of stitching at midpoint of each full width. Pin seams and lines.

8. *Stitch seams and lines,* beginning at lower edge and stitching just above ruffle (match top thread to lining and bobbin thread to face fabric).

9. *Cut a strip of fabric* wide enough to go around rod plus 1 inch and 2 inches longer than rod. Fold in half lengthwise; stitch across one end and along entire length, making a ½-inch seam; trim. Turn right side out, insert rod, and slip-stitch end closed.

10. *With pins,* mark ring positions, placing bottom rings at lower edge stitching and spacing others at chosen distance; align horizontally.

11. *Follow steps 8–9,* "Cloud shade," page 81, to apply and gather shirring tape.

12. *Divide rod* into number of spaces on shade; mark. Using doubled heavy-duty thread to match lining, sew rod to each end of shade at lower stitching, sewing a ring on at same time; direct needle through lining and under stitching without catching face fabric.

Line up remaining marks on rod with vertical stitching; sew rod and rings to shade in same manner. Sew on remaining rings.

13. *Follow first part* of step 15, "Flat Roman shade," page 75, to cover mounting board.

14. *Follow steps 16–18,* "Flat Roman shade," page 75; in step 18, tie together lower four rings in each row to create pouf.

15. *Follow steps 20–21,* "Flat Roman shade," page 75, to finish shade (disregard reference to folds in step 20).

Roller Shade

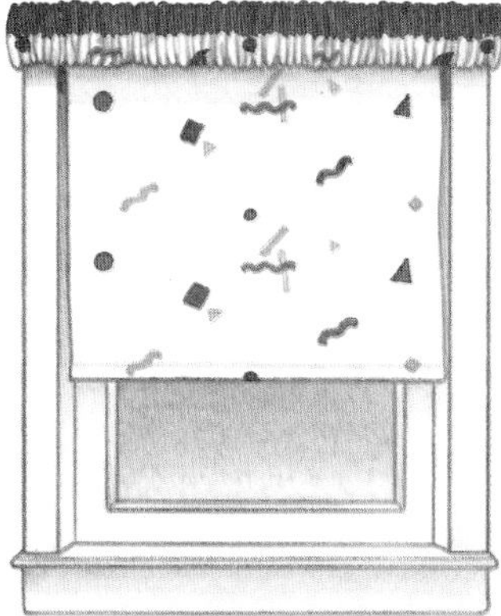

Of all the shade styles, the roller shade requires the least amount of fabric and sewing—there are no seams, side hems, folds, or gathers. And, because the shade is flat, the fabric's pattern shows clearly. A top treatment, such as a valance or narrow cornice, finishes the shade nicely and hides the roller.

Two cautions: The width of the roller shade can't exceed the usable width of your fabric—splicing or seaming is glaringly obvious and interferes with the smooth operation of the shade. Also, roller shades are not recommended for windows more than 5 feet high.

Planning and installation. Choose the type of roll and mounting before you purchase hardware or fabric.

Because you won't know the thickness of the shade until it's finished, make the shade before installing the brackets. When you install them, be sure to position them so the roller will be perfectly level.

For a *conventional-roll shade,* the blade end of the roller should be on your left as you face the window. Mount the slotted bracket on the left side and the other bracket on the right. For a *reverse-roll shade,* reverse the brackets.

Choosing fabric and backing. Look for a firmly woven all-cotton or other natural-fiber fabric that won't fray easily. Avoid fabrics with heavy finishes, which may prevent the backing from adhering to the fabric.

Also, don't use a blend that contains synthetic fibers. To be safe, test the fabric and backing to make sure the fabric bonds well.

Fusible shade backing, a heat-sensitive material made especially for shades, stiffens the fabric and, if it's a blackout backing, blocks light. Backings come in varying widths; look for them in fabric stores.

Calculating yardage. The finished width of your shade is equal to the desired length of the roller. The piece of fabric must be 3 inches wider than the finished shade width and 12 inches longer than the finished length (for wrapping around the roller). If the fabric has repeats, buy enough to place a full repeat just above the slat and to center a repeat horizontally.

Purchase a piece of fusible backing the same size as the fabric.

Roller shade step-by-step

1. ***Choose and prepare*** face fabric (see pages 25–32).

2. ***Square off one cut end*** of face fabric. Measure total length of shade; square and cut other end.

3. ***Fuse shade and backing,*** following manufacturer's instructions.

4. ***Measure and mark*** side edges to finished width, keeping lines straight and corners square. Cut along lines with sharp scissors, making long, clean strokes and keeping fabric perfectly flat.

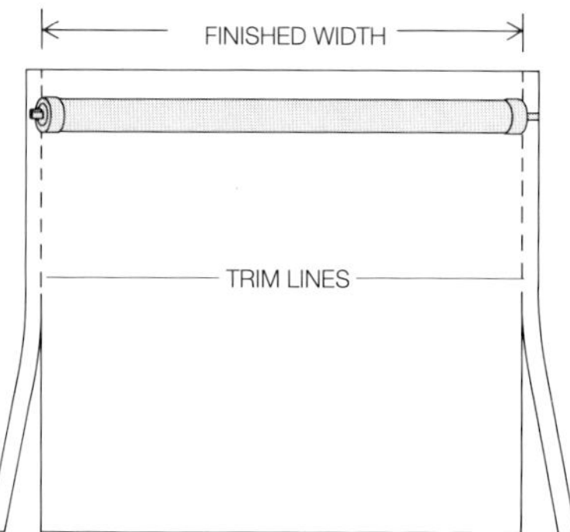

5. ***Turn up lower edge*** 1½ inches, backing sides together; finger-press fold. Stitch 1¼ inches from edge, using longest straight stitch setting. Insert slat in pocket.

6. ***Align top edge*** of shade with guideline on roller (if roller has no guideline, hold roller firmly on a table and, with marker lying flat on table, draw a line along roller).

7. ***Attach shade to roller*** with masking tape, aligning edge with guideline; be sure orientation is correct for either conventional or reverse roll.

To check that shade is straight, roll by hand and insert in brackets. If shade is crooked, unroll and adjust. If roller is wood, staple shade to roller, pounding in staples if necessary.

8. ***To prevent edges*** from fraying, pull shade down and run a bead of liquid fray preventer along each edge; let dry completely before raising shade.

Valances

Simple balloon valances (at right) were stapled to mounting boards. Matching stationary rod-pocket curtains feature 4-inch headings.

Contrast banding on a scalloped valance (below) accentuates its graceful lines. The valance tops stationary drapery panels similarly banded.

WINDOW TREATMENT: MUFFY HOOK

DESIGN: SANDRA MOZART. WINDOW TREATMENT: ROSSETTI & CORRIEA DRAPERIES INC.

DESIGN AND WINDOW TREATMENT: HEIDI EMMETT

Windows in a gentle bay wear tapered valances hung on wide rods. Barely there 12-inch lace panels (sold as valances) slip over tension rods mounted underneath.

In a guest room for the grandkids, a scalloped valance that runs the length of one wall makes a focal point of an angled wall and dormered window.

DESIGNER: BRENDA LYNE

A nautical theme for a lakeside house: The tailored box valance is pieced to resemble a nautical flag in colors that repeat elsewhere in the room.

DESIGNER: ANN PLATZ

A swag valance echoes the form of an arched window. The pleated valance is looped around brackets made by attaching plaster rosettes to short dowel pieces. The jabots, or cascading side panels, provide visual weight and balance.

Simple arched valance gathered with shirring tape and mounted on a board visually unifies beds dressed in the same floral fabric. Gimp trims the canopies.

DESIGN: JUDY HENN INTERIORS
WINDOW TREATMENT: DELTA PI DESIGN

Deep box-pleated valance with contrast trim caps apron-length draperies. The folded banding was topstitched to the face fabric before the lining was attached. Tailored tiebacks draw the panels to the side.

Balloon valance in an old-world tapestry print tops tall bay windows in a country-style kitchen. Tissue in the poufs gives them their shape. Note how the motif is centered in all the spaces.

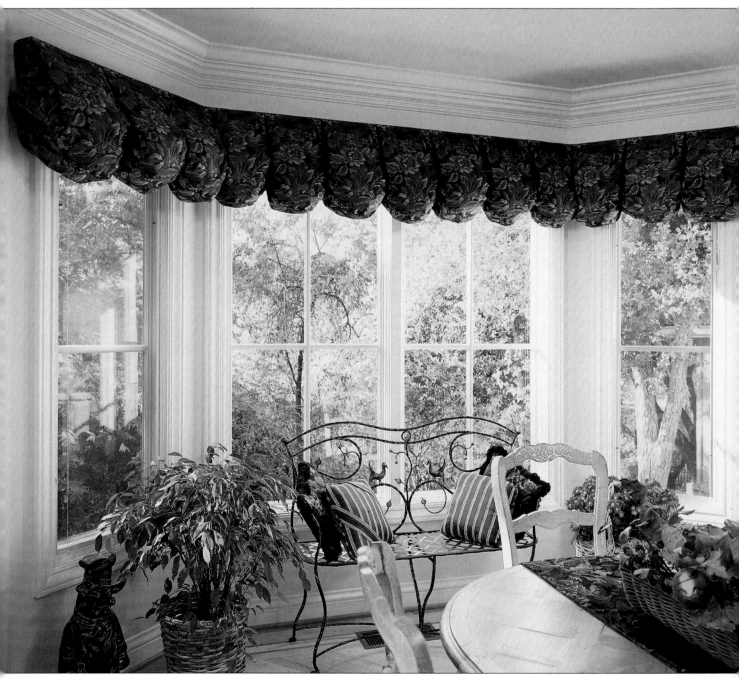

DESIGN: INGELA'S INTERIORS INC. WINDOW TREATMENT: DELTA PI DESIGN

DESIGNER: CHER BEALL, CASHMERE & COMPANY

In this kitchen (above), a box-pleated valance made from a silk-blend fabric conceals mini-blinds. Black synthetic suede ties and silver buttons add detail (at left).

HOW TO MAKE

Valances

Rod-Pocket Valance ■ Pouf Valance ■ Arched Valance ■ Tapered Valance ■ Scalloped Valance ■ Wide-Rod Valance ■ Tailed Roman Valance ■ Balloon & Cloud Valances ■ Box- & Kick-Pleated Valances ■ Tab Stagecoach Valance ■ Rolled Stagecoach Valance ■ Shirred Valance ■ Skirt Valance

Whether used alone or with other treatments, fabric valances soften and frame windows. Some valances, such as rod-pocket and balloon valances, can be thought of simply as shortened curtains or shades; other valances are unique.

Often, you'll use the same fabric for the valance as for the undertreatment. Where there's no undertreatment, follow the fabric guidelines for the longer version. Or see the individual project for specific recommendations.

Though styles may be different, most valances call for an attached lining at the lower hem. Sewing the lining in with the face fabric at the lower edge ensures a neat, professional look.

Length guidelines. Most valances begin 8 inches above the window opening, though this can vary depending on what's underneath. Finished length for straight valances is from 12 to 18 inches; shaped valances can be considerably longer on the sides.

Long valances can reduce light, interfere with the view, and visually shorten windows. If you like the look of a deep valance, consider starting it farther above the window opening.

Hardware. Rod-pocket and related shaped valances hang from curtain rods (see below); install the rod as described on page 43. Other valances, such as pleated and balloon styles, are board mounted. A valance used alone requires a 1½-inch board; one used over other treatments requires a 3½- or 5½-inch board, or whatever is needed to clear the undertreatment.

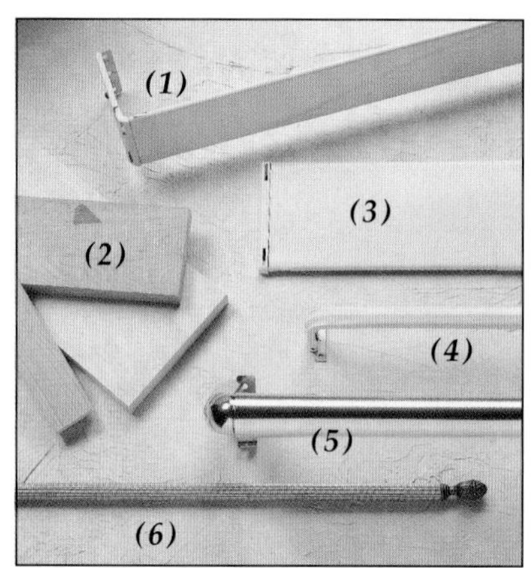

Rods and boards for valances include (1) 2½-inch wide rod, (2) mounting boards, (3) 4½-inch wide rod, (4) flat rod, (5) brass rod, and (6) brass café rod.

Rod-Pocket Valance

This basic valance style looks just like a short rod-pocket curtain, but the order of fabrication is different, and the lining hem is attached. A contrast band emphasizes the lower edge. Directions for a plain valance are also included.

Calculating yardage. Measure your window and fill in the window treatment work sheet (see pages 20–24). For most fabrics, a fullness of 2½ times the finished width is best. For length guidelines, see at left.

Use the following allowances in your calculations. Refer to the chart on page 44 for pocket size. For a contrast band on the lower edge, there's no lower hem allowance on the face fabric. Instead, you'll need contrast fabric equal in length to the total valance width and equal in width to 2 times the desired finished width, plus 3 inches.

	Fabric	*Lining*
Lower hems	None*	1½"
Side hems	3" total	3" total
Top	2 x pocket + 2 x heading (if used)	None

* For a valance without a band, lower hem allowance is 3".

Rod-pocket valance step-by-step

1. *Choose and prepare* face fabric and lining, joining fabric widths as described (see pages 24–33). Press seams open.

2. *For a contrast band,* pin and stitch band to lower edge of face fabric, right sides together, making a seam equal to band's finished width.

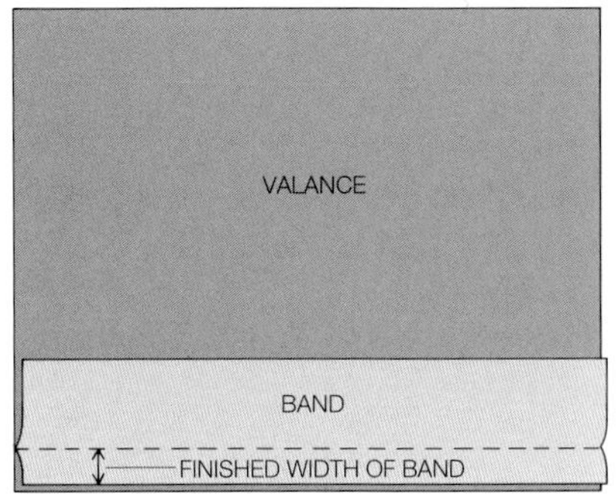

Press seam allowances toward bottom.

3. *With right sides together,* pin and stitch band (or face fabric, if there is no band) and lining at lower edge, making a 1½-inch seam. Press seam allowances toward band (or face fabric). Press lower hem so 1½ inches of band (or face fabric) show on back.

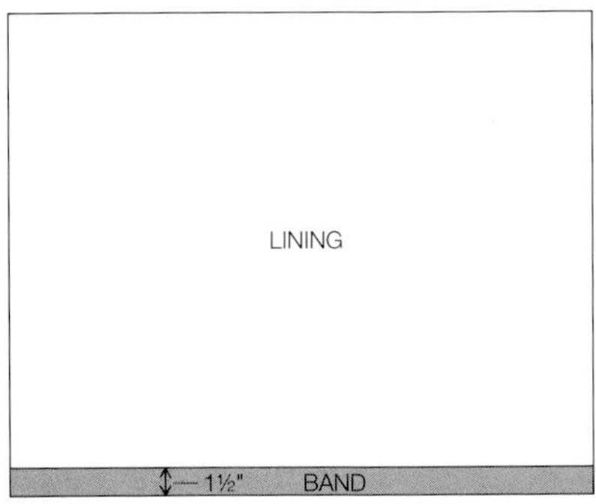

4. *Turn under* 1½-inch side hems on face fabric and lining, rolling under ¼ inch more of lining; starting at lower edge, pin face fabric and lining together about three-quarters of way up sides.

5. *On right side* of face fabric, measure from lower edge a distance equal to finished length and mark with pins every 4 inches across valance. Measure and mark proper top allowance (2 times pocket plus 2 times heading, if used) above pin-marked finished length line. Trim ravel allowance.

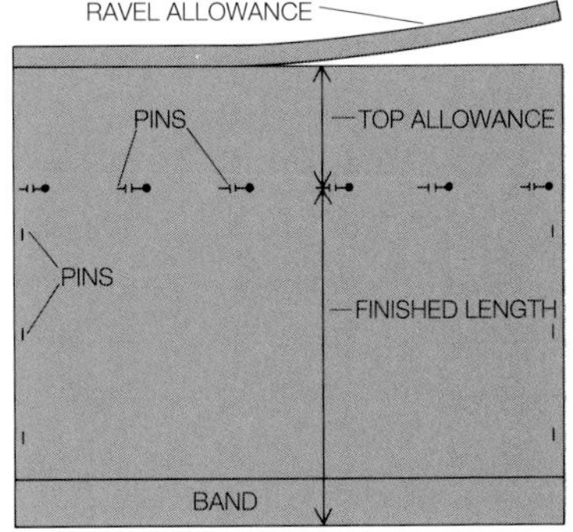

Trim lining so upper edge meets pin-marked finished length line.

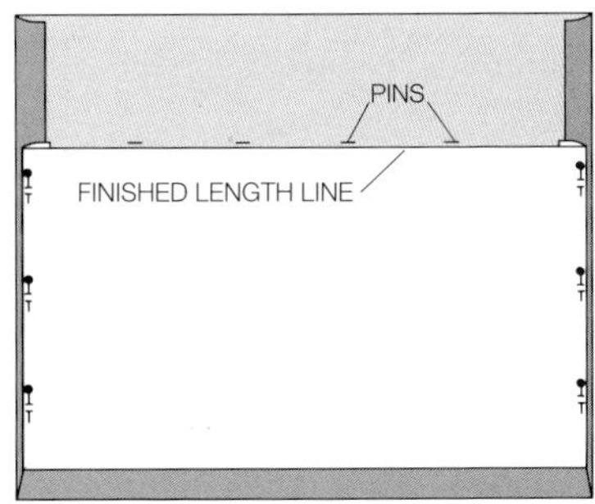

6. *Fold top edge* of fabric, wrong sides together, along finished length line; press. Remove pins. Turn raw edge in to meet pressed fold and press again. Stitch close to second fold. For heading, if used, stitch again from top fold a distance equal to heading depth; press.

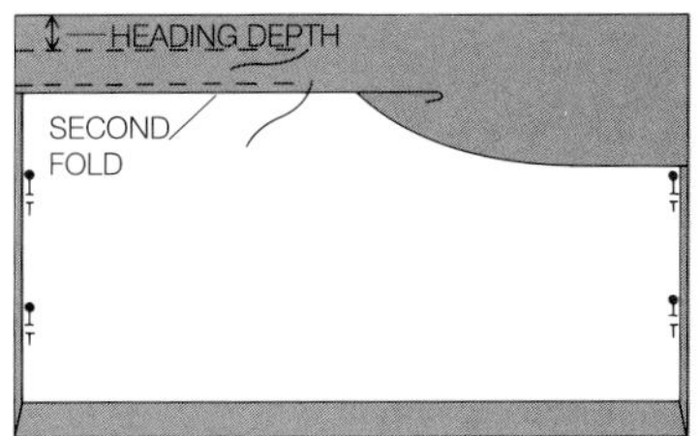

7. *Slip-stitch* side hems closed.

8. *Slip rod through pocket* between back two layers of fabric, gathering fabric evenly.

Pouf Valance

Sometimes called a mock balloon, a pouf valance is a rod-pocket valance with a pocket at the top and bottom. The rod in the bottom pocket is attached under the top rod, creating a pouf at the lower edge. For extra fullness, place crumpled tissue paper in the pouf.

Calculating yardage. Measure your window and fill in the window treatment work sheet (see pages 20–24). For most fabrics, a fullness of 2½ times the finished width is best.

To determine finished length, make a sketch of your window. Finished length is equal to the distance covered above the window opening, plus double the distance the valance goes into the opening (it goes under itself), plus the distance to the point where it ends.

Typically, a valance used alone or over an inside-mounted treatment starts 8 inches above the opening, extends 4 inches into the opening, goes 4 inches under itself, and ends 4 inches above the opening. (Finished length in example is 20 inches.)

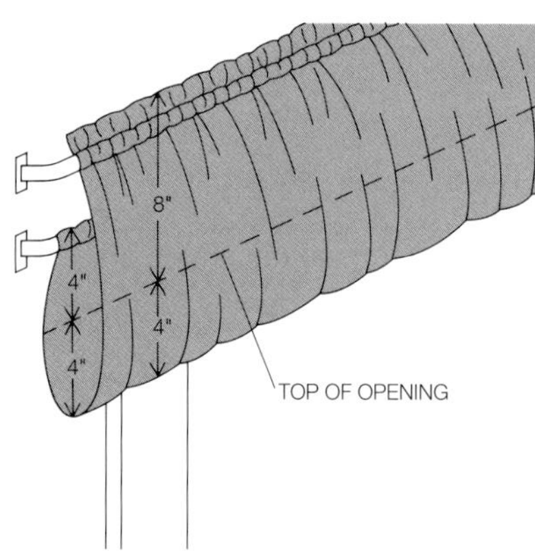

A valance over draperies might start 15 inches above the opening (near or at the ceiling), extend 3 inches into the opening, go 3 inches under itself, and end 7 inches above the opening (enough to cover the 5-inch drapery heading).

Use the following allowances in your calculations. Refer to the chart on page 44 for pocket size.

	Fabric	*Lining*
Lower hems	2 x pocket	None
Side hems	3" total	2½" total
Top	2 x pocket + 2 x heading (if used)	None

Pouf valance step-by-step

1. ***Choose and prepare*** face fabric and lining, joining fabric widths as described (see pages 24–33). Press seams open.

2. ***On right side*** of face fabric, measure from lower edge a distance equal to lower hem (2 times pocket size). Mark with pins every 4 inches across valance. From pin-marked line, measure a distance equal to finished length. Mark with pins every 4 inches across valance.

Measure and mark proper top allowance (2 times pocket plus 2 times heading, if used) above pin-marked finished length line. Trim ravel allowance.

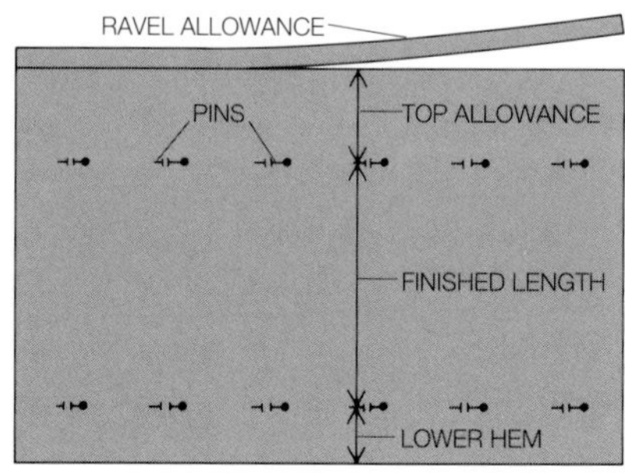

3. ***With right sides together,*** lay lining on face fabric so lower edge of lining is on lower pin-marked finished length line. Trim lining so upper edge meets upper finished length line.

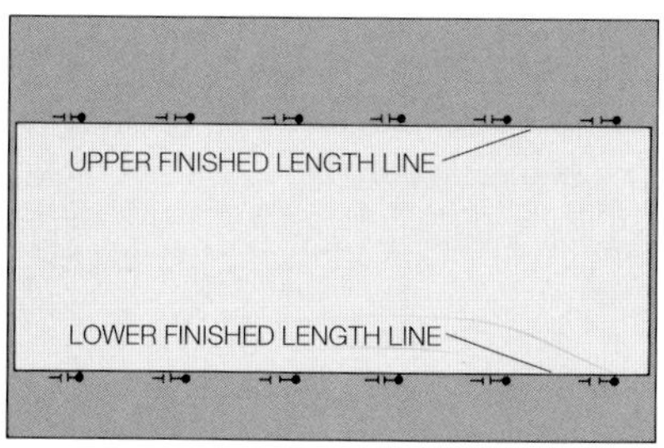

4. ***Pin lining*** to face fabric, right sides together, so edges are aligned at one side (lower edge of lining is on lower pin-marked line).

5. ***Follow steps 8–9,*** "Rod-pocket curtains," page 45, to stitch and press side hems.

6. ***At lower edge,*** fold face fabric, wrong side toward lining, along finished length line; press. Remove pins. Turn raw edge in to meet pressed fold and press again. Stitch close to second fold.

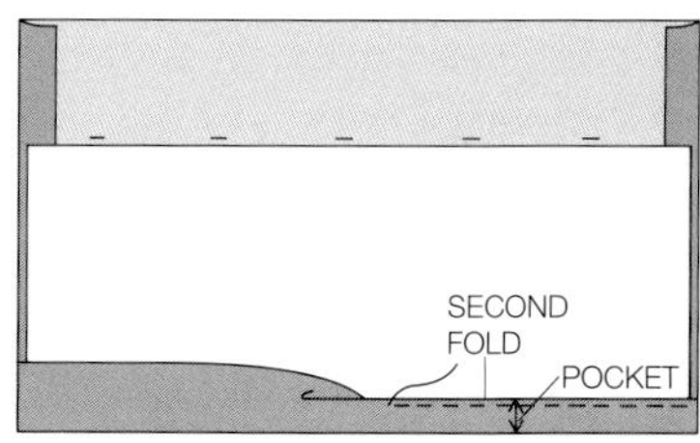

7. ***Follow step 6,*** "Rod-pocket valance," page 91, to fold and stitch top pocket and heading, if used.

8. ***Slip rods through pockets*** between back two layers of fabric, gathering fabric evenly.

Arched Valance

This gathered valance forms a graceful curve along its lower edge. The arch should be gentle; a sharply arched valance, when gathered, won't curve evenly.

Calculating yardage. Measure your window and fill in the window treatment work sheet (see pages 20–24). For most fabrics, a fullness of 2½ times the finished width is best. Finished length is the longest point at the sides.

For best appearance, the difference between the long and short points of the arch should be no more than 8 inches and no less than 3 inches. Typical finished side length is 18 inches, with a center length of 10 inches.

Use the following allowances in your calculations. Refer to the chart on page 44 for pocket size. If you plan to add a ruffle, piping, or facing, buy extra fabric.

	Fabric	*Lining*
Lower hems	½"	½"
Side hems	3" total	3" total
Top	2 x pocket + 2 x heading (if used)	None

Arched valance step-by-step

1. *Choose and prepare* face fabric and lining, joining fabric widths as described (see pages 24–33). Press seams open.

2. *Turn under* and press 1½-inch side hems on face fabric and lining.

3. *On right side* of face fabric, measure from upper edge a distance equal to top allowance (2 times pocket plus 2 times heading, if used). Mark with pins every 4 inches across valance to make finished length line.

4. *With right sides together* and lining facing up, pin face fabric and lining, aligning side hem folds and lower raw edges. Trim lining so upper edge meets pin-marked finished length line.

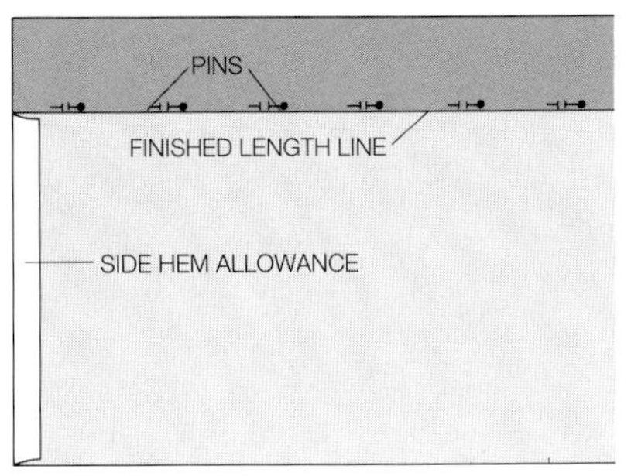

5. *Make a paper pattern* at least ½ inch longer than finished length and half finished width of valance, dividing pattern vertically into fourths.

From top edge, mark shortest point plus ½ inch for hem allowance (10½ inches in example) on center edge; mark finished length (longest point) plus ½ inch (18½ inches in example) on side. Subtract short distance from long and divide by 4 for increment.

Add increment to dimension at center edge and, at next vertical line, mark that distance from top edge with a standing pin. Continue adding increment to previous distance and pinning at vertical lines. Then move middle three pins up to strike a gentle arch, moving middle pin up most. Mark curve.

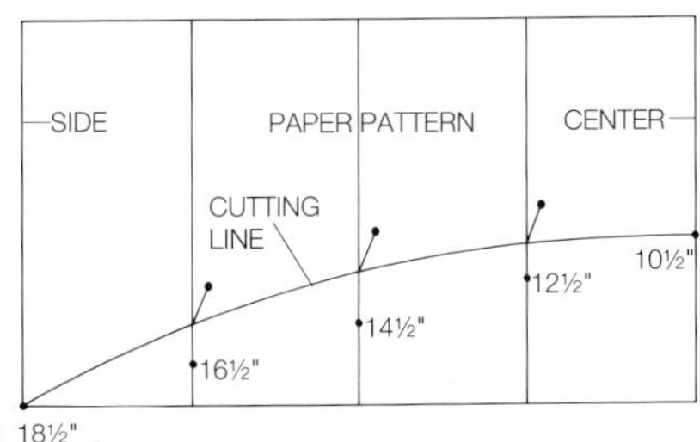

6. *Cut pattern* and lay on half of valance, placing top edge of pattern on finished length line; mark curved cutting line. Flip pattern and mark other half of valance. Cut face fabric and lining on line.

7. *For a same-fabric facing* (see page 94), topstitch facing to lower edge of lining. *For trim* (see page 94), apply to lower edge of face fabric.

8. *Pin lower edges* of face fabric and lining together. Stitch, making a ½-inch seam; trim and clip seam allowances. Turn right side out and press lower edge. Pin sides.

9. *Follow steps 6–8,* "Rod-pocket valance," page 91, to finish valance.

Tapered Valance

This easy-to-make, gathered valance cascades down the sides of a window, framing the view. It uses a minimum of fabric. A contrast lining looks especially nice on a longer valance.

Calculating yardage. Simply allow a full width for each tapered side panel and another full width (or more for especially wide windows) for the center portion.

Measure your window and fill in the window treatment work sheet (see pages 20–24). Fullness is 2½ times the finished width. Divide the total width by the number of widths you're using to get the flat width of the center panel and each tapered side panel. If the number is more than your fabric's usable width, the fullness will be slightly reduced. If the number is less, trim each width; or use full widths, increasing the fullness slightly.

Make the center panel 12 to 18 inches long. Tapered valances look best when the side panels are either a third or two-thirds longer than the center panel. You can save fabric if you allow two long cuts for the side panels and shorter cuts for the center panel.

Use the following allowances in your calculations. Refer to the

Finishing Shaped Valances

Sometimes, the lower edges of arched, tapered, and scalloped valances may reveal a bit of the lining from the front. If you wish to hide or disguise the lining, you have several options.

One easy solution is to line the valance with a contrast fabric. Or you can add a deep ruffle or narrow piping to the lower edge. Still another approach is to topstitch a same-fabric facing to the lower edge of the lining (note that the facing will show from the outside).

You can also topstitch a contrast band to a scalloped valance, but this trim is tricky to apply and adds bulk.

The project will instruct you when to add the trim.

Ruffles

To make a folded ruffle, see page 51.

1. ***With raw edges aligned,*** pin ruffle to lower edge of face fabric, aligning ends of ruffle with side hem folds.

2. ***Baste,*** making a ½-inch seam.

Piping

For ½-inch piping, you'll need a 2-inch strip of contrast fabric equal in length to the total width of the valance. For ¼-inch piping, make the strip 1½ inches wide. (Bias-cut strips work best on curved edges but require more fabric.) Note that the piping won't hide the lining.

1. ***Fold strip*** in half lengthwise, wrong sides together; press. At one end, open strip and turn in ½ inch; finger press.

2. ***With raw edges aligned,*** pin piping to lower edge of face fabric, aligning folded end of strip with side hem fold on valance. Making a ½-inch seam, baste to within a few inches of other side. Trim piping ½ inch beyond side hem fold. Turn in ½ inch; finger press. Finish basting.

Same-fabric facing

For an arched or scalloped valance, add 2 inches more than the difference between the longest and shortest points on the valance to the cut length on your work sheet.

Cut the face fabric to the desired shape, using the leftover fabric for the facing.

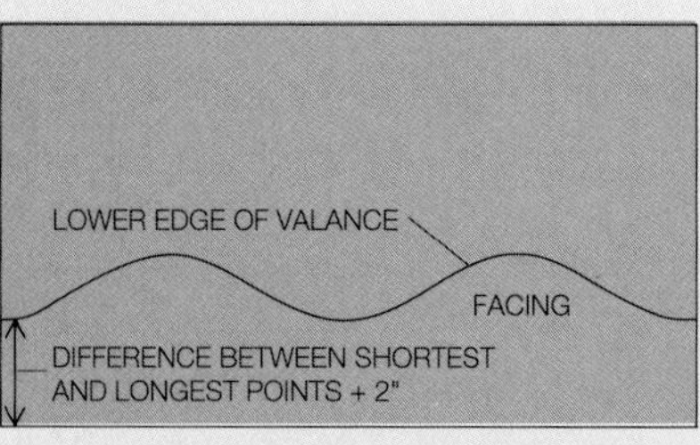

1. ***Turn under*** top ½ inch of facing; press. With right sides up and side hems open, pin facing to lining so lower straight edge of facing aligns with longest points on lining. Baste; topstitch facing to lining close to pressed fold.

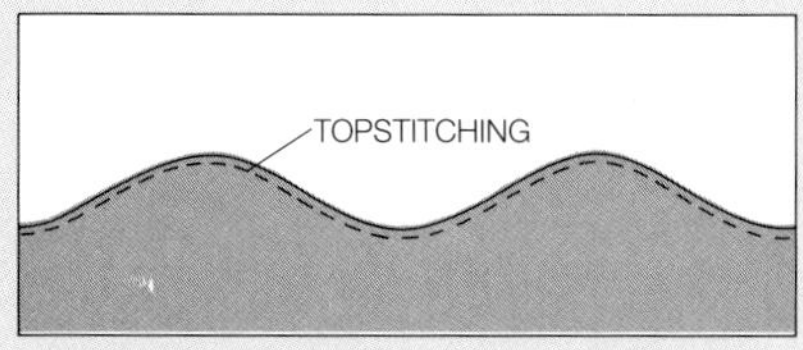

2. ***Trim facing*** along curved edge of lining.

Contrast banding on a scalloped valance

You'll need two strips of fabric, each as long as the total valance width. The width of strips should equal the distance between the high and low points on the lower edge, plus the desired finished width of the banding (typically 1 to 2 inches), plus 1 inch.

1. ***Lay strips*** right sides together, aligning raw edges. Placing pattern 1½ inches from each side, cut lower edges. Move pattern up a distance equal to finished width of band plus 1 inch. Mark upper curve and cut along line.

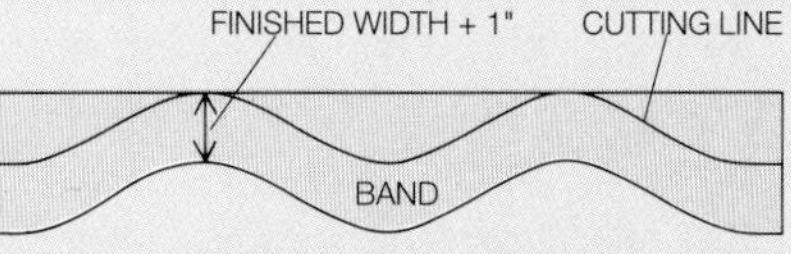

2. ***Pin strips together*** on upper curve and stitch, making a ½-inch seam. Trim and clip seam allowances. Turn right side out; press edge.

3. ***With right sides up*** and side hems open, pin and baste lower raw edge of band to lower edge of valance. Pin and topstitch seamed edge of band to valance.

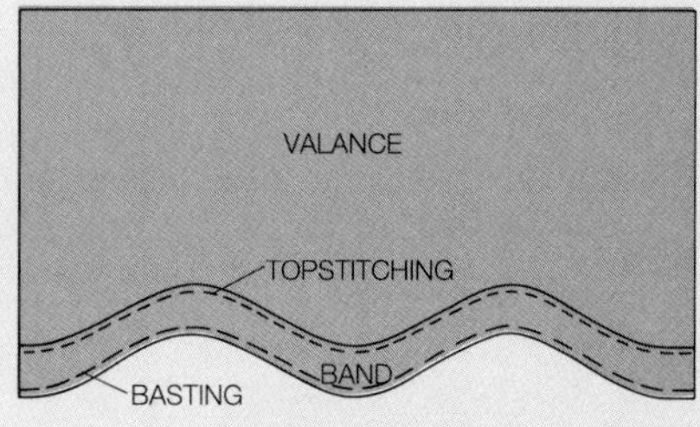

chart on page 44 for pocket size. Purchase extra fabric for a ruffle or piping.

	Fabric	*Lining*
Lower hems	½"	½"
Side hems	3" total	3" total
Top	2 x pocket + 2 x heading (if used)	None

Tapered valance step-by-step

1. *Choose and prepare* face fabric and lining, joining fabric widths as described (see pages 24–33). Press seams open.

2. *Follow steps 2–4,* "Arched valance," page 93, to press side hems, mark top allowance, and trim lining.

3. *At each inner corner* where center and side widths meet, measure and mark finished length at center plus ½ inch from pin-marked finished length line; draw a line connecting inner corners. At ends, measure and mark outer finished length plus ½ inch from finished length line. Measure and mark depth of returns.

Draw a line from each inner corner to return, rounding corners.

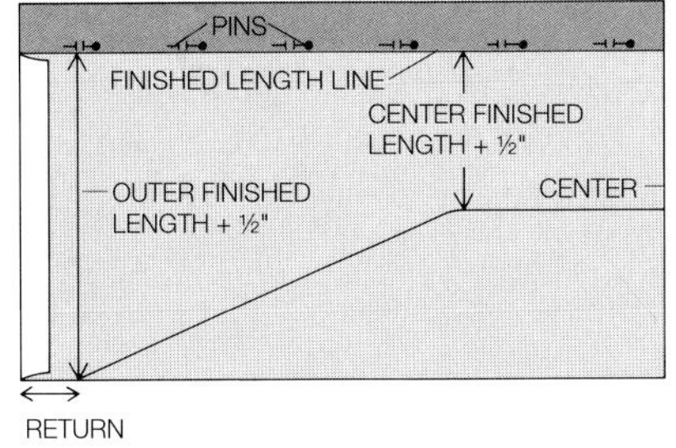

Cut lining and face fabric on lower marked lines.

4. *Follow steps 7–8,* "Arched valance," page 93, to apply trim and stitch lower edge; clip seam allowances at corners.

5. *Follow steps 6–8,* "Rod-pocket valance," page 91, to finish valance.

Scalloped Valance

A gently undulating lower hem sets this valance style apart from other shaped valances.

Calculating yardage. Measure your window and fill in the window treatment work sheet (see pages 20–24). For most fabrics, a fullness of 2½ times the finished width is best.

Finished length is based on the longest points at the sides. For a scalloped valance over traversing draperies or stationary side panels, the sides and center are often the same length. For a valance over blinds, a shade, or café curtains, the sides are often longer.

Follow the same length guidelines as for a tapered valance (see page 93); typically, the difference between the shortest and longest points is 5 inches.

Use the following allowances in your calculations. Refer to the chart on page 44 for pocket size. To add a ruffle, piping, facing, or contrast banding, you'll need more fabric.

	Fabric	*Lining*
Lower hems	½"	½"
Side hems	3" total	3" total
Top	2 x pocket + 2 x heading (if used)	None

Scalloped valance step-by-step

1. *Choose and prepare* face fabric and lining, joining fabric widths as described (see pages 24–33). Press seams open.

2. *Follow steps 2–4,* "Arched valance," page 93, to press side hems, mark top allowance, and trim lining.

3. *Make a paper pattern* at least ½ inch longer than finished length and half finished width of valance, dividing pattern vertically into fourths.

For a valance with sides and center at same length, mark finished length plus ½ inch at side and center lines; connect with a horizontal line. Mark shortest length plus ½ inch at third (middle) line; draw a horizontal line through point across pattern. Add another horizontal line midway between; at remaining vertical lines, mark points where vertical lines intersect middle horizontal line.

Connect points in a gentle curve; cut pattern.

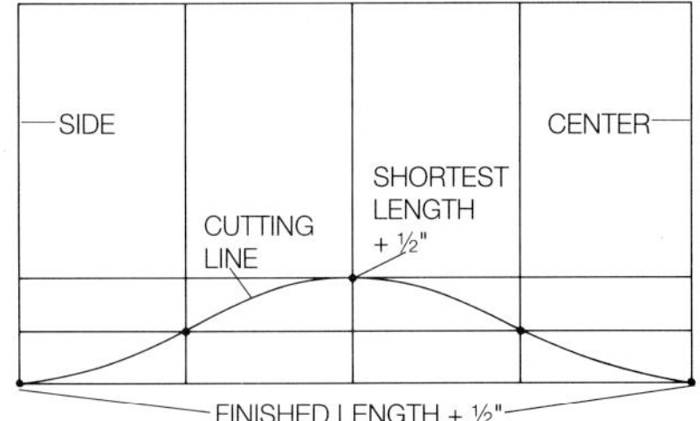

4. *Follow steps 6–8,* "Arched valance," page 93, to cut fabric, apply facing or trim, and stitch lower edge.

Continued on next page

5. Follow steps 6–8, "Rod-pocket valance," page 91, to finish valance.

Wide-Rod Valance

This unlined valance covers inside-mounted blinds or shades. A single valance has one pocket, a double valance two pockets. To add a skirt, make the lower heading 6 to 8 inches deep.

Calculating yardage. Measure your window and fill in the window treatment work sheet (see pages 20–24). For most fabrics, a fullness of 2½ times the finished width is best. The cut length is equal to 2 times the pocket(s) (see page 44 for pocket size) plus 2 times each heading, if used, plus 1 inch.

Wide-rod valance step-by-step

1. *Choose and prepare* fabric, joining widths as described (see pages 25–33). Press seams open.

2. *With wrong sides together,* fold in 1 inch at each end and press. Turn in raw edge to meet pressed fold and press again. Stitch each end close to second fold.

3. *Fold fabric* in half lengthwise, right sides together. Pin and stitch, making a ½-inch seam. Press seam open, being careful not to press edges.

4. *Turn valance* right side out. For a single valance, center seam at back; for a double valance, position seam so it will be at center back of either pocket. Press both long edges.

5. *For each heading,* if used, stitch at a distance equal to heading depth. For a two-pocket valance, stitch lengthwise at middle of valance.

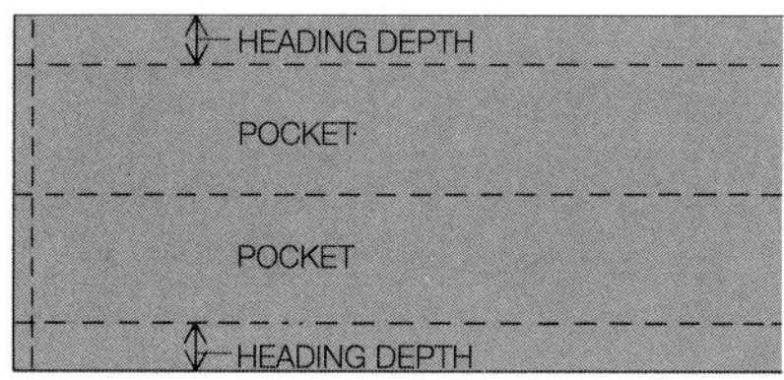

6. *Slip rod(s) through pocket(s),* gathering fabric evenly.

Tailed Roman Valance

In this short, stationary version of a Roman shade, you create tails at the sides by leaving off the outer rows of rings.

Make this valance as you would a flat Roman shade (see page 73), with the following modifications: Finished length equals the distance you want to see when the valance is finished, plus 18 inches. Rings are spaced 6 inches apart vertically and are placed a sixth of the finished width from each side edge. Adjust the cords for the proper tension and tie each cord to each screw eye.

If you like the look of a "relaxed" Roman, that is, a valance that droops slightly in the middle, and your board size is 48 inches or less, use just one row of rings on each side. For a straight lower edge, have rows of rings across the valance, just as on a shade. Insert a rod that extends from outer ring to outer ring; hand-stitch the pocket to keep the rod in place.

Balloon & Cloud Valances

These stationary valances are shortened versions of the shades.

Depending on the valance you want, follow "Balloon shade," page 78, "Cloud shade," page 80, or "Ruffled cloud shade," page 82, with these changes: Add 18 inches to the desired finished length (see page 90 for guidelines) for the permanent pouf. Adjust the cords for the proper tension and tie each cord to each screw eye.

You can also make a cloud valance with a pocket for a wide rod. Instead of the specified top allowance, add enough face fabric above the finished length line for the rod-pocket top allowance (2 times pocket plus 2 times heading, if used; see the chart on page 44 for pocket size). Instead of applying shirring tape, follow step 10, "Rod-pocket curtains," page 45, to stitch the pocket and optional heading.

When you sew on the rings, sew the top rings to the rod-pocket stitching.

Box- & Kick-Pleated Valances

A pleated valance sports deep inverted pleats, lending a tailored look to the window.

When you make the pleats and the spaces between them the same size, you create a classic box-pleated valance. If the pleats are more widely spaced, it's called a kick-pleated valance. Construction is basically the same for both types.

Planning. Pleated valances are board mounted; see the hardware information on page 90 for board sizes. Return size is equal to the width of the board.

It's best to try to hide seams within the pleats. To do this, you must add up spaces and pleats from one end to see where seams will occur and then adjust the seams as necessary.

Start by choosing space and pleat sizes. A good pleat width is 6 inches (12 inches before being pleated); space width can vary from 6 inches for a classic box-pleated valance up to the usable width of the fabric, less the pleat size, for a kick-pleated one.

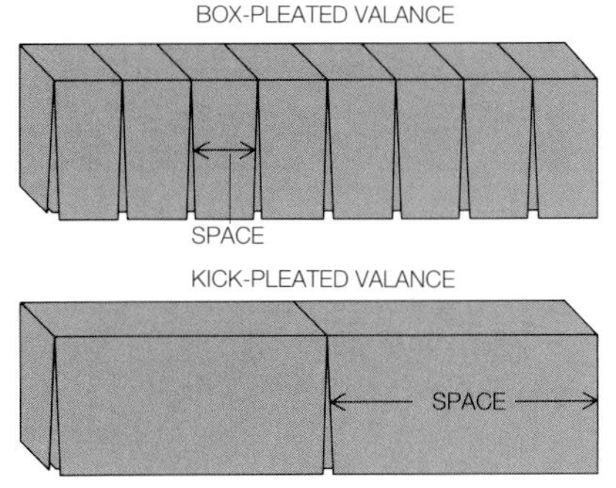

Note that it's easier to plan a kick-pleated valance if the space size is evenly divisible into the board length (three 24-inch spaces for a 72-inch-long board, for example).

Full pleats are usually placed at each corner, with half the pleat on the front and half on the return. If, however, your return is less than half a pleat wide, place a half-pleat, rather than a full one, at each end.

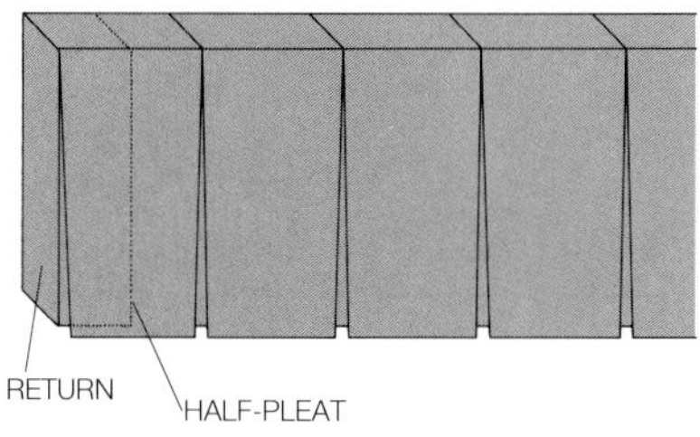

See the valance guidelines on page 90 to choose the finished length, with the following considerations: On a box-pleated valance, the width of the spaces should be less than the finished length of the valance; otherwise, it will appear too square. On a kick-pleated valance, where there are few pleats, the spaces will be much wider than the valance length.

Once you decide on pleat and space sizes, make a sketch of your valance. *For a classic box-pleated style,* start adding up pleats and spaces from one end of the valance, beginning with the 1½-inch side hem and the return. When you reach your usable width figure (52 inches in this example), that's where the first seam will occur. If you're lucky, the seam will fall within a pleat and be hidden.

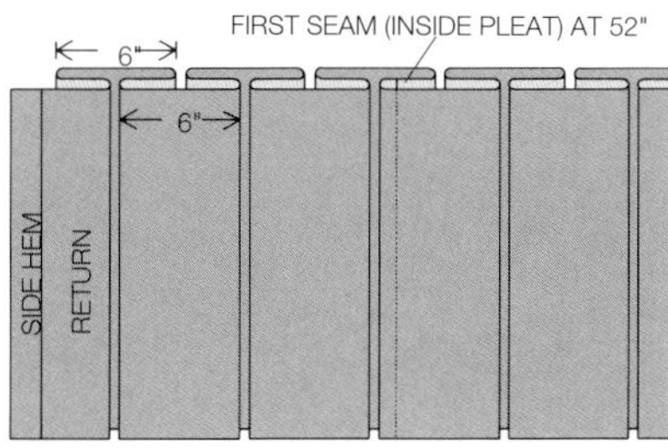

If the seam falls in a space, back up and plan to join widths so the seam falls within the previous pleat.

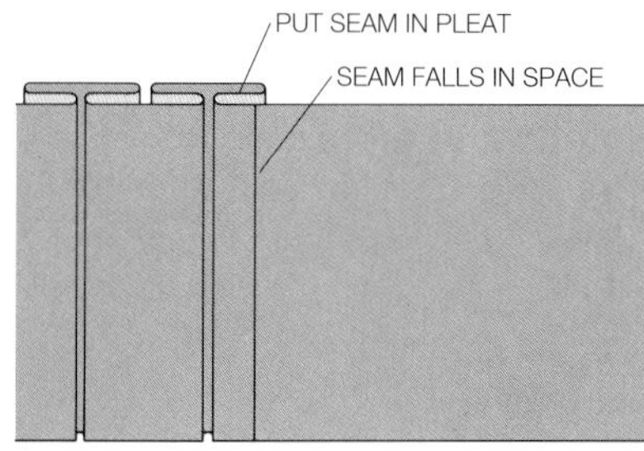

Continue adding spaces and pleats, adjusting seams as necessary and noting their positions on your sketch so you can join widths accurately.

For a kick-pleated valance, follow the same approach. If a seam falls in the first space, you'll need to split a width and seam half to the left side. Shift the fabric to make that seam fall in the first pleat.

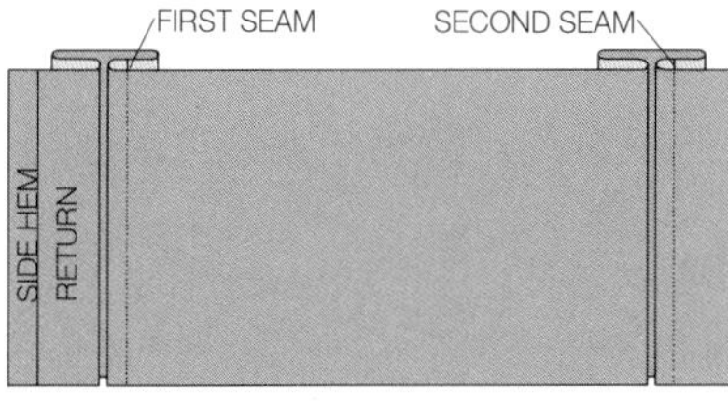

Choosing fabric. Select fabric with enough body both to form a crisp pleat and to hold its shape between pleats.

It's easiest to use an unpatterned fabric for a pleated valance. With patterned fabric, choose a space size that allows the major motifs to be centered in the spaces. Make sure there's enough fabric between horizontal repeats to make the pleats.

Calculating yardage. For either valance, follow these steps:

1. Measure your window and fill in window treatment work sheet (see pages 20–24) to arrive at board size.

2. Divide space size into board size to arrive at number of spaces. If result is a fraction, round down to a full number.

3. Divide number of spaces into board size to get exact space size.

4. Add returns to board size to get finished width.

5. Instead of filling in fullness on work sheet, multiply exact pleat size by number of pleats (1 more than number of spaces; but if you have a half-pleat at each corner, number of pleats is same as number of spaces). Add this figure to finished width. Add side hems for total width. Divide by usable width for number of widths needed. If result is a fraction, round up to next whole number. Add a width.

Use the following allowances in your calculations:

	Fabric	*Lining*
Lower hems	3"	1½"
Side hems	3" total	3" total
Top	3"	3"

Box- & kick-pleated valances step-by-step

1. ***Choose and prepare*** face fabric and lining (see pages 24–33). Join fabric widths, trimming as necessary to make seams fall as desired. (Don't *cut* your widths to measurements on sketch, as each seam requires a ½-inch seam allowance.) Press seams open.

2. ***Follow step 3,*** "Rod-pocket valance," page 91, to stitch lower hem, disregarding references to band.

3. ***On right side*** of face fabric, measure from lower edge a distance equal to finished length and mark with a fabric marker across valance. Measure and mark 3 inches above finished length line on face fabric and lining. Trim ravel allowance.

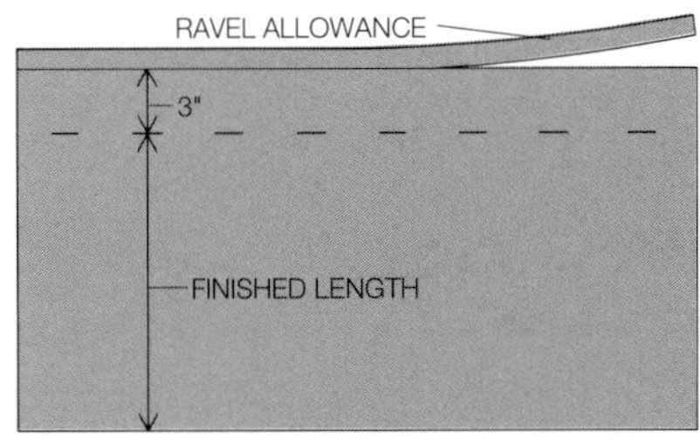

4. ***With face fabric*** right side up, measure 1½-inch side hem plus return at one end and pin vertically on finished length line to mark start of first pleat or half-pleat. Pin same distance on lower edge. Measure and pin first pleat (12 inches for full pleat in example) and first space (6 inches in example).

Continue measuring and pinning pleats and spaces across valance, making sure seams fall within pleats and ending at other return.

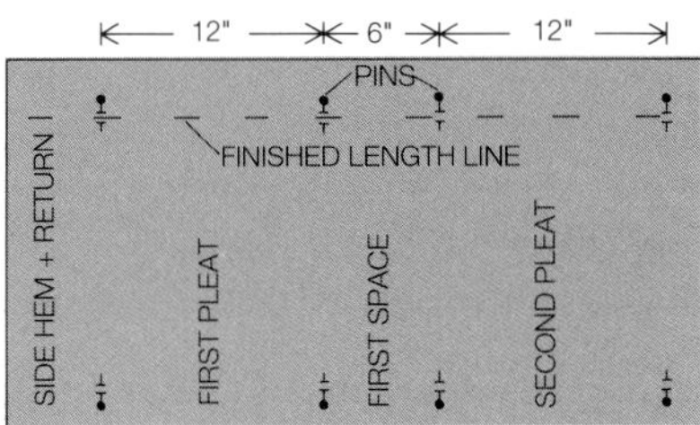

Last pleat should fall just before return.

5. ***Bring pins together*** so pleats form a flattened loop on back and folds "kiss" on front.

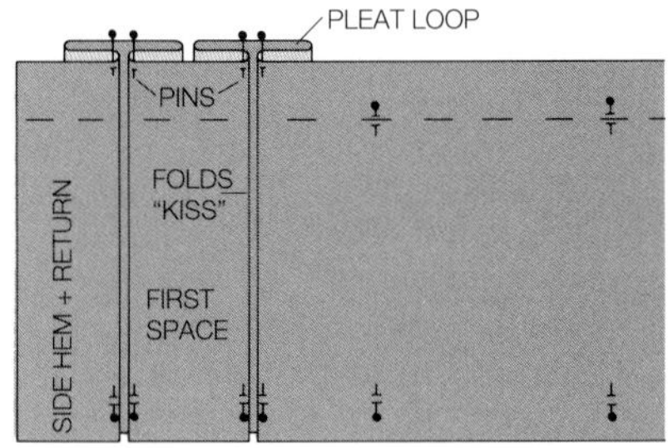

On front and back, pin layers together where pleats form folds.

6. ***Turn under*** 1½-inch side hems on face fabric and lining, rolling under ¼ inch more of lining. Pin face fabric and lining together; slip-stitch side hems closed.

7. ***Follow first part*** of step 15, "Flat Roman shade," page 75, to cover mounting board.

8. ***On right side*** of valance, measure and cut top allowance ¼ inch less than width of board. Fold along finished length line and press. Also press pleats in place above finished length line. Overcast top raw edge with a wide zigzag stitch or serge, joining face fabric and lining.

9. ***Position valance*** right side up over board so finished length fold aligns with top front edge of board and pleats are at corners. Staple top allowance to board; fold and staple returns.

10. ***Follow directions*** for an outside mount in step 21, "Flat Roman shade," page 75, to install valance. Support with angle irons every 40 inches.

Tab Stagecoach Valance

This jaunty valance, which is made in much the same way as a rod-pocket curtain, hangs from a tension rod. Two simple loop tabs hold the valance up at the ends, forming a slightly curved lower edge and tails.

Because this valance hangs from a tension rod and is held up only at the ends, use it only on a narrow window; for a series of narrow windows, make several valances.

This style is self-lined to prevent the wrong side of the valance from showing when the lower edge is folded up on itself.

Choosing fabric. Select a firmly woven fabric that will hold its shape, such as sailcloth or duck. Patterned fabric may show through if the fabric is thin; to test, hold two layers of the fabric up to the light to see the effect.

A striped fabric is ideal because the stripes line up on the front and back. If you choose a striped fabric, consider running the stripes vertically on the valance and horizontally on the tabs.

Calculating yardage. Total width equals the width of the window opening, less ¼ inch, plus 1 inch for two ½-inch side hems. Cut length is equal to 2 times the finished length (12 to 14 inches is a good range for finished length), plus 2 times the pocket size (see the chart on page 44), plus a 1-inch ravel allowance.

For tabs, you'll need two strips of fabric, each twice the desired finished width (1½ to 2 inches, depending on the width of the valance), plus 1 inch for two ½-inch seam allowances. The cut length of each strip is 2 times the finished length.

Tab stagecoach valance step-by-step

1. ***Choose and prepare*** fabric (see pages 25–33).

2. ***On right side*** of fabric, measure from lower edge a distance equal to 2 times finished length and mark with pins every 4 inches across valance width. Then measure and mark 2 times pocket size above finished length line. Trim ravel allowance.

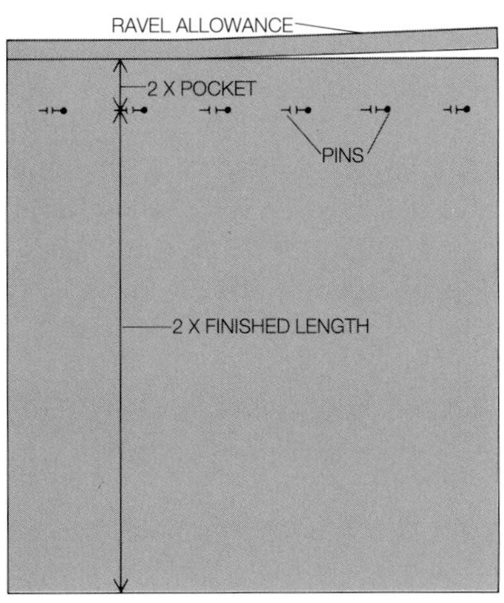

3. ***With right sides together,*** fold panel so lower raw edge is on pin-marked finished length line.

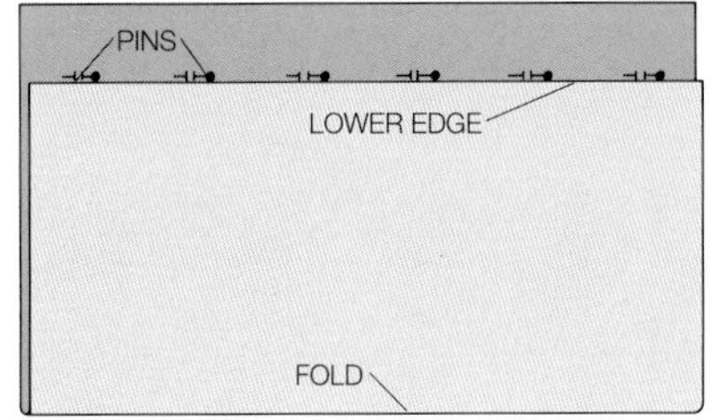

4. ***Pin and stitch*** side hems, making a ½-inch seam. Clip at corners.

5. ***Turn right side out*** and press edges. Fold top edge of fabric, wrong sides together, on finished length line; press. Turn raw edge in to meet pressed fold and press again. Stitch close to second fold.

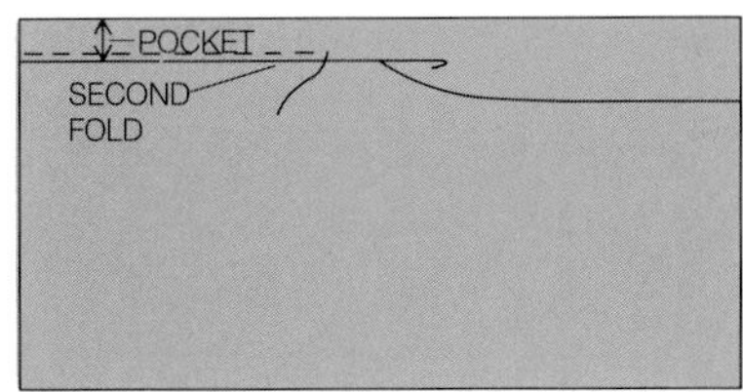

6. ***For tabs,*** cut two strips to desired dimensions. With right sides together, pin and stitch each tab lengthwise, making a ½-inch seam. Turn right side out and press, centering seam at back. Overlap ends and pin.

7. ***Slip rod through pocket*** of valance. Folding up valance, slip tabs over to check length. Adjust length to your liking and repin. Remove tabs and slip-stitch ends. Replace on valance, positioning stitched ends on wrong side near top so ends don't show.

Rolled Stagecoach Valance

This inside-mounted lined valance is stapled to a 1½-inch board, rolled up, and tied in the center. Use this valance only on a narrow window.

Choosing fabric. Any firmly woven fabric that will keep its shape when rolled is appropriate.

Calculating yardage. Total width equals the width of the opening, less ¼ inch, plus 1 inch for two ½-inch side hems. Cut length is equal to the length you want to see (typically 12 to 16 inches), plus 1½ inches for the top allowance, plus ½ inch for the lower hem, plus a 1-inch ravel allowance.

Allow extra length for the roll. Before you buy the fabric, unroll and fold 20 inches over itself; roll up. Experiment until you arrive at a pleasing roll; then measure the fabric and add to the visible length to arrive at the finished length.

For a self-lined valance, double the amount of face fabric. Or line with a contrast fabric. Also, you'll need two lengths of ribbon or two fabric ties, each equal to the visible length of the valance, plus 18 inches for the bow and 1 inch for the attachment.

Rolled stagecoach valance step-by-step

1. ***Choose and prepare*** face fabric and lining (see pages 24–33).

2. ***With right sides together,*** lay lining over face fabric. Pin and stitch side and lower hems, making a ½-inch seam. Clip corners.

3. ***Turn right side out*** and press edges. On right side, measure from lower edge a distance equal to visible finished length plus roll; mark with pins every 4 inches across valance. Measure and mark 1¼ inches above pin-marked finished length line. Trim ravel allowance.

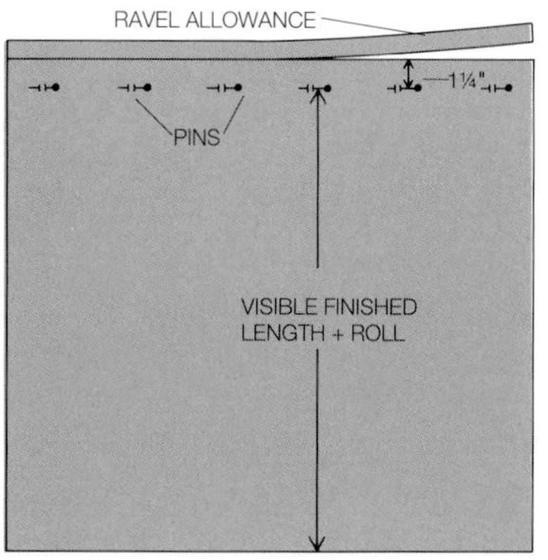

4. ***Fold valance*** on finished length line; press. Remove pins. Overcast top edge.

5. ***Follow first part*** of step 15, "Flat Roman shade," page 75, to cover mounting board.

6. ***Staple a length*** of ribbon or tie, pointing back, to top middle of board. Position valance, right side up, on board so finished length fold aligns with top front edge of board. Staple top allowance to board. Staple remaining length of ribbon or tie, pointing forward.

7. ***Follow directions*** for an inside mount in step 21, "Flat Roman shade," page 75, to install valance.

Shirred Valance

Shirring tape creates well-mannered pleats and gathers on arched, tapered, or scalloped valances.

Calculating yardage. For yardage, see the desired valance style, except that the top allowance on the face fabric is equal to the heading (see "Cloud shades," page 80), plus ½ inch. Buy shirring tape equal in length to the total valance width.

Shirred valance step-by-step

1. ***Depending on your style,*** follow steps 1–8, "Arched valance," page 93; steps 1–4, "Tapered valance," page 95; or steps 1–4, "Scalloped valance," page 95.

2. ***Follow step 9,*** "Cloud shade," page 81, to apply shirring tape.

3. ***Follow first part*** of step 15, "Flat Roman shade," page 75, to cover mounting board.

4. ***Staple valance*** to face of board, placing staples vertically.

5. ***Follow directions*** for an outside mount in step 21, "Flat Roman shade," page 75, to install valance.

Skirt Valance

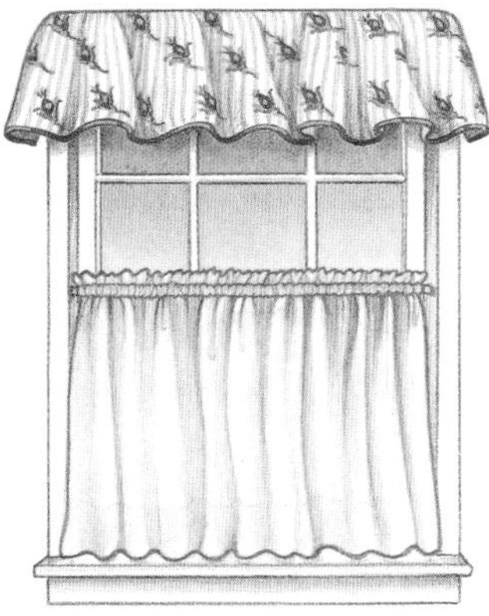

Made from a square of fabric, this unseamed valance hangs in bias folds from a board. Welt accentuates the undulating lower edge. Or you can use narrow piping.

Choosing fabric. The fabric must be crisp enough to keep from stretching at the top but supple enough to form graceful folds.

Calculating yardage. One 48- or 54-inch square of fabric will cover a board approximately 48 inches long, including returns. For the welt, buy contrast fabric.

The valance can be from 16 to 20 inches long (the shorter the valance, the wider it will be). To be safe, cut a trial valance from scrap fabric to determine the length you like and how much welt you'll need (measure the circumference and plan to piece strips cut from contrast fabric).

Skirt valance step-by-step

1. ***Choose and prepare*** face fabric and lining (see pages 24–33). Cut face fabric and lining into squares.

2. ***Fold face fabric square*** in half from selvage to selvage; fold again to make a smaller square. With a fabric marker, mark fold opposite selvages.

3. ***Position square*** as shown below. Measure distance between center point and left corner. Using a tape measure like a compass with "point" on center point, mark that distance across bottom; connect marks to form a curve.

From left corner, measure and mark toward center point a distance equal to finished length plus 2 inches. From that mark, measure distance to center point. Using tape measure as before, mark that distance across top; connect marks to form curve.

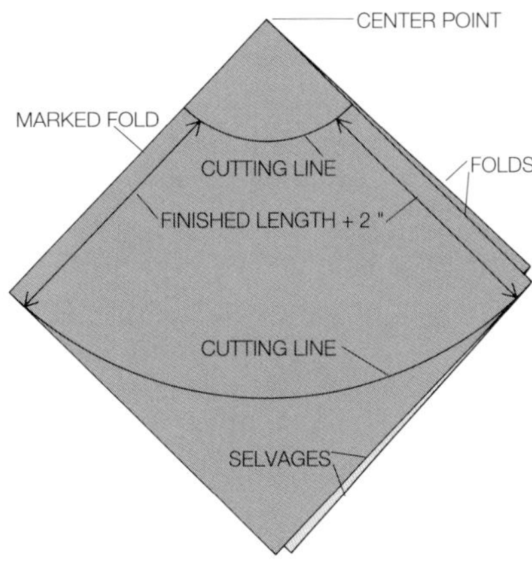

Cut on both curves. Using fabric as a pattern, cut lining.

4. ***Open circle of fabric*** and lay flat. Cut on marked fold.

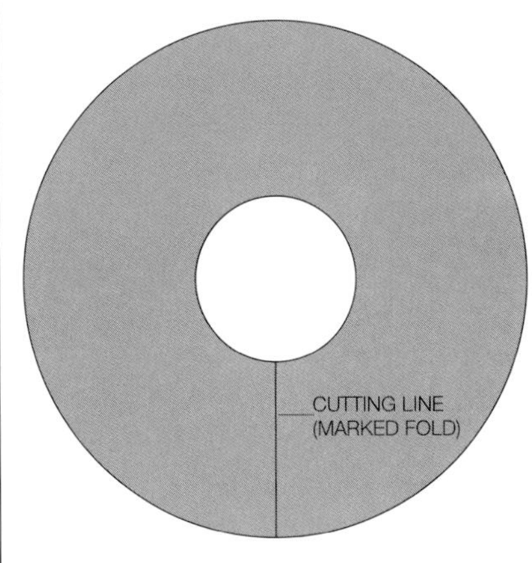

Repeat on lining.

5. ***For welt,*** see page 47 to determine width of strips. Cut and piece strips for required length. Stitch welt. With raw edges aligned, pin welt to lower edge of face fabric; baste.

6. ***With right sides together,*** pin face fabric and lining together along lower edge. Stitch just inside basting; trim seam allowances. Turn right side out and press lower edge. Pin face fabric and lining together at top edge.

7. ***Follow first part*** of step 15, "Flat Roman shade," page 75, to cover mounting board. Mark midpoint of board.

8. ***Align midpoint*** of valance with midpoint of board, placing raw edges of valance 1½ inches from front edge of board. Pin valance, including returns, to board. With pins, mark end of each return at ends of board.

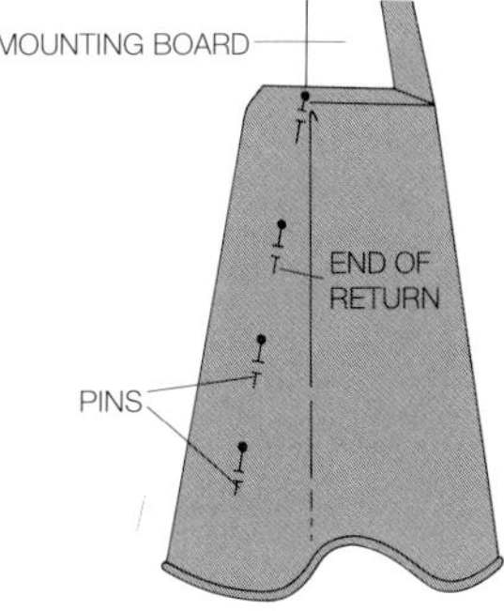

Remove valance. Trim 1½ inches beyond side pins. Pull out and cut 1½ inches of cording from each end of welt.

9. ***Turn under*** face fabric and lining 1½ inches on sides, rolling under ¼ inch more of lining and folding in welt. Slip-stitch side hems closed.

10. ***Overcast top edges*** with a wide zigzag stitch or serge, joining lining and face fabric. Pin valance to board as before; staple.

Cornices

Grand motif takes center stage on a small shaped cornice (at right). Welt accentuates the graceful curves of the cornice. An already dramatic fabric gets extra visual punch from the sinuous curves of a formal upholstered cornice (below).

DESIGN: NICOLE PATTON INTERIORS. WINDOW TREATMENT: ROSSETTI & CORRIEA DRAPERIES INC.

DESIGN: BARBARA MACK, FLEECE TO FIBERS INTERIOR DESIGN. WINDOW TREATMENT: PINK'S CUSTOM DRAPERIES

Straight cornices with self-welt along the lower edges dress up miniblinds and unify corner windows. The contemporary cotton print brings out the color in the custom tile.

Although upholstered to frames, these cornices seem to hang in fluid folds like a swag valance because of their shape.

HOW TO MAKE

Straight & Scalloped Cornices

A fabric-covered wood cornice mounted over curtains, draperies, or a shade neatly frames a window and adds architectural interest to a room. A cornice is practical, too— it hides the heading and the hardware at the top of the undertreatment and blocks cold drafts.

You make a scalloped cornice in much the same way that you make a straight cornice; where steps differ, special instructions for the scalloped version are given.

Tools & supplies

To make a straight or scalloped welted cornice, obtain the following supplies from a lumberyard: 1-inch No. 2 kiln-dried pine (width and length depend on cornice dimensions) and ⅜-inch interior fir plywood (amount depends on cornice dimensions).

You'll also need a saber saw or handsaw, cement-coated box nails, shelf paper or newsprint (for scalloped cornice only), white or craft glue, a wood rasp, a paint brush, a razor or utility knife, C-clamps, a staple gun, angle irons, and fasteners.

Additional supplies include ½-inch foam (enough to wrap around the legs and face board, plus 1 inch on all edges); T-pins or push pins; fabric for the cornice, welt, and lining; upholstery tack strips; ⅜-inch cord; and gimp.

Planning your cornice

The dimensions of your cornice depend on the size of your window and the coverage you need.

Measure the width of your window opening (see page 20), adding the window frame, if any. Then decide how far to extend the cornice on either side. The top board must be a minimum of 1½ inches longer than the width of the opening (including the window frame) or than the treatment the cornice will cover.

The recommended minimum distance above the opening is 8 inches; the recommended distance into the window opening is 4 inches. If you're running a patterned fabric vertically, the vertical repeat (see page 23) must fit within the desired cornice height.

On a scalloped cornice, the difference between the short and long points should be at least 3 inches. The short points must cover the heading of any undertreatment.

The width of the horizontal board on top depends on what will hang underneath. If it's an inside-mounted treatment, such as miniblinds or a shade, the top board can be 3½ inches wide. But if the cornice will top an outside-mounted treatment, make the top board at least 5½ inches wide.

The boards that form the legs are the same width as the top board. Their length is equal to the desired height of the cornice minus ¾ inch. The plywood face board needs to be as long as the top board; its width is equal to the length of the legs, plus ¾ inch.

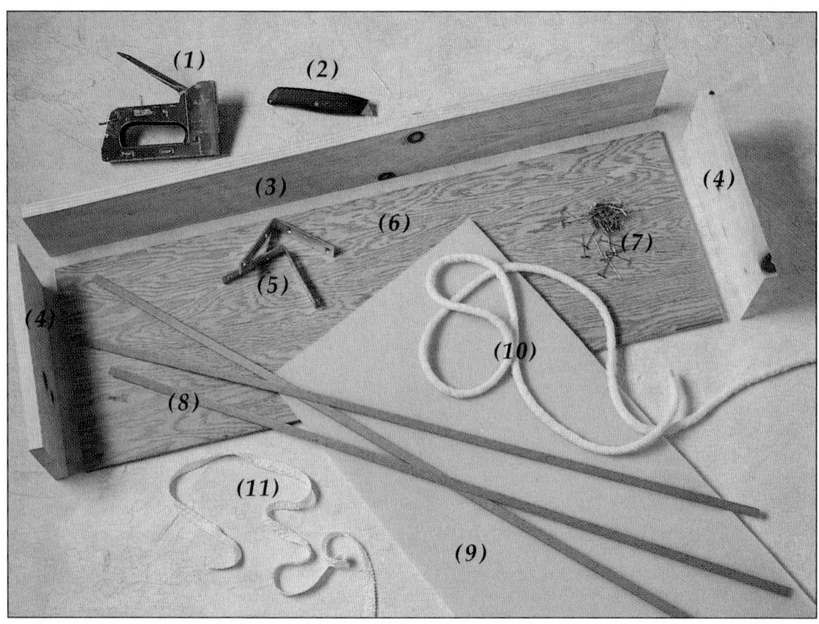

Tools and supplies for making a cornice include (1) staple gun, (2) utility knife, (3) top board, (4) legs, (5) angle irons, (6) face board, (7) T-pins, (8) tack strips, (9) foam, (10) cord, and (11) gimp.

Straight & Scalloped Cornices

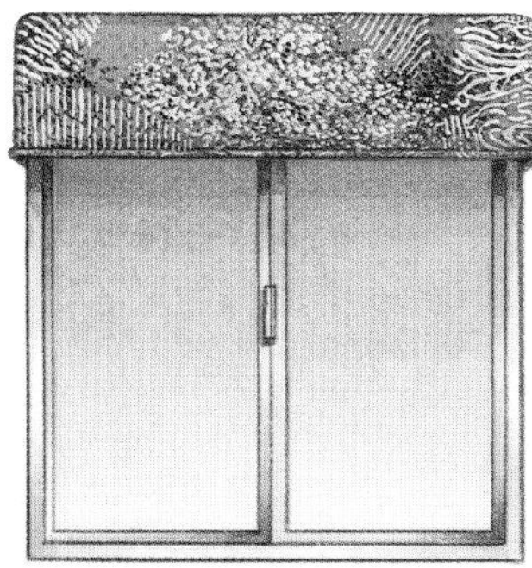

For a simple, tailored top treatment, make a cornice with a straight lower edge. A scalloped cornice creates a softer look.

Select a firmly woven fabric that won't lose its shape.

Calculating yardage. If possible, railroad your fabric (run selvages parallel to the floor) to avoid seams. Most patterned fabric must be run vertically.

Add together the long dimension of the cornice, the returns (depth of legs), and 6 inches for wrapping the fabric around the legs.

For railroaded fabric, divide by 36 to arrive at yards needed (the fabric will be wide enough to cover the height of the cornice).

For fabric run vertically, divide by the usable fabric width (less selvages and seams) for the number of widths needed. The cut length is equal to the height of the cornice plus 6 inches. To figure the repeat cut length for patterned fabric, see page 24. Multiply the cut length (or repeat cut length) by the number of widths; divide by 36 for yards needed.

Railroad the lining, figuring it as you would face fabric.

Add extra fabric for same-fabric or contrast welt (see step 17, page 106, to determine the length).

Straight & scalloped cornices step-by-step

1. ***Using 1-by lumber*** for top board and legs and plywood for face board, measure and cut boards to your specifications. Make cuts precise: ends of all boards must be perfectly square. Lay out pieces.

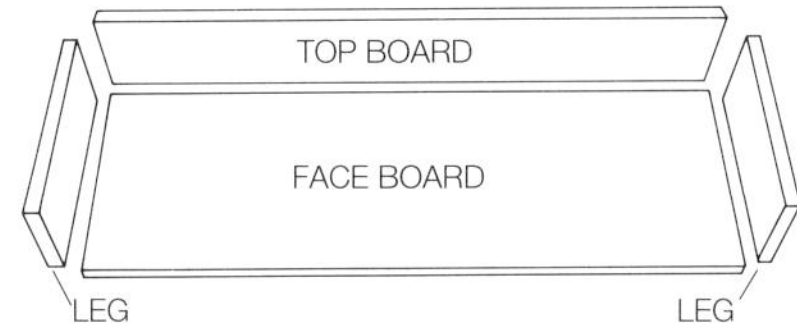

2. ***Start nails*** at ends of top board for legs. Glue legs to underside of board at ends; finish nailing. Apply glue to front edge of top board and legs. Lay face board over frame.

Using nails, tack face board to top board at corners; tack to legs, pulling them out slightly to straighten, if necessary. Finish nailing.

Round corners and edges of face board with a wood rasp. Measure and mark vertical line at midpoint on face board.

3. ***For a straight cornice,*** continue to step 4.

For a scalloped cornice, make a paper pattern, using a sheet of paper equal to half long dimension of cornice and deep enough to accommodate short and long points.

Draw half of design, cut, and tape to face board. Mark outline; flip pattern and mark other half. Cut face board on marked line.

4. ***Lay cornice,*** face board up, on sawhorses. On foam, mark midpoint at top and bottom. Dilute glue with water to consistency of heavy cream and use to paint face board. Lay foam on top, aligning marks on board and foam. Let dry.

5. ***Paint legs*** with glue and wrap foam around, pinning to inside of legs with T-pins or push pins until glue is dry. Using a razor or utility knife, trim foam even with top, lower, and back leg edges.

6. ***For fabric run vertically,*** join widths, as described on page 33; press seams toward center. To avoid a center seam on an even number of widths, cut off half a width and seam to opposite side.

7. ***Center fabric,*** right side up, on face board. Smooth over top board; measure and mark fabric 3 inches beyond top front edge. Remove fabric, mark line, and cut on line.

8. ***Hang cornice,*** top board up, over sawhorses. On top board, measure and mark a line 2 inches from front edge.

9. ***Center fabric,*** wrong side up, on top board so edge of fabric is at marked line and fabric is toward back. Starting at midpoint of top board, lay a tack strip over fabric, aligning edge with raw edge of fabric. Staple strip.

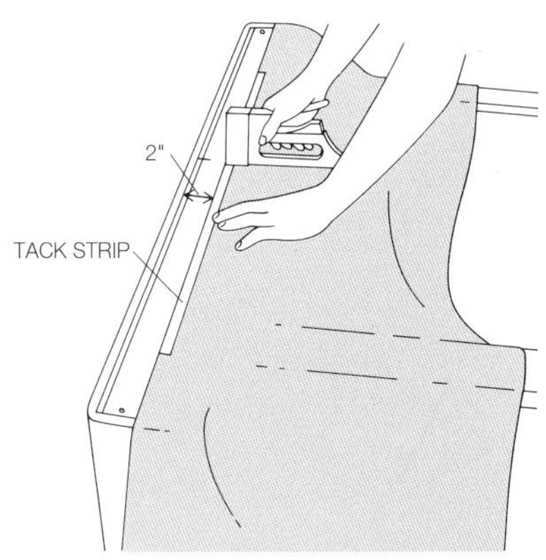

Continued on next page

Continue stapling, placing staples 3½ inches apart and adding strips as needed, to within 1 inch of ends of cornice; trim ends.

10. *Flip fabric forward;* if any staple has pulled a thread, remove and restaple. Smooth fabric down face board and up underneath. Roll cornice back so top board is down. Clamp to sawhorses.

11. *On a straight cornice,* pull fabric taut at midpoint of face board and, keeping grain straight, wrap around bottom of face board. Staple to inside about 1½ inches from edge, placing staples about 6 inches apart (staples are temporary).

On a scalloped cornice, pull fabric taut and staple at longest point or points (staples are temporary).

For either cornice, pull fabric around legs and staple to inside in several places.

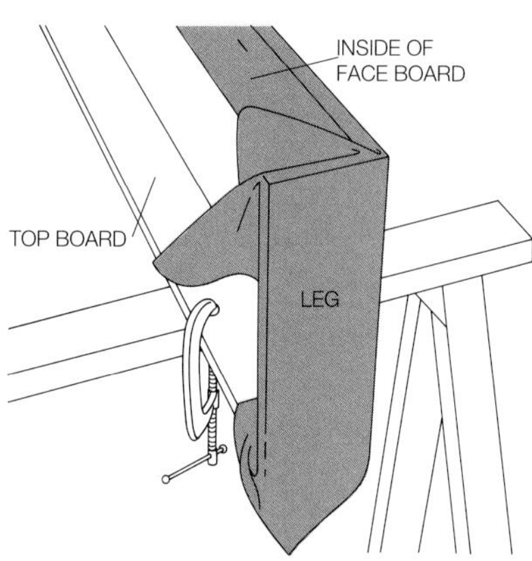

12. *Starting at midpoint* of face board on a straight cornice or at long points on a scalloped cornice, remove a temporary staple. Pull fabric taut enough to see edge of board and staple about 1½ inches from edge.

On a straight cornice, continue removing temporary staples, one at a time, pulling fabric taut, and restapling; keep grain straight and place staples about ½ inch apart. Staple to within 4 inches of ends.

On a scalloped cornice, remove temporary staples, one at a time, pull fabric taut, and restaple. Cut into fabric at curves almost to front edge of face board. Pull each flap of fabric taut and staple to inside. If curve meets a straight edge, fold fabric carefully and staple.

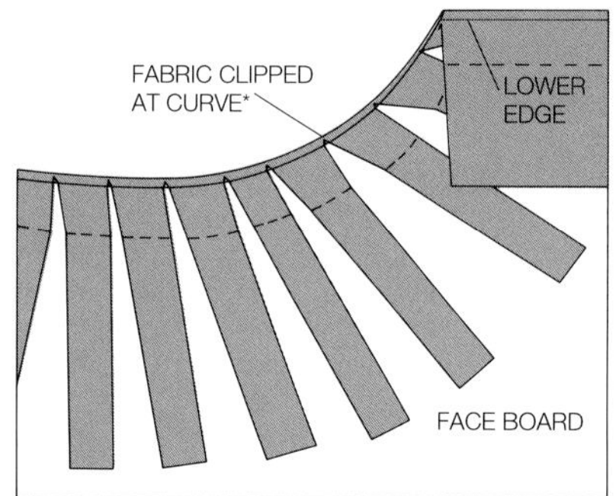

13. *Restaple legs* in same manner, stapling fabric to inside.

14. *Roll cornice* so top board is up. Fold fabric at top corners, forming miters; staple to top board. Trim close to staples.

15. *Roll cornice* so top board is down. At corners, cut fabric to inside edge of face board; staple up to inside corners.

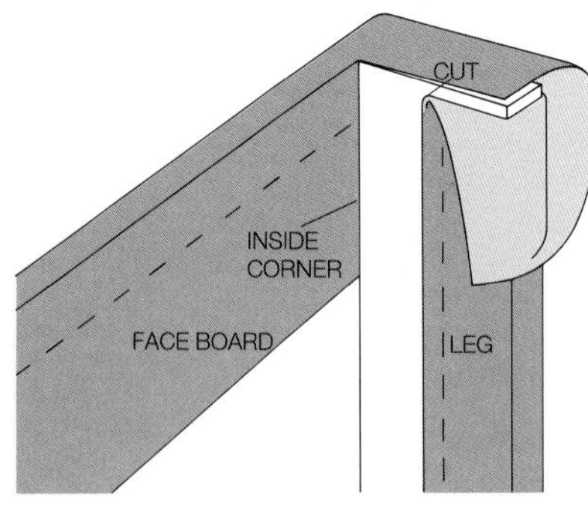

Smooth fabric up outside of legs, across bottom, and to inside. At corners and back of legs, neatly fold fabric under; staple to inside.

16. *Trim fabric* on inside of face board and legs close to staples.

17. *Measure, mark,* and cut enough 6-inch-wide strips of fabric to cover lower edge of face board and legs and, if it's same-fabric welt, extend up back edge of each leg, plus 2 inches for each end, plus 6 inches for each seam. Seam strips on bias; trim seam allowances and press open.

Lay cord on wrong side of strip. Fold strip over cord, making one seam allowance 1½ inches wider than other. Stitch close to cord (don't crowd cord).

18. *Trim tack strips* to ⅜ inch.

19. *Starting at end* of face board and leaving enough welt to cover adjoining leg and, for same-fabric welt, back of leg, lay welt on edge of face board with narrow seam allowance underneath. Miter end of a tack strip; open welt and lay strip on top.

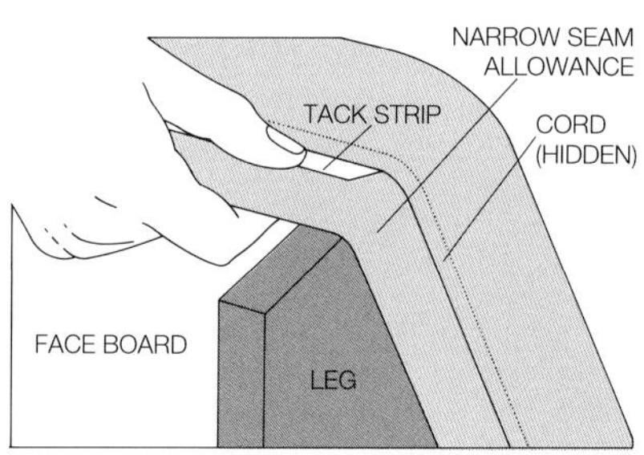

Push strip against welt stitching; at same time, gently pull on bottom seam allowance so stitching is drawn slightly under strip.

20. *Staple tack strip* to edge of face board, placing staples about 1 inch apart and adding strips as needed. *For a scalloped cornice,* clip welt seam allowances to within ½ inch of welt stitching and stretch welt slightly around curves.

At opposite corner, miter strip.

21. *Miter another tack strip* and use to staple welt along bottom of leg. Flatten and staple excess fabric in corner.

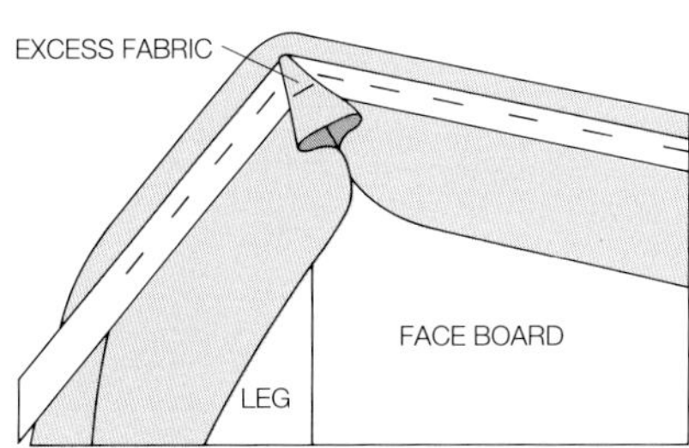

For same-fabric welt, continue stapling strip and welt up back of leg; trim strip even with edge.

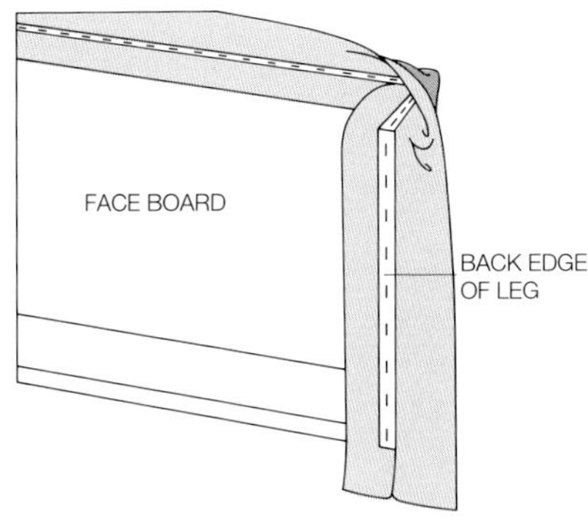

For contrast welt, trim strip at back corner of leg.

Repeat on other leg.

22. ***Trim narrower*** welt seam allowance close to tack strip.

23. ***Roll cornice*** so top board is up. Cut welt 1½ inches beyond end of tack strip. Rip out stitching and cut cord even with top board.

For same-fabric welt, fold fabric strip and staple to top board.

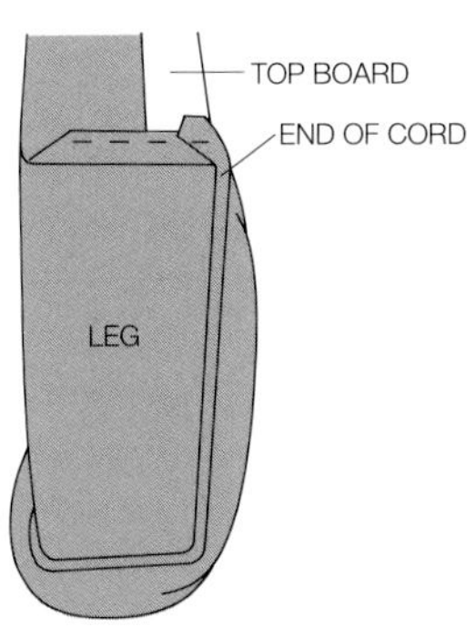

For contrast welt, fold strip and staple to inside of leg.

24. ***Roll cornice*** so top board is down. Starting on face board, gently pull wider welt seam allowance down and staple just below previous staples, placing staples 1 inch apart.

At inside corners, cut into seam allowance as before, forming a fabric flap. Miter seam allowance at back edge of leg and staple.

Fold fabric flap down and staple to inside corner.

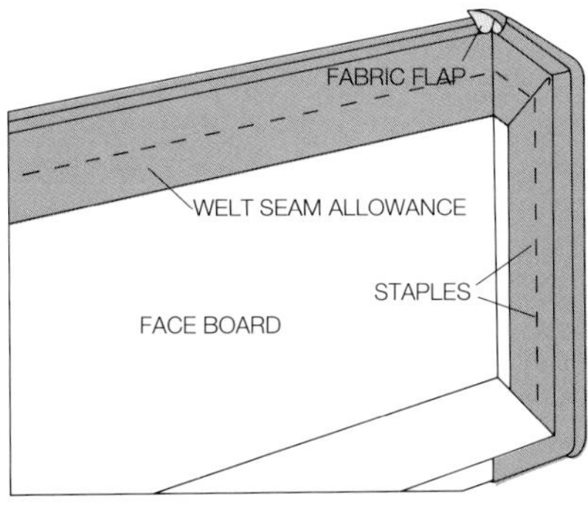

25. ***Roll cornice*** so top board is up. Center lining over top board with fabric toward front and raw edge of lining aligned with front edge of first tack strip (hidden). Lay another strip on lining so edge of strip is snug against first strip; staple strip along length. Trim ends of strip.

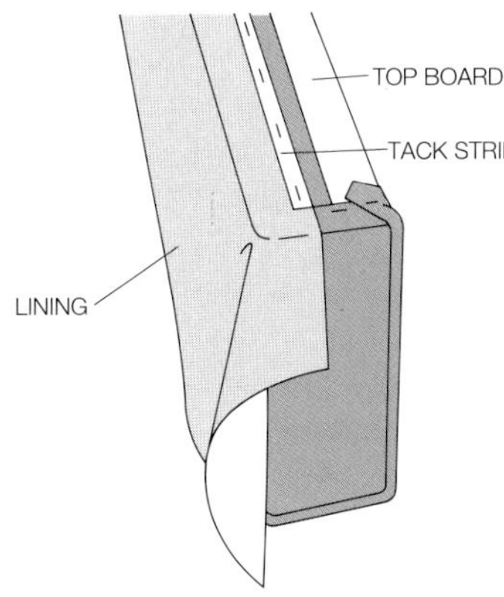

26. ***Flip lining*** to back and trim even with each end of top board. At back edge, cut lining at an angle so you can fold lining under.

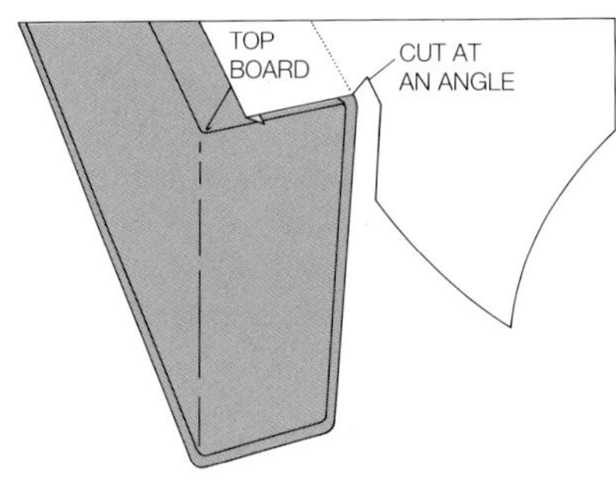

Turn under raw edge of lining and staple to top board.

27. ***Roll cornice*** so top board is down. Smooth lining to inside and staple long edge where top board meets face board.

28. ***At inside leg,*** fold lining over itself and cut ½ inch beyond where leg meets top board; fold lining under and staple to underside of top board.

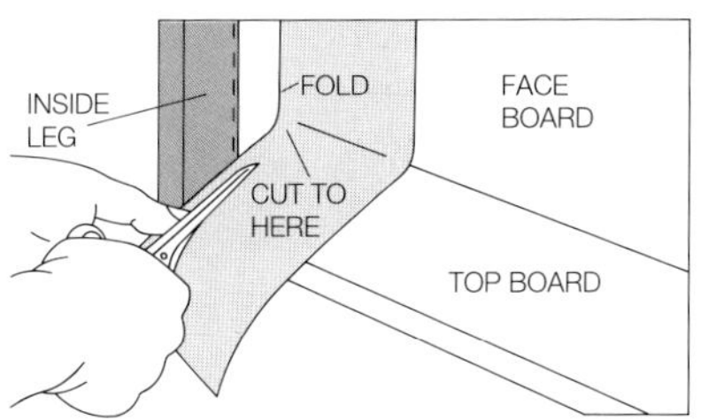

29. ***Staple inside edge*** where face board meets leg. Smooth fabric over inside of leg. Trim remaining flap of fabric to ½ inch; turn under and staple to inside of leg.

30. ***Trim lining*** 1 inch beyond back edge of leg; turn under and staple leg. Repeat on other leg.

31. ***Staple lining*** to lower edge of cornice, stapling just above previous staples. Trim close to staples. Glue gimp over raw edges.

32. ***Follow directions*** for an outside mount in step 21, "Flat Roman shade," page 75, to install cornice. Support with angle irons every 40 inches.

Swags & Cascades

WINDOW TREATMENT: ROSSETTI & CORRIEA DRAPERIES INC.

Traditional swags (at right) take on a look of easy elegance when made of crisp chintz. Full-length pleated side panels held back by bows fan at the floor. The bold checks of this dramatic swag (below), gathered in a pouf, reverse to a rich rose colored fabric, used for the cascades. A heavy fringe unites the elements.

DESIGNER: CLIFFORD MCALPIN

Cascades and jabots lined in a contrast fabric accent overlapping traditional swags. Because these swags hang on the bias, the striped fabric creates an unusual effect. Simple rosettes embellish the treatment.

DESIGN: JUDITH APPEL, APPEL DECORATING DEN. WINDOW TREATMENT: DELTA PI DESIGN

Garden-fresh cutout swags trimmed with tassel fringe are attached to a 2-inch fluted wood pole. Pleated side panels (each is made from one width) have returns, like some cascades. Underneath, sheers close to filter light and provide privacy.

DESIGN: NICOLE PATTON INTERIORS. WINDOW TREATMENT: ROSSETTI & CORRIEA DRAPERIES INC.

DESIGN: NICOLE PATTON INTERIORS. WINDOW TREATMENT: ROSSETTI & CORRIEA DRAPERIES INC.

In an unusual pairing, cutout swags and cascades are mounted on a cornice. Starting the taper high on the cascades reveals more of the contrast lining; the narrow spaces between the pleats create the tight stack on the cascades and jabot. Choux add the finishing touch.

Cutout swags and self-lined cascades attach to a wood pole by means of hook-and-loop fastener tape. Returns on the cascades cover the space between the treatment and the window.

DESIGN: ALLISON KOESTER. WINDOW TREATMENT: DELTA PI DESIGN

Sensational pouf swags (below) dramatically frame a window and French doors. Each pouf was pulled through a tulip-shaped swag holder and then pushed into the center to form a rosette. Tissue gives the swags their fullness. Sheer sash curtains filter light. Hand-painted silk fabric (detail at right) puddles luxuriously on the floor; hidden rope tie-backs cinch the panels to form bishop's sleeves.

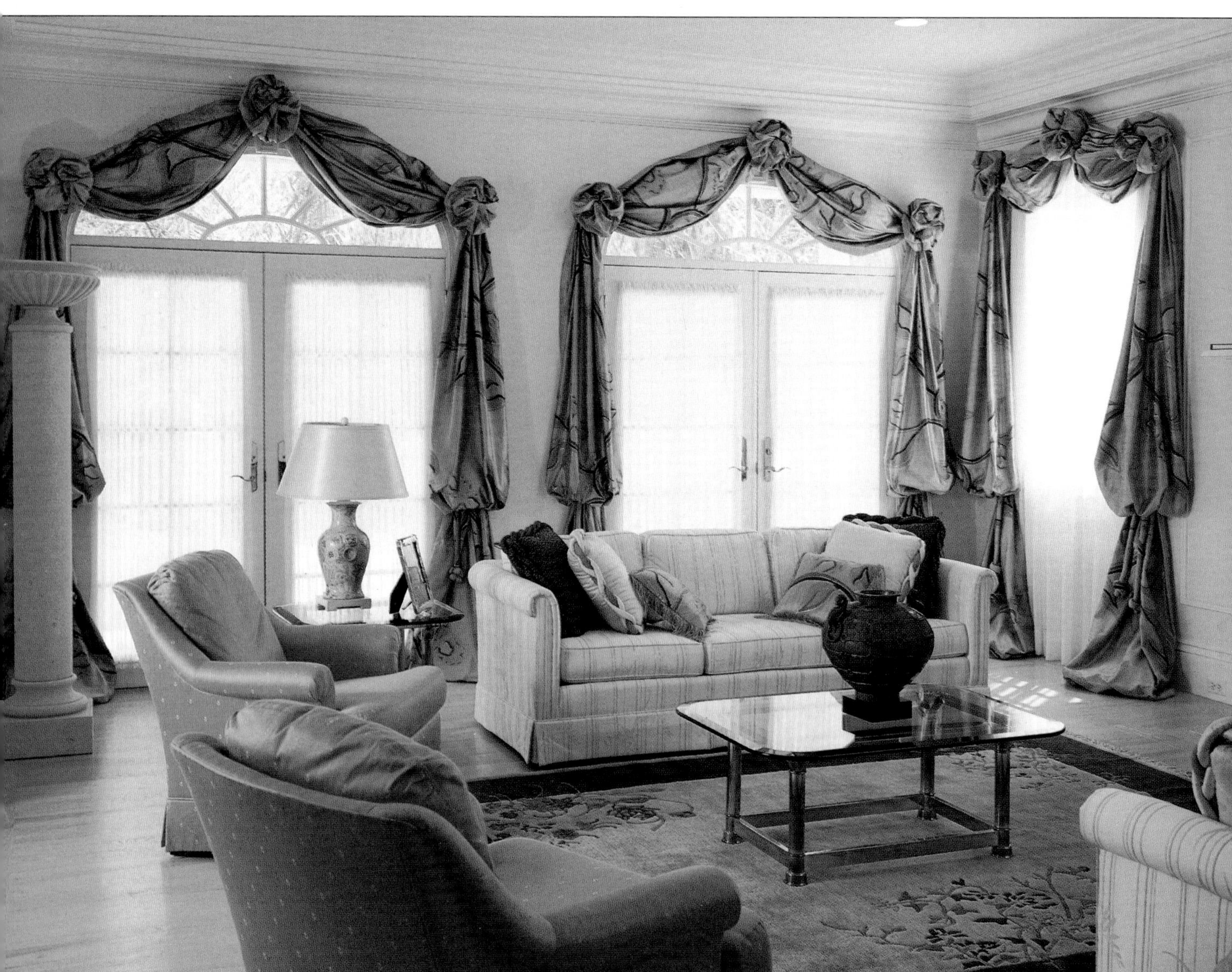

DESIGN: DIANNA CLOOS, CLOOS INTERIOR DESIGN. WINDOW TREATMENT: ROSSETTI & CORRIEA DRAPERIES INC.

You almost have to touch this wooden lambrequin to believe it's not fabric. Cut from thin plywood and artfully painted, this decorative window treatment duplicates swags and cascades.

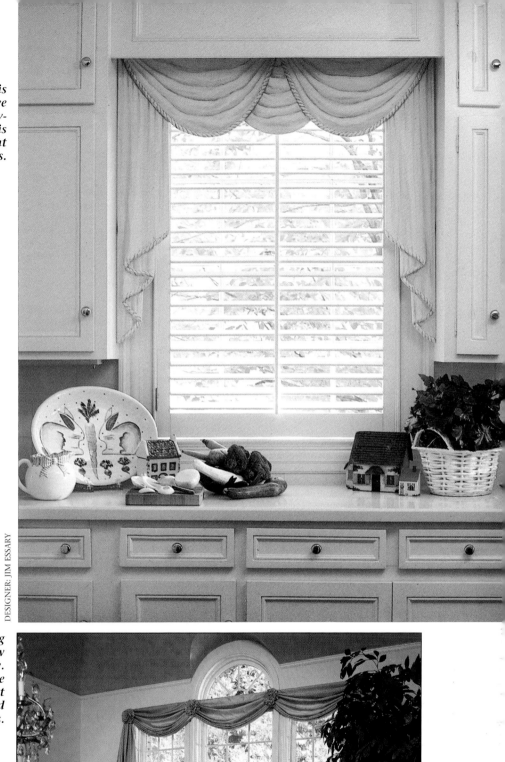

DESIGNER: JIM ESSARY

Board-mounted tab running swag dresses a noteworthy window without diminishing the view. Narrow tabs hold the folds close to the board; two-tone flat rosettes, made of contrast-lined ruffle strips, cover the tabs.

DESIGN: JEANNE TEPPER. WINDOW TREATMENT: HARDING'S INTERIORS

HOW TO MAKE

Traditional Swags & Cascades ▪ Cutout Swags & Cascades ▪ Cutout Swags & Cascades with Returns ▪ Pouf Swags ▪ Tab & Knotted Swags ▪ Scarf Swags ▪ Wrapped Swags

Whether casual or formal, swags and cascades impart a look of timeless beauty. Some styles are simple to make; others are more difficult.

Simply put, swags are top treatments that are board mounted, placed in swag holders, or wrapped around a pole. They're almost always paired with cascades or other side treatments, such as tied-back curtains or straight panels.

You can make swags in a variety of styles. Traditional swags possess a simplicity that belies their construction. What appear to be swathes of fabric nonchalantly draped over boards are, in fact, structured, precise window treatments. Closely related are cutout swags, which also hang on the bias but are open at the top.

Cascades are pleated side panels that flank traditional or cutout swags. Because all lines are straight, they're simple to make.

If you like the look of swags and cascades but prefer an easier project, consider a running swag. Made from one length of fabric, a running swag offers a less structured look than traditional or cutout swags and cascades.

Rosettes, choux, and jabots (see pages 126–127) embellish swags and cascades. Rosettes and choux also lend sophistication to other window treatments, such as cloud shades and tied-back curtains.

Swag hardware

Traditional swags and cascades are mounted on boards (shown at right). For swags used with cascades, a 3½-inch board is best. For swags used over additional treatments, measure the width needed and choose a board that will clear the heading and hardware below.

Cutout swags are attached to decorative rods with hook-and-loop fastener tape. You can use a decorative traverse rod without the rings; the flat back on these rods makes it easy to attach the tape. Or attach the fastener tape to a 1³/₈-inch wood pole.

Running swags can hang from decorative poles, tulip-shaped or circular swag holders, medallion or scarf swag holders, or swag rings. Running swags with knots or ties are mounted on boards.

Many holdbacks (see page 43) also work as swag holders.

Choosing fabric

Since a successful swag depends on the fabric's draping qualities, make sure your fabric is soft enough to drape yet firm enough to form and retain folds.

To test a fabric's draping qualities, unroll several yards and fold the cut edge to one selvage. Grasp the diagonal corners and hold the fabric up to see how it falls. If it drapes nicely, it will make softly rounded swags. If the fabric breaks rather than drapes, you can still use it, but you'll have to work harder to form the pleats.

If you suspect that a fabric doesn't have enough body, try draping it with lining.

Some running swags can be made from firmly woven fabrics, such as chintz, since the hardware determines the swag's form. Wrapped swags lend themselves to sateen and other soft fabrics. Avoid fabrics with obvious one-way patterns because the cascades will run in opposite directions.

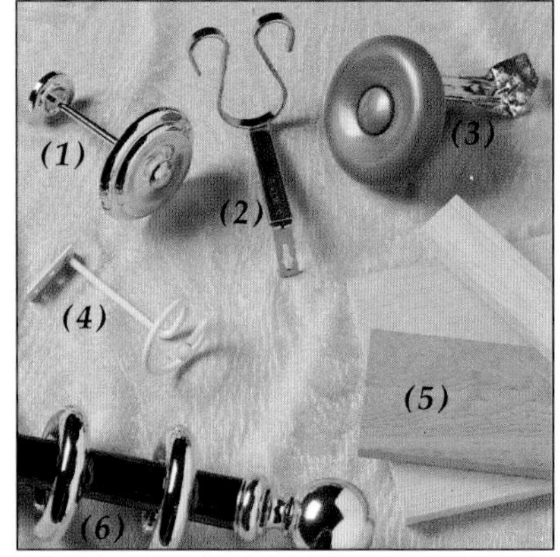

A selection of swag hardware shows (1) scarf swag holder, (2) tulip-shaped swag holder, (3) disk swag holder, (4) spiral swag holder, (5) mounting boards, and (6) ring-and-pole set.

Traditional Swags & Cascades

Making beautiful swags takes time, as well as some creativity. Before you commit to yards of fabric, make a sample swag using the fabric and lining you like to get a feel for how the swags are made and what they'll look like.

The swags and cascades in this project are pleated; directions are also given for a version with soft gathers at the top.

Planning traditional swags

Swags start with a square of fabric 6 inches larger than the desired finished width, which can range from 32 to 48 inches, depending on your fabric's width. Length varies; in general, it will be about a third the size of the fabric square.

Swags can be used singly or in a series; the number depends on both board size and swag size. Swags often overlap by half the swag width, an arrangement called a classic swag. Swags can also meet, or "kiss."

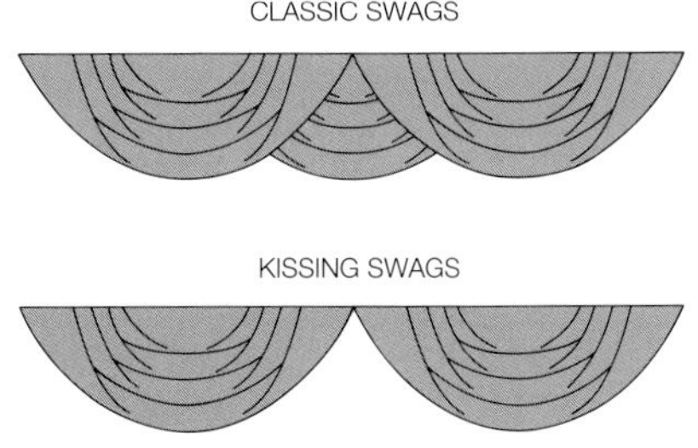

Swags are usually installed 8 inches above the top of the window opening or at ceiling height. For a series of swags, the point where the swags cross should reach 2 to 4 inches into the window area.

Typically, swags used with cascades extend 4 to 6 inches beyond the opening, with a portion of each cascade covering the window. If you're planning tied-back side panels, place half the panel on the window. For straight panels, place most of each panel off the window.

To plan a swag treatment, complete the following steps:

1. Measure your window width and add extensions (see pages 20–21) to arrive at board size. (In example, swags overlap and board size is 90 inches.)

2. *For swags that meet rather than overlap,* divide board size by 40 and round up to next whole number to arrive at number of swags. *For overlapping swags,* multiply board size by 1½ and divide by 40; round up to next whole number (in example, 90 x 1½ = 135 ÷ 40 = 3.38, rounded to 4).

3. Sketch your arrangement, showing full swags and half-swags, if swags overlap. Add number of full and half-swags that you see (1 full swag + 3 half-swags = 2½).

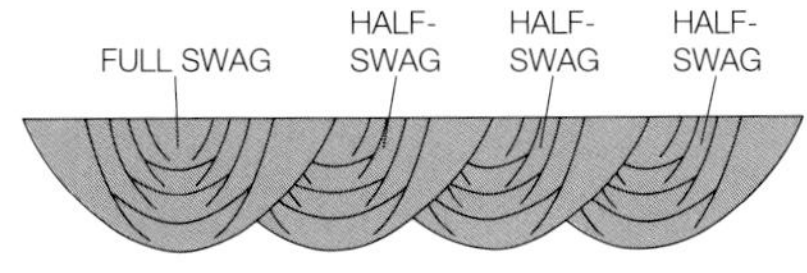

4. Divide board size by result in step 3 for swag width (90 ÷ 2½ = 36).

Calculating yardage. Add 6 inches to the desired finished width to arrive at the cut length of each square. For patterned fabric, figure the repeat cut length following steps 2–3 on page 24. For a single swag, cut only one length; for more than one swag, multiply the cut length or repeat cut length by the number of swags.

Use lining the same width as your fabric; buy the same amount.

Swag tips. When pleating your swag, have a helper stand on the other side of your work area. Otherwise, make and pin pleats one at a time on each side. Either way, you'll need to make adjustments to achieve uniformly rounded folds.

A grid cardboard cutting board is helpful for pleating the swag to the correct finished width.

Traditional swags step-by-step

1. ***Choose and prepare*** face fabric and lining (see pages 24–33).

2. ***Measure, mark, and cut*** a square of lining equal to finished swag width plus 6 inches (42 inches in example).

3. ***Fold lining vertically,*** wrong sides together, into a triangle; fold again, bringing first fold to side. Finger-press folds.

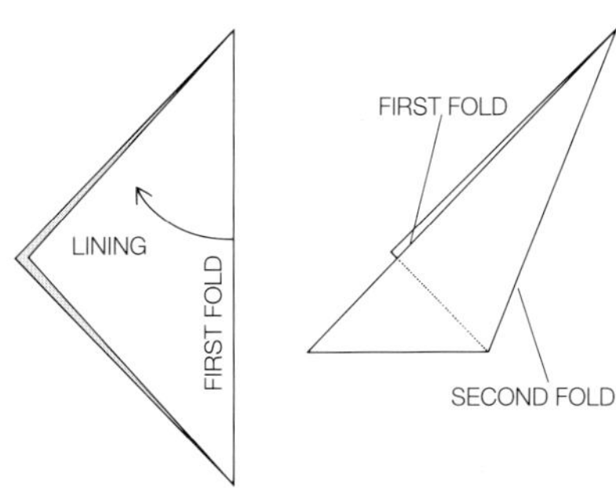

Continued on next page

4. *Unfold lining,* wrong side up, and mark a point on center fold 1 inch longer than side of square (43 inches in example). Also, mark points on quarter folds ½ inch longer than side of square (42½ inches in example). Strike a curve through marks from one corner to other corner.

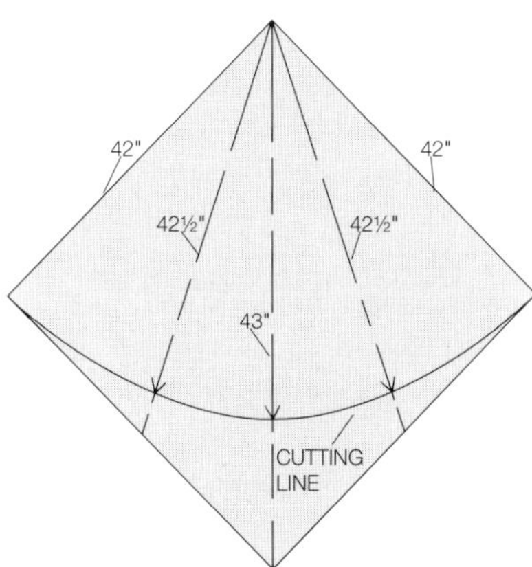

Cut curve. If you've made a sample swag, cut linings for additional swags now, using first piece as a pattern.

5. *Position face fabric* right side up and determine top point of swag (make sure motifs on patterned fabric are going in right direction). Lay lining over face fabric, right sides together, aligning sides. If fabric is patterned, move lining until repeat is centered as desired.

Pin layers together 1 inch above curve; cut face fabric along curve. Stitch, making a ½-inch seam.

6. *Turn right side out* and under-stitch through lining and seam allowances ⅛ inch from seam. Press curve, turning ⅛ inch of face fabric to lining side.

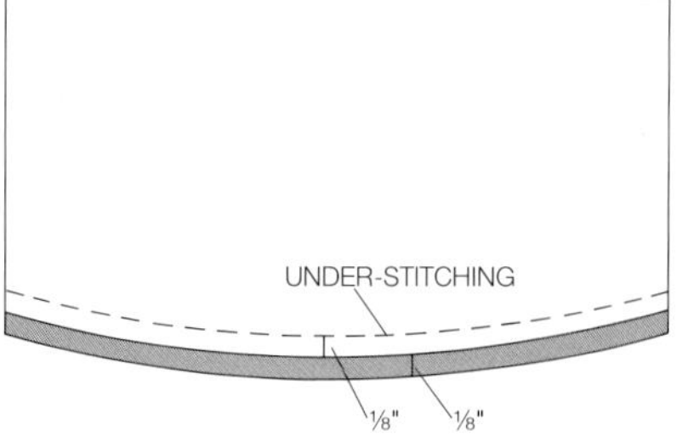

Pin face fabric and lining together up center.

7. *With face fabric* right side up, measure from top point down each side a distance equal to a third finished swag width (12 inches in example); pin perpendicular to side. Using chalk, mark a horizontal line between pins; mark a dot ¾ inch from edge on each side. Measure and mark another horizontal line 3 inches below first line.

If finished swag width is 42 inches or less, add 1 inch to distance along edge below first marked line and divide by 5. *If finished swag width is 43 inches or more,* add 1 inch to distance and divide by 6. Measure that distance along edge and mark with pins for pleat positions (last pleat will be slightly smaller).

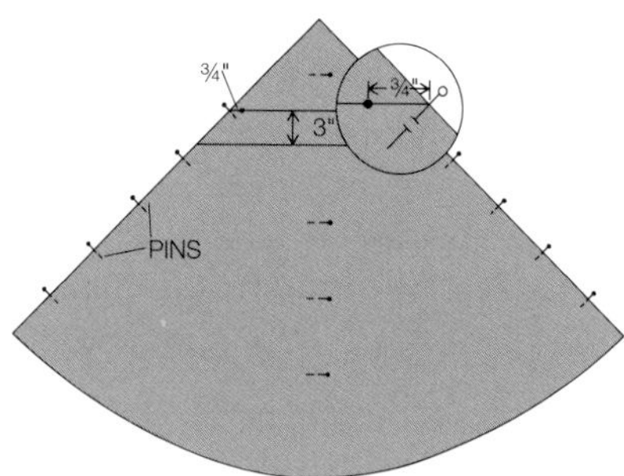

8. *Directly on work surface* or cutting board, measure and mark with tape or pins a vertical line for center of swag; from that line in each direction, measure and mark vertical lines at half the finished swag width (18 inches in example).

9. *Lay swag,* right side up, on work surface, lining up top point with center line and placing lower horizontal line on front edge of work surface; pin.

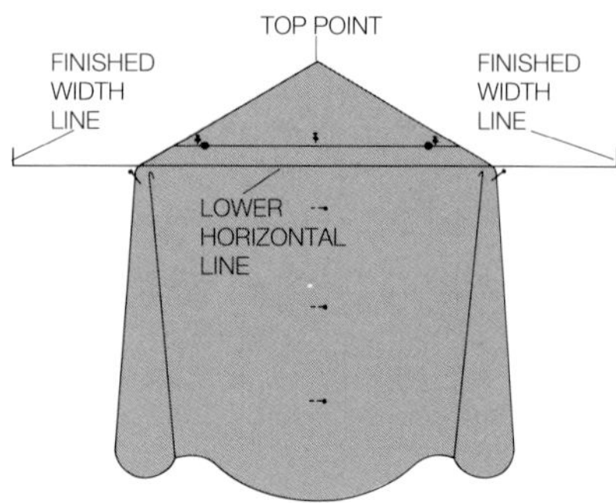

10. *On one edge,* grasp fabric at second pin and, angling pleat, bring to ¾-inch dot; pin.

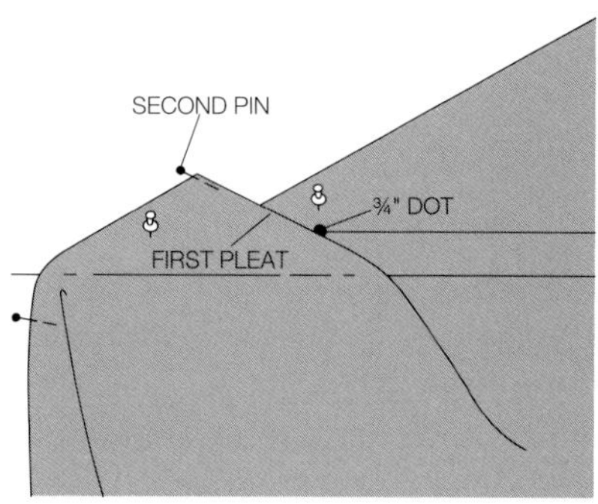

Repeat on other side.

11. *Continue making* and pinning pleats, keeping spacing even and stair-stepping pleats. Make last pleat so cut edge is parallel to edge of work surface and hem meets finished width lines. Adjust pleats as necessary.

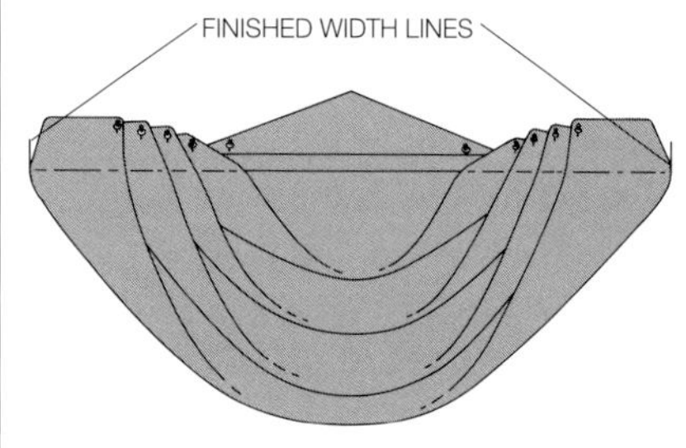

Working from both sides, coax pleats into rounded folds; adjust and repin as necessary.

Pin pleats together. Check swag length; if too long, remove anchoring pins and move entire swag back from edge, adjusting pleats as needed.

For a gathered swag, unpin pleats, one at a time, and make small tucks; using a long gathering stitch, hand-stitch tucks 1½ inches from edge of work surface. Hem should meet finished width lines.

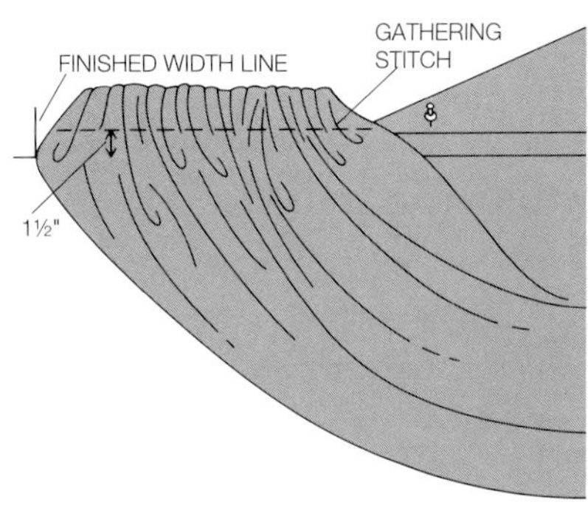

12. ***Mark a line*** on swag parallel to and 1½ inches from edge of work surface. Place lower edge of 1-inch masking tape on marked line.

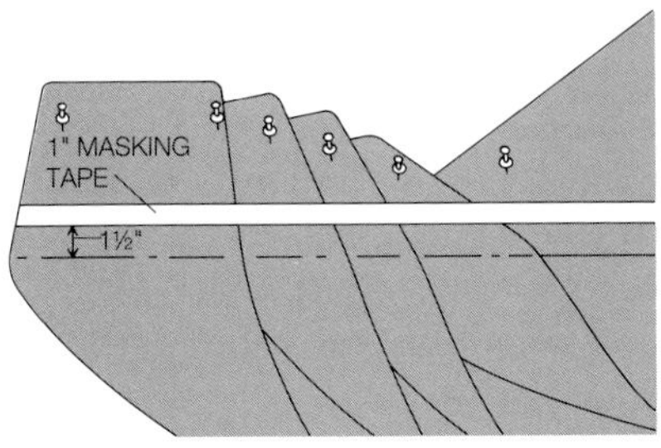

Stitch on line through all layers; remove pins. Trim swag along upper edge of tape; remove tape.

13. ***Cut a lining strip*** 4 inches wide and equal in length to width of swag; have a selvage along one long edge or finish one edge. Fold strip, wrong sides together, 1½ inches from finished edge and press. Turn in raw edge on other side to meet fold and press again.

14. ***With finished edge*** of strip underneath, sandwich swag between lining strip. Topstitch close to fold through all layers.

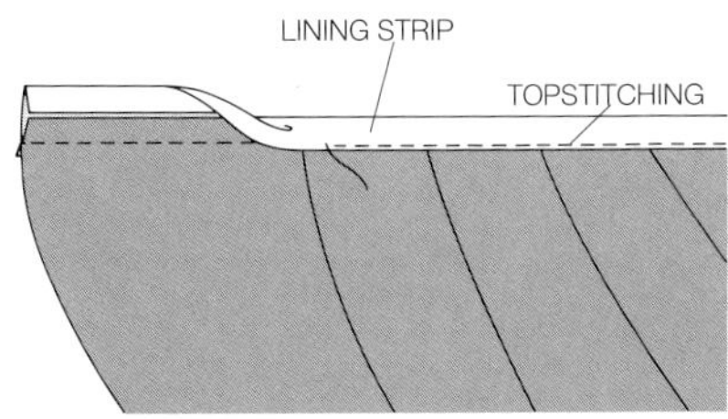

Planning cascades

For color and pattern continuity, self-line cascades. But if you want to see another color or pattern from the front where the pleats break, line the cascades with a contrast fabric. Cascades can go over or under a swag.

Cut a sample cascade from lining or scrap fabric and experiment with length and pleat and space sizes before you cut your face fabric.

Traditional cascades are pleated, though you can gather them to match gathered swags. On a gathered cascade, the inside edge appears scalloped.

Length varies, depending on the look you want to achieve. As a rule, the cascade at its longest point is at least twice as long as the swag. When cascades extend to the sill or apron, the look is usually casual.

Where you begin the taper on a cascade is important. The higher the taper, the more lining you'll see. Begin the taper above or several inches below the longest point on the swag; avoid beginning the taper even with the long point of the swag.

Each cascade is made from one width of fabric. A typical cascade has a 4-inch leading edge space, four 6-inch pleats alternating with three 2-inch spaces, and a return; finished width is 10 inches, not including the return.

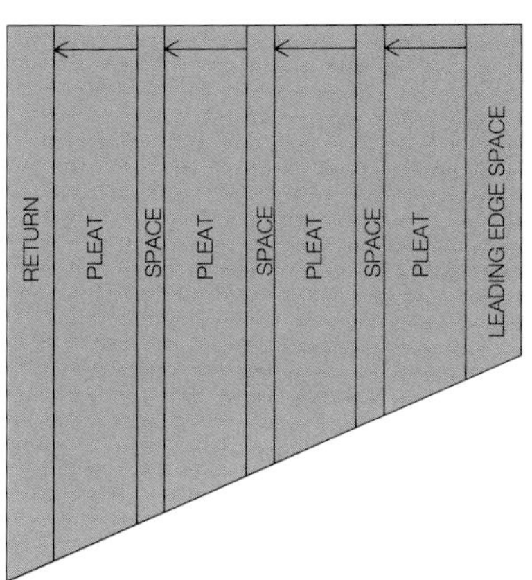

For a narrower cascade, make the pleats 7 inches and the spaces 1 inch for a finished width of 7 inches. The spaces can be narrower than 1 inch for an even more tightly stacked cascade.

Sketch your cascade and add up the sizes of the pleats and spaces to determine where to trim the fabric width; be sure to add a ½-inch seam allowance on each side.

For a gathered cascade, multiply the desired finished width by 2½ and add seam allowances to arrive at the cut width.

Calculating yardage. Each cascade requires one width of fabric the desired finished length (measured at the longest point), plus 4 inches total for seam allowances and an allowance to go over the top of the mounting board.

Take into account repeats on patterned fabric: cascades look best if a full repeat is at the top, just below where the cascades break over the board. Or you can center one repeat on the cascade, splitting repeats above and below. Don't put a full repeat at the bottom—most of the design will be cut away when the cascade is tapered. Place repeats at the same level on cascades; they won't be mirror images of each other, but the color arrangement will be the same.

If your fabric doesn't have a directional pattern and you're making self-lined cascades, you can save fabric by cutting cascades as shown below. You can then use the lower portion of fabric to line the opposite cascade.

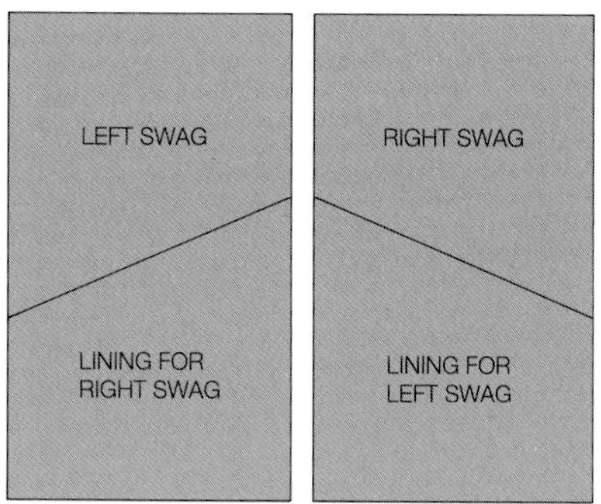

Cascades step-by-step

1. ***Lay lining*** and face fabric right sides together; trim both to finished flat width plus 1 inch. On leading edge of each cascade, measure and mark from top a distance equal to start of taper plus 4 inches. Using a straightedge, draw a line from mark to opposite lower corner. Cut on line.

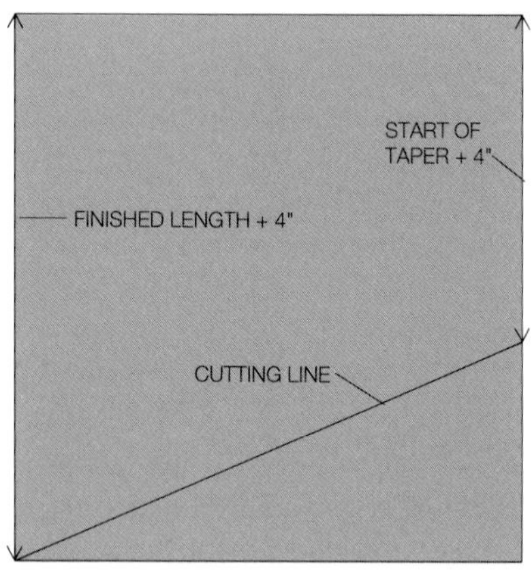

2. ***Pin lining*** and face fabric together on all edges except top. Stitch, making a ½-inch seam; trim seam allowances at corners. Turn right side out and lightly press edges. If fabric is heavy, zigzag or serge top raw edges together.

3. ***Lay cascade*** on work surface. At return edge, measure and mark finished length line; extend line across top.

4. ***For a pleated cascade,*** measure and mark pleats and spaces with pins.

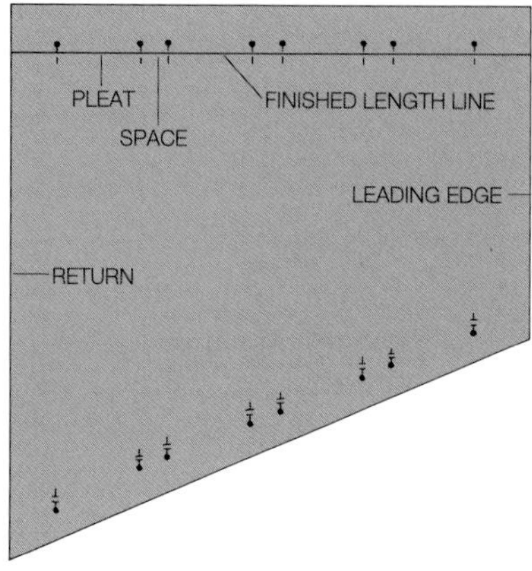

Form pleats, working from return to leading edge. Pin in place at top edge and along finished length line.

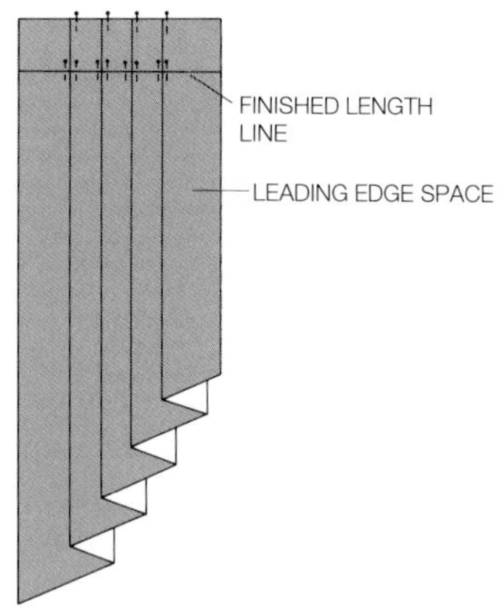

For a gathered cascade, run a long gathering stitch by hand 1½ inches beyond finished length line. Gather to desired finished width.

5. ***With right side up,*** place lower edge of 1-inch masking tape on finished length line. Stitch pleats or gathers in place along top edge of tape. Measure 1½ inches beyond stitching and mark another line; cut on line. Remove tape.

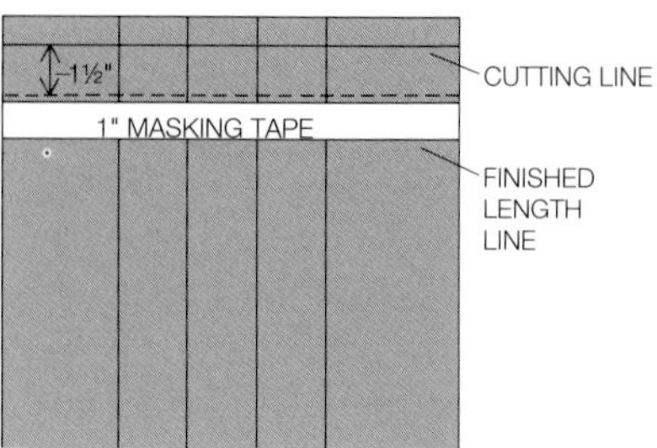

Overcast top edge with a wide zigzag stitch or serge, joining face fabric and lining.

Mounting traditional swags & cascades

Stapling traditional swags and cascades to a mounting board is the most common method of attachment. To make removal easier, you can use hook-and-loop fastener tape instead, but it adds bulk.

1. ***Follow first part*** of step 15, "Flat Roman shade," page 75, to cover mounting board.

2. ***Pin swag or cascade,*** whichever goes under, to board first, placing edge so finished length line is at front edge of board; check finished length and adjust if necessary. Repeat for other treatment. Fold cascade at corner for return.

3. ***Staple to board,*** placing staples about 2 inches apart. Staple jabots (see page 127), if used.

4. ***Follow directions*** for an outside mount in step 21, "Flat Roman shade," page 75, to install. Support with angle irons every 40 inches.

Cutout Swags & Cascades

Attached to decorative poles and often combined with sheers, miniblinds, or pleated shades, cutout swags and cascades are a lighter alternative to traditional swags and cascades. The only difference between them is that cutout swags have an open area at the top.

Because cutout swags are open at the top, the coverage they provide for an undertreatment is shallow. If you're planning an undertreatment other than cascades, such as floor-length or puddled side panels, be sure to mount the swags so they conceal the undertreatment's heading.

Making these swags takes time and a willingness to experiment with fabric. Make a sample cutout swag first to get a feel for how the swags are made and to see if you like the look.

Because of the way they're attached, cutout swags and cascades are the most difficult to make of all the swag treatments. This project gives instructions for swags and cascades without returns. If you want to cover the gap between the treatment and the window, make them with returns (see page 122).

Planning cutout swags. For guidelines in choosing fabric, see pages 24–33.

Cutout swags appear to flow across the pole; cascades can go behind or over the pole at the ends. The swags shown below overlap each other (in the example, each is 36 inches wide, with a 16-inch cutout and two 10-inch overlaps). The cascades are behind the pole.

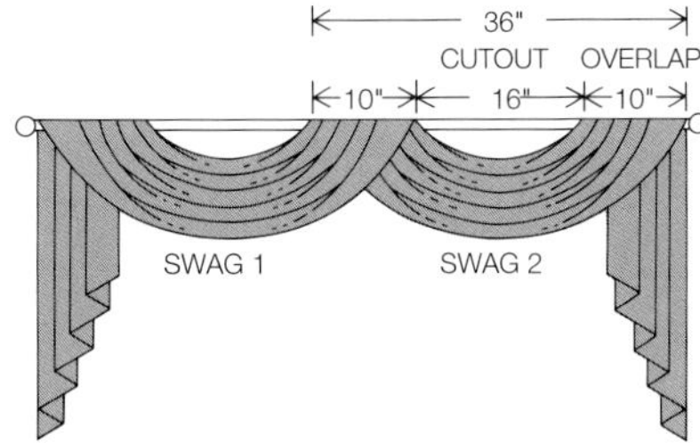

Swags start with a square of fabric 6 inches larger than the desired finished width, which can range from 32 to 48 inches, depending on your fabric's width. The cutout should be between 16 and 20 inches wide. Overlaps are from 8 to 12 inches; 10 inches is standard.

The rod or pole is usually installed 8 inches above the top of the window opening. Extensions for swags used with cascades are typically 4 to 6 inches, allowing a portion of each cascade to cover the window. If you're planning tied-back side panels rather than cascades, place half of each panel on the window and half off. For straight panels, place most of each panel off the window.

Because rods and poles hang from brackets placed near or at the ends, the treatment will cover only the distance from the inside of one bracket to the inside of the other.

To figure the number of swags and their width, complete the following steps. If you want one more swag than this method yields, return to step 3 and refigure, using the new number of swags.

1. Measure your window width and add extensions (see pages 20–21) to arrive at rod or pole size. (In following example, rod or pole size, bracket to bracket, is 62 inches.)

2. Divide rod or pole size by a trial swag size of 35 and round off to nearest whole number to arrive at number of swags (62 ÷ 35 = 1.8, rounded to 2).

3. Multiply number of overlaps (one more than number of swags) by 10 inches, a trial overlap size (3 x 10 = 30 inches).

4. Subtract result in step 3 from rod or pole size; divide by number of swags to arrive at cutout size of each swag (62 - 30 = 32 ÷ 2 = 16 inches).

If cutout size is less than 16 inches, reduce overlap to 9 inches and refigure; if cutout is still less than 16, reduce overlap to 8 and refigure. If cutout size is greater than 24 inches, increase overlap to 11 or 12 and refigure.

5. To cutout size, add 2 times overlap size to arrive at swag width (16 + 20 = 36 inches). Sketch your treatment.

Calculating yardage. Calculate yardage for cutout swags in the same way as for traditional swags (see page 115).

Swag tips. It's easiest to pleat a swag if you have a helper on one side. If you work alone, make and pin pleats one at a time on each side. Either way, you'll need to adjust pleats and repin a bit to make uniformly rounded folds.

A grid cardboard cutting board is helpful for pleating the swag to the correct finished width.

Continued on next page

Cutout swags & cascades step-by-step

1. *Choose and prepare* face fabric and lining (see pages 24–33).

2. *Follow steps 2–4,* "Traditional swags," pages 115–116, to cut lining and lower curve.

3. *With lining* right side up, measure and mark from top point down each side a distance equal to cutout size plus 3 inches (19 inches in example). Measure and mark from top point down center a distance equal to cutout size plus 2 inches (18 inches in example). Strike a gentle curve from side marks to center mark; cut along curve.

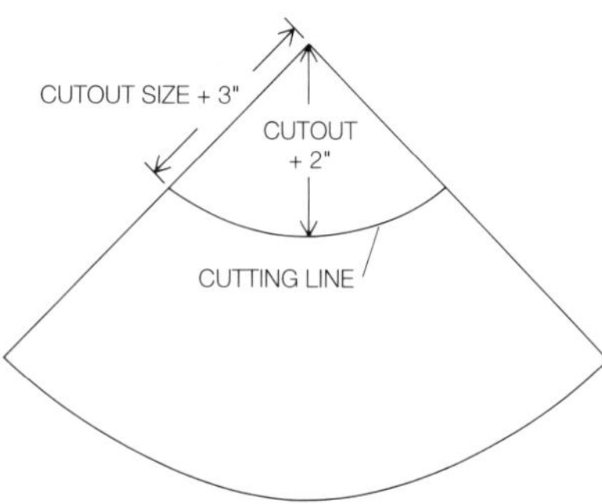

4. *Position face fabric* right side up and determine top of swag (make sure motifs on patterned fabric are going in right direction). Lay lining over face fabric, right sides together, aligning sides. If fabric is patterned, move lining until repeat is centered as desired.

Pin layers together along curves; cut face fabric along curves. Pin and stitch lower curve only, making a ½-inch seam.

5. *Follow step 6,* "Traditional swags," page 116, to under-stitch lower curve, disregarding instruction to pin swag up center.

Turn right sides together again. Pin and stitch upper curve, making a ½-inch seam. Turn right side out and press.

6. *Measure distance* along each side and divide by 5 to arrive at pleat size. If less than 5 inches, divide distance by 4. Measure that distance along edges and mark with pins for pleat positions.

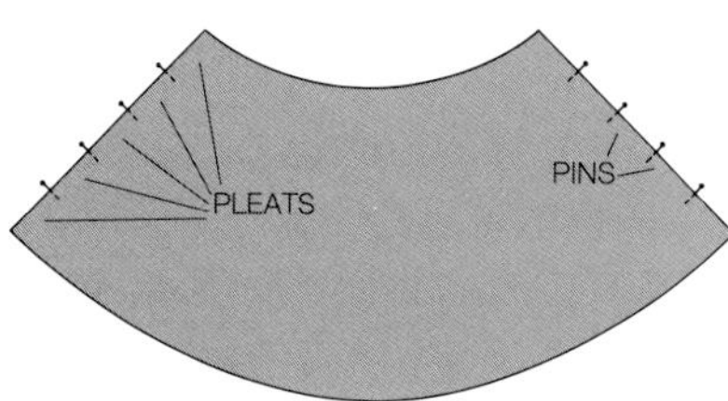

7. *Directly on work surface* or cutting board, measure and mark with tape or pins finished swag width (36 inches in example); mark midpoint (18 inches). On each side of midpoint, mark half the cutout size (8 inches).

8. *At upper curve,* turn under 1½ inches just on sides. On each side, pin first pleat to work surface, angling and aligning with cutout lines. Secure with pins.

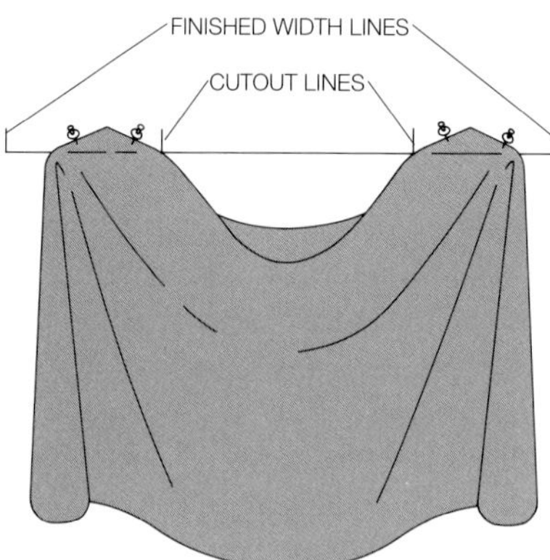

9. *Continue making* and pinning pleats, keeping spacing even and stair-stepping pleats. Make last pleat so cut edge is parallel to edge of work surface and hem meets finished width lines. Adjust pleats as necessary.

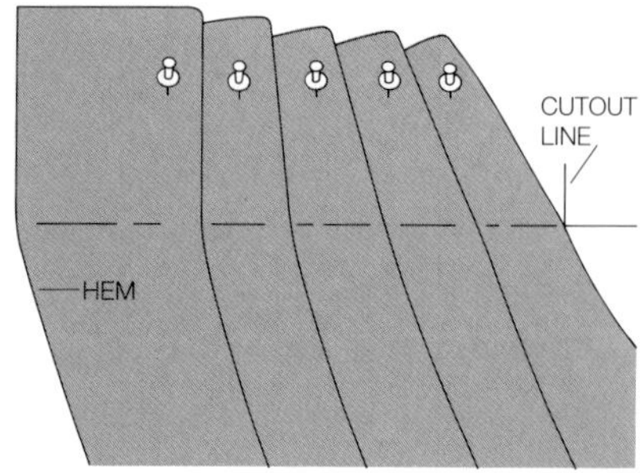

Starting at top and working from both sides, form pleats into rounded folds; adjust and repin as necessary.

Pin pleats together. Check swag length; if too long, remove anchoring pins and move entire swag back from edge, adjusting pleats as needed.

For a gathered swag, unpin pleats, one at a time, and make small tucks; using a long gathering stitch, hand-stitch tucks 1½ inches from work surface edge. Hem should meet finished width marks.

10. *To make cascades,* follow directions that begin on page 117 through step 4, page 118, disregarding references to returns. With cutout swags, cascades can go over or behind pole. Make finished width equal to size of overlaps (10 inches in example).

11. *To determine length* of hook-and-loop fastener tape, multiply number of swag overlaps by 2; multiply result by size of each overlap plus 1 inch (in example, 3 x 2 = 6 x 11 = 66 inches).

12. *Cut two strips* of hook-and-loop fastener tape equal to overlap size plus 1 inch.

On a rod with a flat back, glue hook (stiff) strips to rod at ends.

On a round pole, have a helper hold pole securely on work surface. Using a board laid against pole as a guide, attach masking tape in a straight line. Align hook strips with masking tape and glue at ends.

For more than one swag, attach other strips at overlap positions.

13. *For a swag or cascade that goes over rod,* proceed to step 14.

For a swag or cascade that goes behind rod, measure distance from bottom of rod to top of hook strip.

On treatment, measure and mark finished length line; pin perpendicular to line and baste. Measure and mark another line beyond finished length line at distance just determined. Place top edge of masking tape on top line.

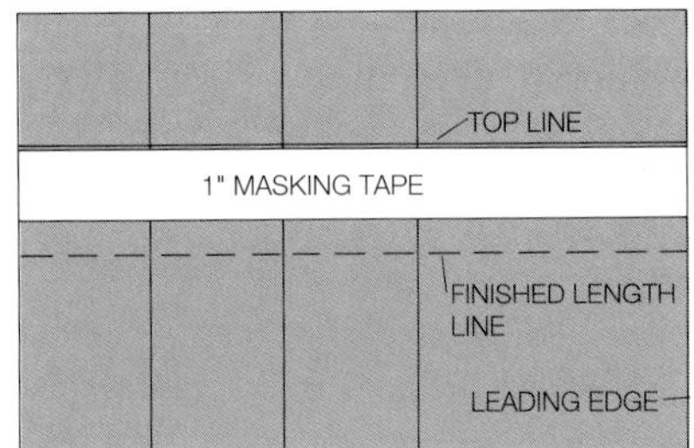

Stitch on top line; trim ¼ inch beyond stitching. Remove masking tape and basting.

14. *For a swag or cascade that goes over rod,* determine distance over rod to bottom of hook strip on back (typically 2½ to 3 inches) by having a helper hold a straightedge vertically behind rod so finished length measurement (16 inches in example) is at top of rod. With a flexible tape measure, measure from bottom of hook strip on back of rod, up and over rod, to bottom of straightedge.

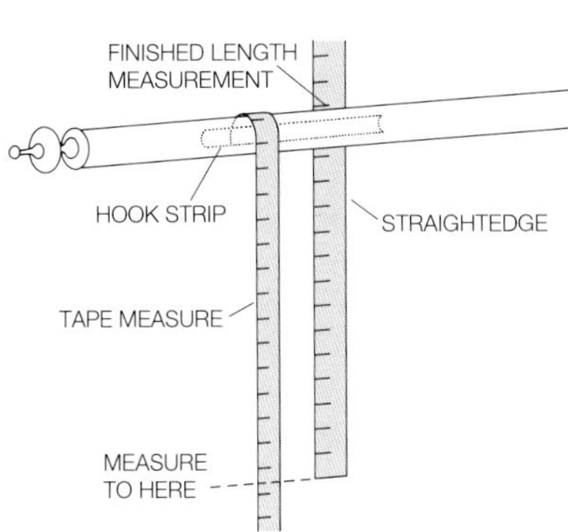

From this figure, subtract finished length of swag or cascade for distance needed beyond finished length line.

On treatment, mark finished length line; pin along line and baste. Measure and mark another line beyond finished length line at distance just determined. Place top edge of masking tape on top line.

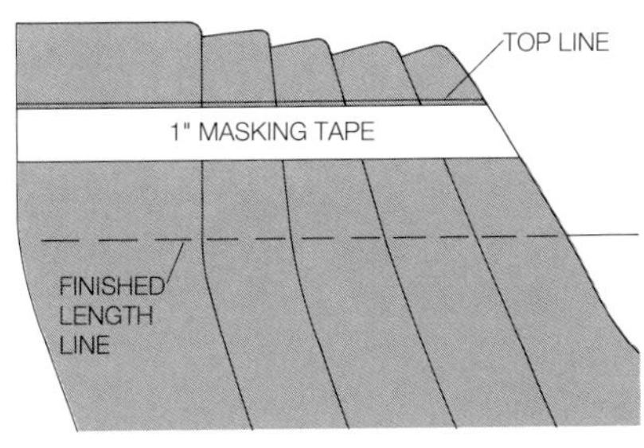

Stitch on top line; trim ¼ inch beyond stitching. Remove tape and basting.

Mounting cutout swags & cascades

Review the arrangement shown on page 119, if used (directions that follow are for that arrangement). A helpful hint in determining which strip to use: hook strips face the wall; loop strips face the room.

For other arrangements, sketch the treatment to help you plan the order of attachment. Swags and cascades should give the illusion of being a continuous piece of fabric. Attach the swags or cascades that go behind the rod before those that go over the rod.

1. *Install rod* (see pages 60–61) or pole (see page 43).

2. *On front* of each cascade, sew a loop strip, aligning top of strip with top row of stitching.

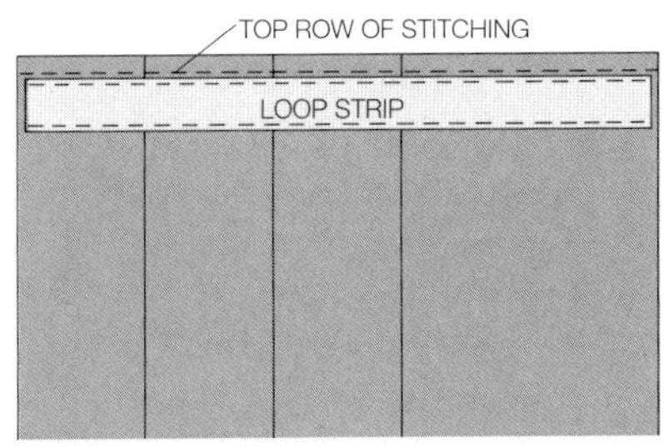

On back, sew a hook strip.

3. *On outer overlaps* of swags 1 and 2, which go over rod, sew a loop strip to back, aligning top of strip with row of stitching. Repeat at center overlap of swag 1.

4. *On center overlap* of swag 2, which goes behind rod, sew a loop strip to front of swag and a hook strip to back.

5. *Attach cascades* to rod. At ends, place swags over rod and attach to cascades.

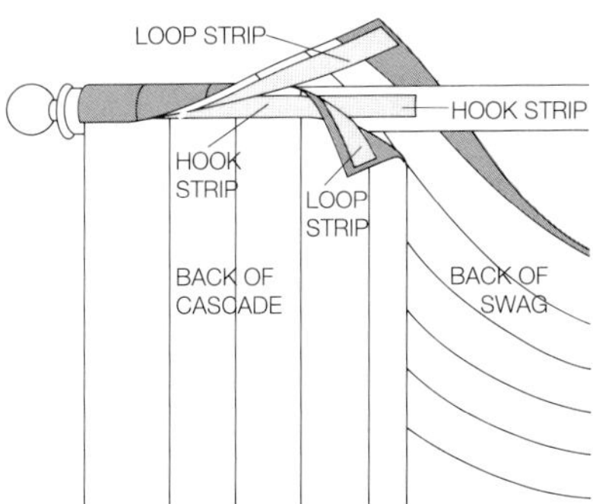

6. *At center,* attach swag 2 behind rod; lift swag 1 over rod and attach to back of swag 2.

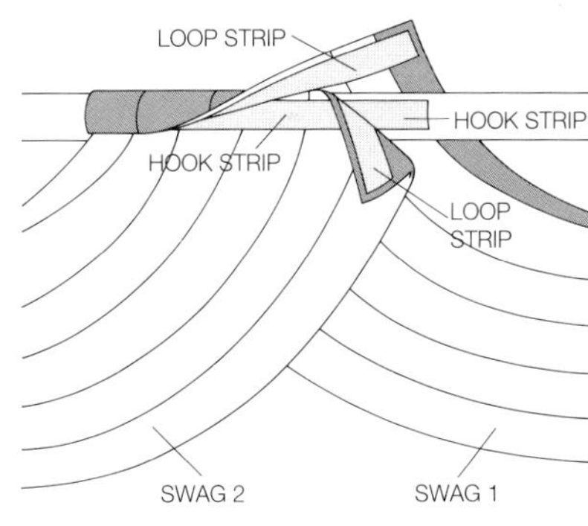

Cutout Swags & Cascades with Returns

Returns cover the gap between the window and the treatment at the sides. A notch at the top of each cascade allows the return to attach to the top of the bracket (use metal rather than wood brackets).

Cutout swags & cascades with returns step-by-step

1. *Follow directions* for "Cutout swags & cascades," pages 119–120, through step 9 to make swags.

2. *Follow directions* that begin on page 117 through step 4, page 118, to make cascades; return size equals distance from back of bracket to front of rod. Finished width of each cascade, not counting return, should equal size of overlaps (10 inches in example).

3. *Make a paper pattern* for notch equal to finished width before cutting fabric. Mark return.

On a cascade that goes behind rod, trim top edge of cascade face 1 inch shorter than return portion. Where return begins, cut a V-shaped notch extending into cascade a depth equal to width of hook-and-loop fastener tape.

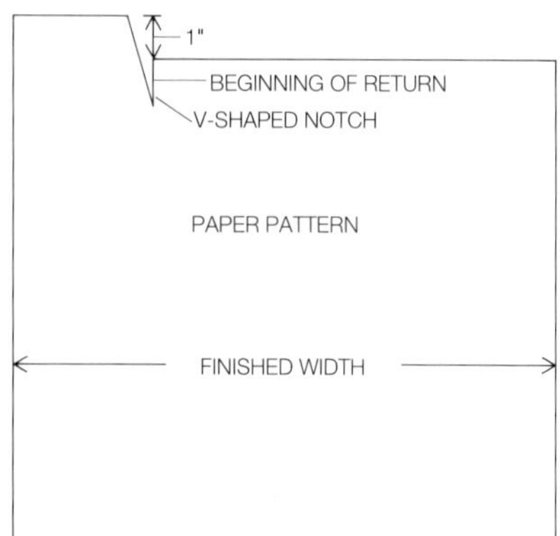

On a cascade that goes over rod, trim top edge of return 1 inch shorter than face. Where return begins, cut a J-shaped notch as deep as circumference of rod plus 2 inches and as wide as rod diameter.

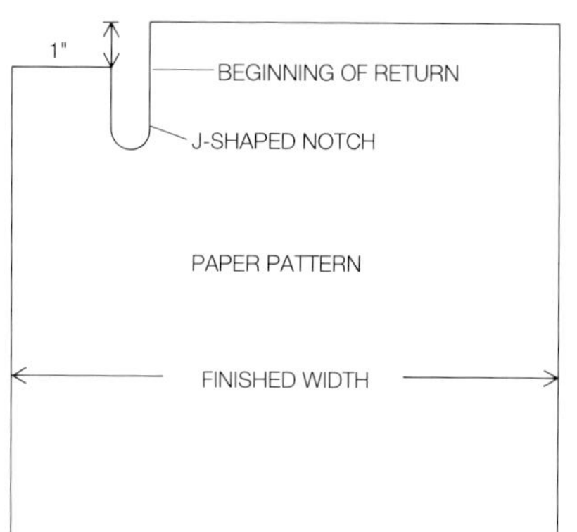

Make a fabric pattern, altering depth of notch if necessary.

4. *Follow steps 11–12,* "Cutout swags & cascades," pages 120–121, to attach fastener tape to rod.

5. *For a swag that goes behind rod,* follow step 13, "Cutout swags & cascades," page 121.

For a cascade that goes behind rod, measure distance from bottom of rod to top of hook strip (typically 1 to 1½ inches). Measure and mark another line on cascade beyond finished length line at distance just determined. Place top edge of masking tape along that line just up to return. On return, place top edge of tape 1 inch above that line.

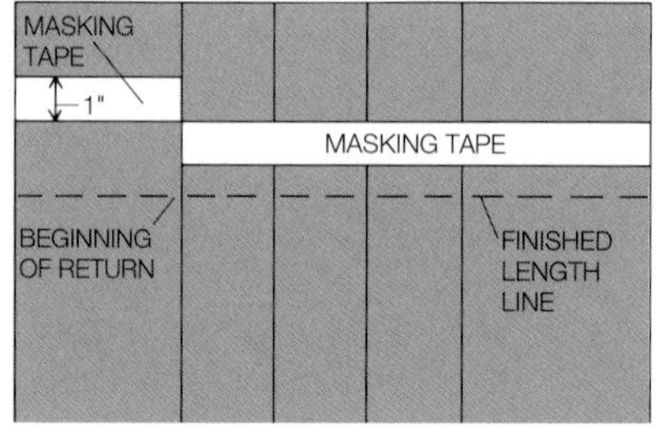

Stitch along top edges of tape; trim ¼ inch beyond stitching. Trim fabric flap where return begins. Remove tape.

6. *For a swag that goes over rod,* follow step 14, "Cutout swags & cascades," page 121.

For a cascade that goes over rod, follow first two paragraphs of step 14, "Cutout swags & cascades," page 121. Measure and mark finished length line; pin and baste. Measure and mark another line beyond finished length line at distance just determined. Place top edge of masking tape on top line.

Stitch on top line; trim ¼ inch beyond stitching. Remove tape.

Trim return portion 1 inch shorter than cascade face; overcast top edges together.

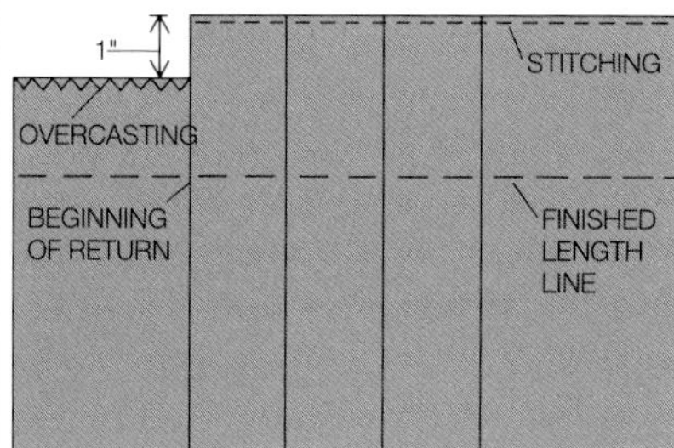

7. *Using pattern,* cut notches in returns. Zigzag raw edges together or serge, using thread to match face fabric. Remove basting.

8. *Follow steps 1–6,* "Mounting cutout swags & cascades," page 121, to mount treatments, with these additional considerations for cascades: On a cascade that goes behind rod, loop strips are attached to front of cascade and back of return; on one that goes over rod, loop strips are attached to back of cascade and return; for either, attach a hook strip to top of each bracket.

Running Swags

Running swags offer a less structured look than traditional or cut-out swags and cascades. Use them alone to frame a window or combine them with other treatments for a soft effect.

Several different styles are presented here. What makes each distinctive is the method of attachment. A running swag can be pulled through or draped over swag holders, held up by tabs or separate knots, or wrapped around a decorative rod or pole. The basic swag is the same for each style.

Planning running swags. For most swags, two fabric widths are best, unless the window is small; then you can use one fabric width. If your fabric is sheer, consider using three widths.

The following simple swag consists of two widths tapered and seamed to form a tube. A self-lined swag requires two lengths of the same fabric; a contrast-lined swag requires one length each of face fabric and contrast fabric.

Directions for determining the cut length accompany each project. The portion of the swag that becomes the cascades can vary from a third to two-thirds the window length. Long cascades can be made into bishop's sleeves (add 8 to 12 inches) or puddled on the floor (add 12 inches). Avoid exact floor-length cascades—it's difficult to get the cascades even.

If you choose asymmetrical cascades, make sure lengths differ significantly—slight variations just look like mistakes.

1. Measure your window width and add extensions (see pages 20–21). Recommended width for each swag is 35 to 50 inches.

2. For two or more swags, divide rod or board size or distance between holders by desired swag width to arrive at number of swags; round off to nearest whole number to arrive at number of swags.

3. Divide rod or board size or distance between holders by number of swags for exact swag size. For number of swag holders, add 1 to number of swags.

Running swags step-by-step

1. ***Choose and prepare*** face fabric and lining (see pages 24–33).

2. ***Measure and cut*** lengths according to specific project. Cut two lengths for self-lined swag; for contrast swag, cut one length each of face and contrast fabric.

3. ***With right sides together,*** measure in 15 inches from each end along one long edge; mark. Draw a line connecting each mark with corner on opposite edge, forming a taper.

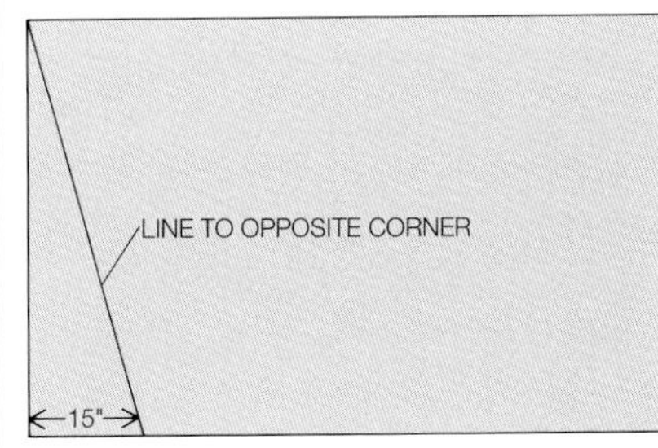

Cut along marked line.

4. ***With right sides together,*** pin edges, leaving an 8-inch opening on one long edge. Stitch all around, making a ½-inch seam. Clip points. Press seams open. Turn swag right side out and press edges; slip-stitch opening closed.

5. ***For attachment,*** see one of following variations.

Pouf Swags

Rounded poufs accent this running swag treatment. You achieve the poufs, also called rosettes, by pulling a basic swag through harp-shaped, tulip-shaped, or circular swag holders. Add bishop's sleeves, if you like.

The cut length equals 1¼ times the distance between the holders, plus 30 inches for each pouf, plus 2 times the cascade length, plus 1 inch.

Pouf swags step-by-step

1. ***Follow directions*** for "Running swags," at left, to make swag.

2. ***Mount swag holders*** according to manufacturer's instructions.

3. ***Lay swag flat*** on work surface, lining side up, and fold accordion style so short and long edges face in same direction. Folded swag should be about 4 inches wide.

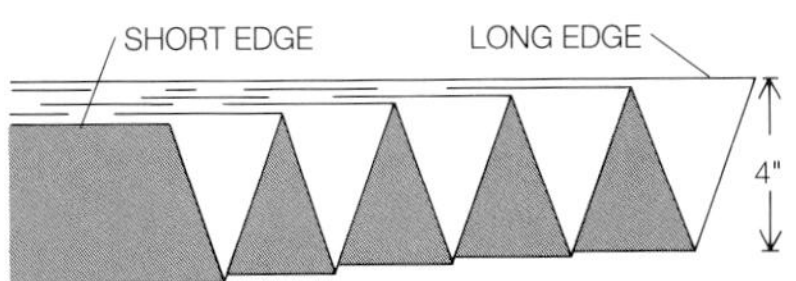

Using fabric scraps, tie swag loosely every 2 feet to keep folds in place.

Continued on next page

4. *From each end,* measure finished length of cascade and slide rubber bands to this point. With short end facing center of window, drape swag over swag holders so rubber bands are behind holders. Remove ties.

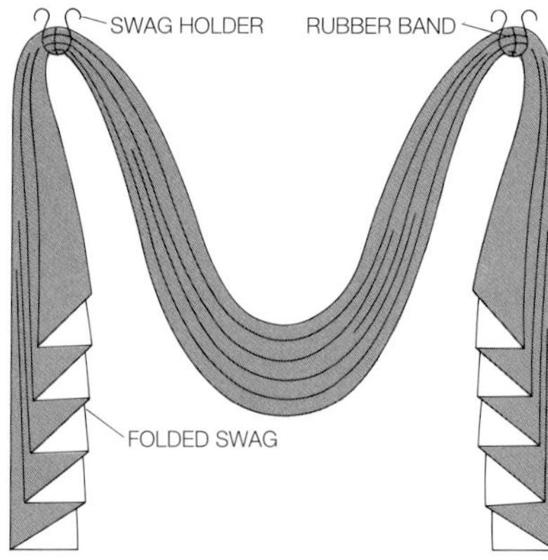

5. *From each holder,* measure toward center 15 inches and mark with tape. Form a 30-inch loop so tape is at bottom of loop; place loop in holder. Remove rubber bands.

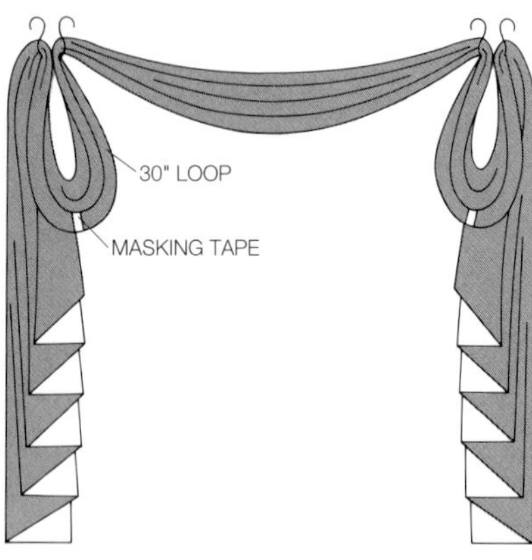

6. *Adjust folds,* pulling gently on lower folds to lengthen swag in center and on upper folds to keep top nearly straight.

7. *To form each pouf,* gently pull up inner folds of loop, fanning fabric.

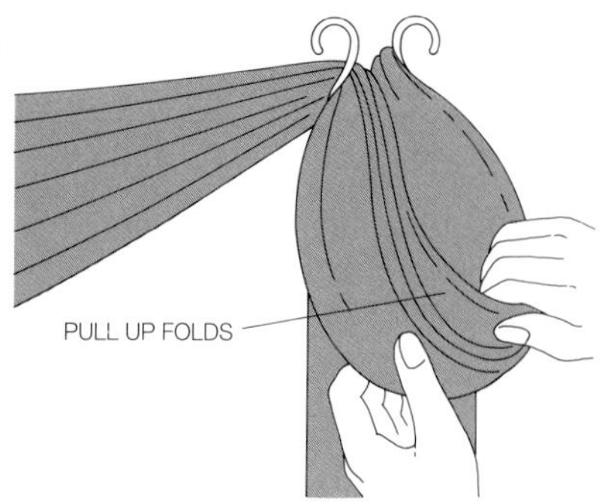

Continue pulling folds until pouf is full and rounded; tuck top and bottom of pouf back into holder. Secure pouf with pins. Adjust folds in swag and cascades.

8. *For two swags* (three holders), mark midpoint of swag. Measure and mark cascades as for a single swag. Match swag midpoint to center holder. Measure 15 inches on each side of midpoint for center 30-inch loop; form center pouf. Form corner poufs as you would for a single swag.

For three swags (four holders), match swag midpoint to center of window.

Tab & Knotted Swags

Though they look very different, both tab and knotted swags are mounted on a board and held up at the corners in the same way. With a tab swag, simple bands of fabric do the job; on a knotted swag, separate knots secure the swag and add visual interest.

For either style, the cut length equals the board size, plus 2 times the cascade length, plus 1 inch.

Tabs. You can make self- or contrast-fabric tabs. Standard finished width of each tab is 2 inches. Finished length is 20 inches (two 2-inch ends that attach to the board and 16 inches for the loop).

Knots. For medium-weight fabric, you need 1 yard for each knot; for sheer fabric, 48 inches. For a contrast-fabric knot, buy ½ yard of each fabric.

Tab & knotted swags step-by-step

1. *Follow directions* for "Running swags," page 123, to make swag.

2. *Follow first part* of step 15, "Flat Roman shade," page 75, to cover mounting board.

3. *To make knots,* proceed to step 4.

For tabs, cut strips of fabric 5 inches wide and 20 inches long. With right sides together, pin and stitch long edges, making a ½-inch seam. Turn right side out, center seam at back, and press. Staple one end of each tab, seam up, to board 2 inches from front and side.

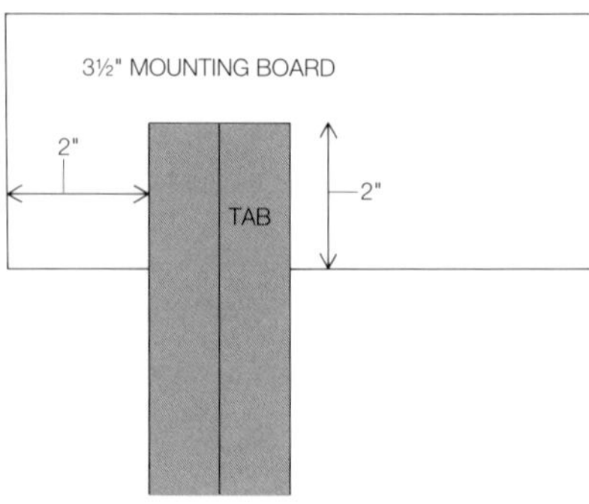

For more than one swag, measure space between tabs and divide by number of swags; mark spaces. Staple remaining tabs over space marks.

4. *For a self-lined knot,* pin cut edges, right sides together; stitch, making a ½-inch seam, to form a tube (selvages will be at ends).

For a contrast knot, pin and stitch two 18-inch pieces.

Turn knot right side out and press lightly. Center seam on self-lined knot.

Tie tube in a single knot so knot is slightly closer to one end than other. With front of knot facing down, staple long end of each knotted tube to board about 2 inches from front and side.

For more than one swag, measure space between knots and divide by number of swags; mark spaces. Staple remaining knots over space marks.

5. *Find midpoint of swag* and match to center of board. Staple swag to board at back edge, working from center to each end.

6. *Gather swag* in your hands, forming soft pleats. Pull tabs or knots up and over swag, angling end tabs or knots outward; pin to top of board, adjusting length as desired. Staple to board; trim. Adjust cascades.

7. *Follow directions* for an outside mount in step 21, "Flat Roman shade," page 75, to install. Support with angle irons every 40 inches.

Scarf Swags

Decorative rings and medallion swag holders are designed to hold graceful scarf swags. Ring-and-pole sets hold the swag in place by means of self-adhesive hook-and-loop fastener tape on the back of the pole; follow the manufacturer's instructions.

The cut length equals 1¼ times the distance between holders or the pole length, plus 2 times cascade length, plus 1 inch.

Scarf swags step-by-step

1. *Follow directions* for "Running swags," page 123, to make swag.

2. *Mount swag holders* according to manufacturer's instructions.

3. *Follow step 3,* "Pouf swag," page 123, to fold swag. Or, for a softer look, gather swag in your hands.

4. *Mark midpoints* on swag and window. Lay swag over holders, lining up marks. Adjust folds, pulling gently on lower folds to lengthen swag at center and on upper folds to keep top nearly straight. Adjust cascades.

Wrapped Swags

This swag and cascade treatment "snakes" around the pole, forming two or more shallow swags with cascades. Single knots on either end secure the swag to the pole. You can knot the cascades also.

A wrapped swag can cover any window more than 36 inches wide. The cut length equals 1½ times the pole size, plus 2 times cascade length, plus 1 inch, plus the knots (experiment to find the length needed).

Wrapped swags step-by-step

1. *Follow directions* for "Running swags," page 123, to make swag.

2. *Install pole* according to manufacturer's instructions.

3. *Follow step 3,* "Pouf swag," page 123, to fold swag. Or, for a softer look, gather swag.

4. *Mark midpoints* on swag and pole. Lining up marks, drape swag over pole at center, with half of swag in front and half behind. Tie a loose knot around pole at each end. Adjust folds in swag, pulling gently on lower folds to lengthen. Adjust knots and cascades.

Decorative Accents: Rosettes, Choux & Jabots

Rosettes, choux, and jabots dress up a variety of window treatments.

Rosettes and choux can be used where swags meet, at the upper corners of cloud shades, or at the ends of tiebacks. Jabots accent swags where they meet or overlap and are often trimmed with rosettes or choux.

Rosettes

To make a rosette with a rounded effect, you sew two ruffles out of contrast fabric and simply roll and stitch them. For a plain, flat rosette, you stitch swirls of gathered fabric to a circle of crinoline.

It's most economical to cut strips crosswise, unless your fabric's pattern demands lengthwise strips. For a plaid fabric, consider cutting strips on the bias.

1. *For a 6-inch, two-color rounded rosette,* cut one 7-inch-wide strip from each of two fabrics. *For a 4-inch flat rosette,* cut one 3½-inch-wide strip and one 2-inch circle of crinoline. Cut length should be approximately 54 inches.

2. *Fold strip(s)* in half lengthwise, wrong sides together, and press. To gather, place one end of cord (buttonhole twist or crochet cotton) ½ inch from lengthwise fold. Zigzag over cord, tapering for 6 inches until cord is ½ inch from lengthwise raw edges; continue zigzagging ½ inch from raw edge down length of strip.

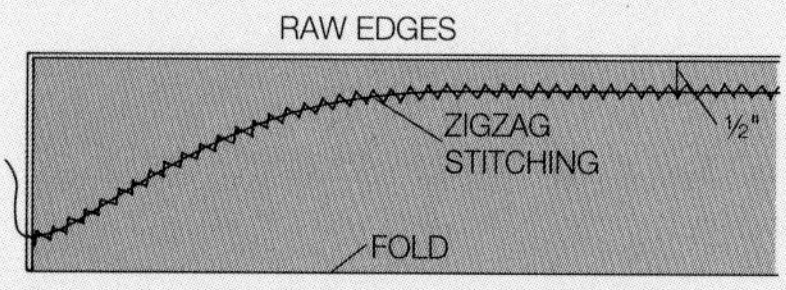

On curve, trim excess fabric to ½ inch. Gather strip(s) to approximately 22 inches.

3. *For a rounded rosette,* layer ruffles so folded edge of bottom ruffle extends ¼ inch beyond edge of top ruffle. Starting at tapered ends, begin rolling ruffles tightly; using a long needle and a thimble, stitch through gathers at base as you go.

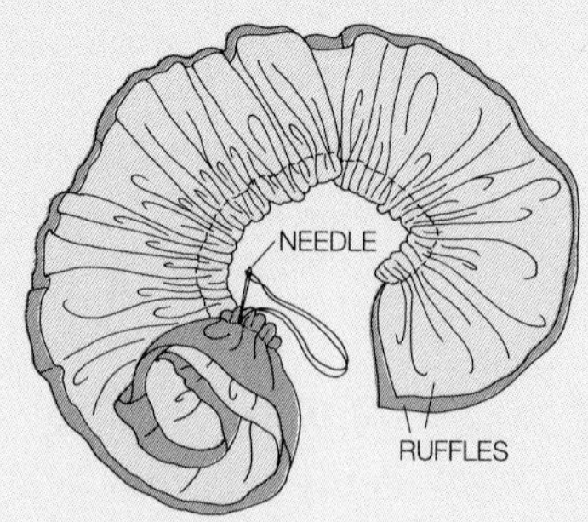

Continue rolling and stitching rosette, sewing through sides as rosette increases and folding under ends to conceal. If desired, cut and stitch a fabric circle to cover raw edges.

For a flat rosette, position square end of ruffle on circle; tack.

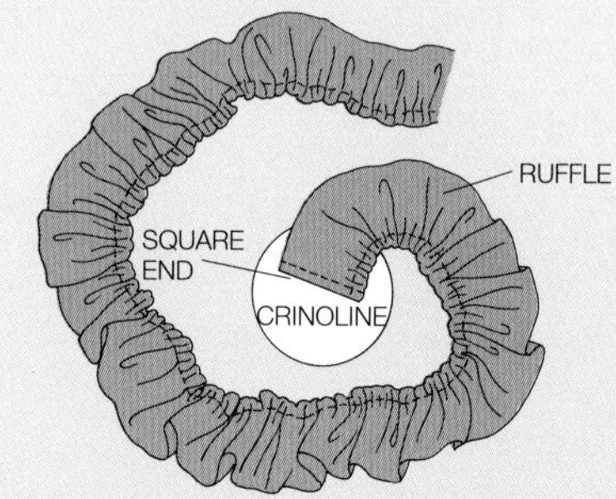

Stitch ruffle to edge of crinoline, letting folded edge overlap crinoline 1 inch. Continue stitching, working inward (ruffle will naturally coil). Push tapered end of ruffle into center; stitch to secure.

4. *Pin, stitch, or glue* in place.

Choux

These decorative trimmings possess an old-fashioned charm. Choux can be made from the same or a contrast fabric.

1. ***For a 5-inch choux,*** cut a 14-inch circle of fabric and a 4-inch circle of crinoline.

2. ***Run a gathering stitch*** around edge of fabric circle; gather like a shower cap until opening is a little less than 4 inches. Overcast crinoline circle to gathered fabric circle.

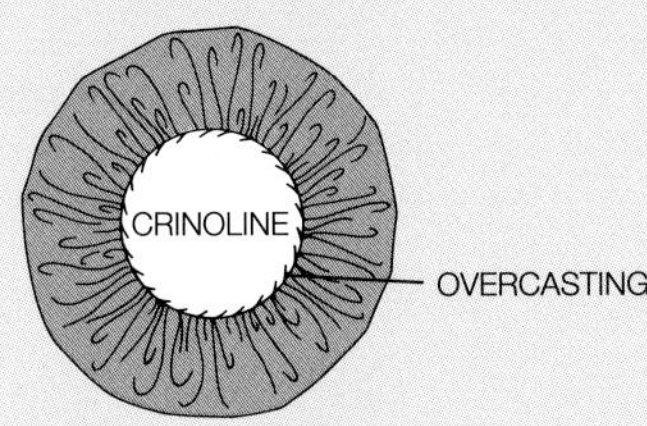

3. ***Turn choux over*** and, at center, stitch up and down one time through crinoline and fabric. Push fabric toward center and take one stitch about halfway between center and edge. Take three more stitches, spacing them evenly around circle.

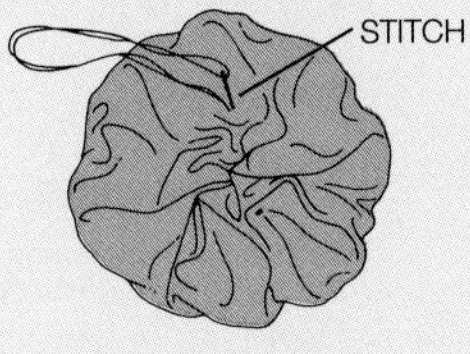

Continue stitching, distributing fabric evenly, to create small folds. Take a few stitches on back to secure.

4. ***Pin, stitch, or glue*** in place.

Jabots

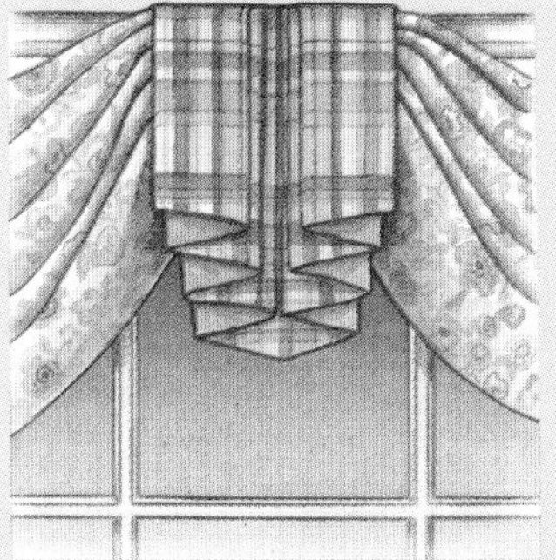

Because the lining will show when the jabot is pleated, line it with the same fabric used on the face or with a contrast fabric. Note that this jabot is used with board-mounted swags.

Make a sample jabot to see if you like the look. Be sure to add 4 inches total to the length for a ½-inch seam allowance and an allowance to go over the top of the mounting board.

On a short jabot, the longest point should be shorter than the swag. Typically, the side taper begins 5 to 8 inches above the longest point, pleats are 6 inches wide, spaces between pleats are 1 inch (½ inch for a tight stack), and side spaces are 3 inches. Typical finished width is 10 inches.

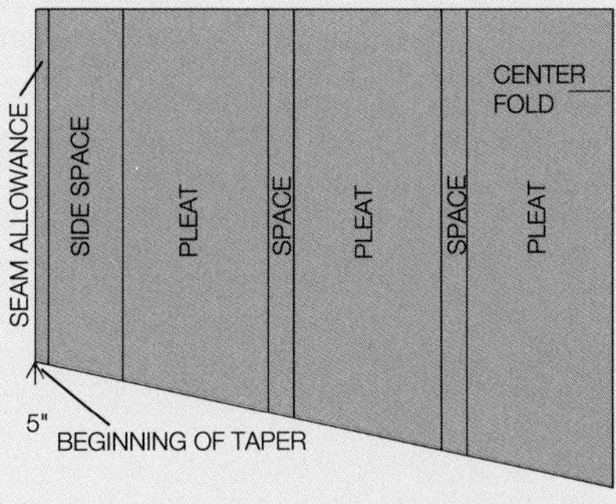

On a longer jabot, the side taper begins at the longest point of the swag or below; finished length depends on the look you want. Pleats are 6 inches wide, spaces between pleats are 2 inches, and side spaces are 4 inches. Finished width is 16 inches.

Sketch your jabot, showing pleats and spaces, to help you determine the width needed.

1. ***Measure, mark, and cut*** face fabric and lining to finished length (longest point) plus 4 inches and flat width plus 1 inch.

2. ***Fold lining*** in half lengthwise, right sides together. At outer edges, measure and mark from top a distance equal to beginning of taper plus 4 inches. With lining still folded, mark longest point plus 4 inches on center fold. Using a straightedge, mark a line from beginning of taper to point on fold. Cut through both layers along line.

Using lining as a pattern, mark and cut face fabric.

3. ***Place face fabric*** and lining right sides together, aligning raw edges. Pin and stitch all edges except top, making a ½-inch seam. Trim seam allowances at corners. Turn right side out and lightly press.

4. ***Lay jabot*** on work surface. At longest point, measure and mark finished length line; extend line across top. Measure and mark pleats and spaces near top and bottom edges with pins.

5. ***Form pleats,*** working from center to outer edges. Pin pleats in place near top and bottom edges.

6. ***On right side of jabot,*** place lower edge of 1-inch masking tape on finished length line. Stitch pleats in place along top edge of tape; remove tape. From finished length line measure and mark a line at a distance equal to width of board less ½ inch. Stitch on line; trim ¼ inch beyond stitching.

7. ***Pin jabot*** to mounting board so finished length line is at front edge of board; adjust length as desired. Staple to board.

Index

Boldface nunmbers refer to photographs.